How To Speak TV,
Print & Radio

How To Speak TV,
Print & Radio

A Self-Defense Manual

When You're The News

By
CLARENCE JONES

FOURTH EDITION

Published and distributed by:
    Video Consultants, Inc.
    5220 S. Russell Street # 40
    Tampa, Florida 33611

To order additional copies, see last page.

ISBN 0-9619603-2-9

Printing history:

Fourth Edition published May, 1993

Third Edition published January, 1991

Second Edition Titled "How to Speak TV"
published February, 1988

First Edition Titled "How to Speak TV"
published September, 1983

Printed in the United States of America

HOW TO USE THIS BOOK

You Can Quickly Find What You're Looking For

We designed this book so you can quickly find what you're looking for. It's divided into three parts—Skills, Strategies, and Inside the Media. Within each part, the chapters are in alphabetic order. Throughout, there are frequent sub-heads to help you find what you need by flipping through.

Part 1—SKILLS

Personal skills you need in dealing with the news media. Read chapters here if the reporter is waiting outside your door. In this part, you'll find interview skills and defensive techniques; news releases and news conferences. How to talk to reporters off-the-record. Writing speeches and delivering them so they'll be reported. How to be acceptably rude on radio and TV talk shows.

Part 2—STRATEGY

This part will help you understand how reporters and editors think. What you should be doing within your organization to cope effectively with the news media. The need for a written media policy, and suggested samples. The ethics media people subscribe to. Fighting back when they do you wrong. What editors are looking for, and how to sell your story to them. Deciding whether you need a public information officer, how to choose one, and the PIO's function. Ten Commandments for better media relations.

Part 3—INSIDE THE MEDIA

The chapters in this part take you behind the scenes. How they'll edit what you say. How networks and local stations split the money and the power. How they know who's reading, watching and listening. The legalities of libel, privacy and fairness.

How To Speak TV, Print & Radio

Gadgets that create electronic illusions, and how they work. The future of the news media in America. A chapter on media jargon that will help you understand the strange dialects media people speak.

TABLE OF CONTENTS

Part 1
SKILLS

How To Speak TV, Print & Radio

Technology

What Will They
Think of Next?

*The battle for TV delivery by air, cable, satellite,
phone lines. Fax newspapers. Inter-active video
catalogs. The decline of old empires as newer, faster
systems emerge.*

Part 4

ORDERS AND SEMINARS

Seminars

On-Camera Training In
Media Skills & Strategy

*How to obtain more details on the author's seminars
for executives in government, the professions and
private industry.*

Order Form

If You'd Like More
Copies of This Book

*A handy order form to obtain more copies. Shipping
and handling charges and carton-lot discounts.*

FOREWORD

What Do You Dislike About the Media?

The first time you face a TV news camera, it is like standing before a firing squad as they load and slam the bolts forward.

Ready

You feel naked. It seems the whole world is watching, listening. Your mind races, trying to form your last words. Words that will live after they fire.

Aim

You sweat. You keep your hands out of sight. They shake. Your mouth goes dry. You hear yourself stuttering. Before the words are out, you wish you'd said it differently.

Why this panic? You've done nothing wrong. Yet you feel guilty. Clumsy. Cornered.

Fire

This kid asking the question, pushing, jabbing, seems to think of himself as a bush leaguer destined for "60 Minutes." There he goes again, twisting what you just said. His smirk says you're lying.

THIS IS NOT FAIR! You want to scream.

But you can't.

For more than 40 years, television reporters have been conning or cornering people to play this traumatic game: **Interview Poker.**

"I don't know how to play," the interview target gamely says.

Trust Me

"That's all right," the reporter smiles, "Trust me. I'll explain the rules to you as we go along."

How To Speak TV, Print & Radio

Interviews for newspapers and magazines date back to the first printing presses.

For some reason, a reporter with a pen or pencil is not as threatening as a camera or microphone. Curious. Because at least the audio or videotape will contain your words exactly as you spoke them.

Print reporters' shorthand is not always that accurate. Editing and quoting out of context can occur with any of the media.

You Don't Know the Rules

Part of your uneasiness in encounters with reporters is the result of your inexperience. You don't know how to do this. You don't know the rules.

This book is designed to teach you the rules, and some of the basics of print and broadcast news. Hopefully, it will make the odds more even, the game more fair.

The media speak another language.

Is That Me?

When you see the published or broadcast version of the interview, you may wonder if the words you're seeing, hearing, or reading were spoken by someone else. An impersonator.

While the camera was rolling, if you were able to control your panic, you thought you were straightforward, concise—maybe even witty and well organized.

But when you gather your friends and family to watch your debut on the six o'clock news, you look evasive, long winded, downright stupid.

Each Day, 35,000 Interviews

Every day in the United States, about 15,000 people are interviewed for television news. Newspapers and magazines will probably top that. Radio, perhaps 5,000 interviews per day.

Many of those interviewed are unhappy with the results. If you work in government or law enforcement or certain types of high-profile industries, you know the feeling.

If you're a top corporate executive, school administrator, judge, hospital administrator or union official, there's a good chance you'll be talking to a reporter. You probably won't have much warning or time to prepare for that conversation or confrontation.

Simple Formulas

There's no great mystery to it. News stories follow simple formulas and techniques.

But if you don't understand how to speak Media, they must pick from the few usable phrases you scatter through your conversation. They didn't quote you out of context. They used the only sentence you spoke that was understandable. The rest—for news story purposes—was pure gibberish.

You Take My Soul

Primitive tribes often feared that if you took their picture, you carried away in the camera a part of their soul. That fear still lives in the gleaming high-rises of metropolitan America.

When the TV crew packs up the camera gear after the interview—when the newspaper reporter folds the shorthand pad, shakes your hand and says goodbye—you watch them leave with a sinking feeling. Your entire career—your income, your reputation—may hinge on that part of your soul that is now on their videocassette or shorthand pad.

You hold your breath until the six o'clock news, or tomorrow's newspaper, almost afraid to watch or read.

What Will They Do To Me?

What are they going to do to me?

If you have been burned, you begin to think of them as the enemy. It becomes a war. And if you adopt that attitude, you will almost surely lose. Richard Nixon and the generals who lost Vietnam thought of the media in that way. They lost.

To be successful, you must look at it the way a professional athlete does. It is a game. Your role in that game is to play as well as you can. To do that, you scout the other team, develop some basic skills, do your homework, keep yourself in good mental and physical condition, and play with energy and vitality.

No Guarantees

I give no guarantees or warranties with this book, or my seminars. But if you will learn how the game is played, and some of its basic strategies; if you will work to overcome your natural weaknesses and handicaps, you will win more than you lose. You will win a *lot* more than you lose.

In most of your encounters with the media, the reporter is not out to get you. The reporter needs a good quote from you if he or she is to succeed. You have not understood what they need, and how they will use it. Your fear and distrust have often made you look incompetent or evasive or guilty.

There Will Be Hard Knocks

Make no mistake—if you play the game, you will take some hard knocks. Getting hurt last week does not keep the professional athlete from playing again this week. If he is good, he learns from last week's mistakes, and plays even harder this week.

The media have changed the way humans receive, remember, and react to information. They have developed state-of-the-art techniques for:

• Grabbing your attention.
• Condensing complex issues.
• Making the information visual and memorable.
• Stimulating an emotional response.
• Motivating you to act.

Because the society has been conditioned by these media techniques, they also work when you communicate with your staff, your board of directors, a jury, a legislative committee, the Kiwanis Club.

If you ever expect to be interviewed by the news media . . . if you want to change things . . . if you need to be an effective leader—communicator—spokesperson . . . if you expect to be quoted accurately and fairly . . . you MUST learn this new language.

Media language. How to speak TV, print and radio.

PREFACE

The Power to Create, Destroy, or Change

The news media have become the most powerful force in this society. I can think of no other institution, no other group, with the power of the media. Is Congress more powerful? No. The President? The courts? The Church? I think not. The media have the power to create—the power to destroy. And—unlike those other forces in our culture—they can do it almost overnight. They are the instruments of change.

They set the agenda for us as a people. We do not get around to discussing or solving a problem we have known about for years until 'the media put it at the top of our priority list.

As a result of that power, there is a great deal of fear and mistrust of the media. And, sometimes, hate.

I Did Not Understand

I spent 30 years as a reporter, but did not truly understand how people feel about my old profession until I published the first edition of this book and began, in 1984, teaching people how to cope with reporters, editors, cameras and microphones. How to play the game.

All across the broad range of my clients—whether they be bank presidents, social workers, corporate CEOs, attorneys, police officers, public officials or university administrators—the fear and mistrust are there.

They Are Afraid

They fear being misquoted—deliberately, inadvertently, or out of context.

They are concerned about reporters who come with the story already set in their heads, simply looking for a quote that will fit that preconception.

There is the terrible vulnerability of having no control whatever over the process and what the reporter will do to you.

And so, many people choose to avoid the media game.

If you choose not to play, you are passing up the most powerful tool in the world.

What Do You Want?

What do you want? A successful business? Election to public office? Community support? New legislation? Understanding for your cause?

The media can bring all that about. In many cases, they are the only way to reach those goals.

I spent the first 16 years of my reporting career in newspapers. When I switched to television in 1970, I was astounded at the impact of my new medium. Like most newspaper people, I had not liked my TV competition.

In my newspaper days, I thought TV was bland and shallow and fleeting. Its reporters were not nearly as experienced or knowledgeable as most newspaper reporters. I suspect that I also hated television because I realized, even then, how truly powerful it can be.

Each Medium is Different

I was dismayed, after I made the switch, at how few people I interviewed had any glimmer of TV's requirements and restrictions. They related to me as though I still worked for a newspaper. They did not understand that television is different. Newspapers, television and radio approach a story from completely different directions. Magazines use still another technique. Each medium demands a different kind of mind-set if you are to communicate effectively.

To be successful in dealing with the news media, you must understand how reporters and editors think. And have some knowledge of what it takes to gather, publish and broadcast information. You need to be aware of the struggles for money and power that take place behind the scenes, and how they shape the final version of the story. And you should be less fearful. You can influence the process more than you realize.

That's what this book is about. I hope it helps.

Clarence Jones

Part 1
SKILLS

Accuracy

Defending Yourself

Interviews-Broadcast

Interviews-General

Interviews-Print

Media Morality

News Conferences

News Releases

Off-the-Record

Speeches

Talk Shows

SKILLS

ACCURACY

If That's the Story, I'm Not Sure I Was There

I often begin a media relations workshop by asking the group to write on a sheet of paper the three things they most fear when they deal with the media. What do you dread? I ask. What concerns you most? The results are remarkably the same. No matter where the seminar is held—no matter what they do for a living. Bank presidents, police chiefs, social workers, doctors, lawyers and accountants all have the same response.

Fear of Being Misquoted

So much so that I make a bet with them, when they have finished writing, but before I know what they have written. Two thirds of you, I tell them—maybe three-fourths—will have as one of your fears the fear of being misquoted.

There are sly smiles, as if I had some psychic power. Or a mirror in the ceiling. They look at each other and at their neighbors' lists. Then I ask for a show of hands. How many of you have as one of your primary concerns the fear of being misquoted?

Sometimes, the count is unanimous. Everyone will have on his list some version of being misquoted or taken out of context.

Incompetence or Bad Motives?

Are inaccurate stories the result of reporter incompetence, insensitivity, or bad motives?

Sometimes one, sometimes the other. Sometimes all three.

Some reporters get tunnel vision pursuing their story. They don't let the facts derail them.

The preconceived story is a major factor in media inaccuracy. Sometimes it is a young reporter, sent out to get a specific story by a strong editor. Remember, each of us views the world from our own, isolated cubicle. Editors are no different. To get ahead in the news business, you do your best to please the boss.

Preconceived Assignments

I once worked for a newspaper editor who was terrible about assigning preconceived stories. I'll disguise his identity and call him Dave.

Dave would stop off at the City Desk when he arrived in the morning, sneezing and blowing his nose. His voice would be hoarse.

"We need a story on the flu epidemic," Dave would tell the city editor.

"Is there an epidemic?" the city editor would ask. He had quickly learned that the boss' story ideas did not always pan out.

The Flu Epidemic Story

"I've got the flu," Dave would say. "My wife and kids have the flu. Everybody at the club has the flu. Can't remember when so many people were sick at one time."

And so a young reporter would be assigned the flu epidemic. His first stop would be the county health department. Lowest reports of flu in 20 years, they'd say. When the reporter's findings were put on Dave's desk, he'd shake his head. "Can't rely on those damned bureaucrats over at the health department," he'd grumble. "Put a more experienced reporter on it."

Sizing Up the Reporter

When a reporter approaches you on a story, your first job is to size up the reporter. Intelligence. Experience. Knowledge of the subject. Prejudices. Attitude toward you and your organization. (See more on the pre-interview interview in **SKILLS/ Interviews-General**)

You may quickly discover the reporter is working on a preconception that is all wrong. You need to set the facts straight IMMEDIATELY. How strongly you object to the false preconception will often determine whether the reporter changes course on the story idea.

Your first approach should be friendly and informative. "A lot of people assume that's the reason for our action, but they're all wrong. Let me tell you what really happened behind the scenes."

Suggest a Replacement

Remember, the editor has invested time, and the time of the reporter and photographer in this preconceived story. If the reporter comes back and says there's no story, the boss may think this is not a very good or aggressive reporter. Most newsrooms are understaffed. They can't afford to waste a reporter's time.

So always suggest another story to replace the false preconception. That way, the reporter doesn't go back empty-handed. It will be a lot easier to tell the boss the original story idea didn't work out.

Become More Aggressive

The reporter may persist with the original concept. Your response should become more aggressive. Lay out your case to show what really happened. Suggest others who can substantiate what you're saying. Produce records and documents that refute the preconception. Provide copies to help the reporter convince the editor the story idea is wrong.

If the reporter is not convinced, make sure your quotes make it clear you disagree, and effectively argue your point of view. You may discover, in that pre-interview conversation, that the reporter knows almost nothing about the subject matter.

Don't Tell Everything

Don't try to teach everything you know about the subject. You'll just confuse the reporter. You increase the chance that the story will be inaccurate, the quotes distorted. The reporter is not expert enough, after a brief visit with you, to sort out what you've unloaded and choose the most important points.

In a seminar for university administrators, one of my students was the public relations director for a very prestigious medical school in the Northeast. "I've given up on television reporters," he told the group. "They send reporters who know nothing about medicine.

"At our school, we're on the cutting edge of research. We're using extremely sophisticated, complex techniques. We work with radiation and lasers and genetic engineering. It takes us a whole day just to give the reporter a basic education in the field. And what do we get for our trouble? Maybe 90 seconds, often inaccurate. Not worth the effort."

What Time Is It?

You're telling reporters too much, I suggested. They only need to know what time it is. You've been insisting they understand atomic clocks. The reporter's only knowledge of the subject may be a newspaper or magazine clipping the editor handed out with the assignment.

Once you realize the scope of the reporter's ignorance, PROVIDE ONLY WHAT IT TAKES TO WRITE THE STORY. Draw the final conclusions. Get to the bottom line. Sum it all up in one or two sentences.

It gives you an opportunity to control—to a large extent—what will appear in print, or on the air. (See **SKILLS/Defending Yourself** and the sections on **SKILLS/Interviews**)

Misquotes—Your Fault

Reporters have been conditioned to look for quotes that fit a certain formula. If you haven't learned to speak Media Language, you may discover that the reporter stitches together a phrase you spoke here, another there, as if they were spoken at one time, in one sentence. (See **INSIDE THE MEDIA/Editing**)

You need to learn how to say what you want quoted in one, quick sentence. Otherwise, you might as well be speaking German or Chinese. Don't make the reporter act as interpreter. Many quotes get lost or distorted if they have to be translated into Mediaspeak.

(See **SKILLS/Interviews** for crafting quotes that will be used and quoted accurately)

If your experience with a specific reporter leads you to believe there is an accuracy problem, a suggestion:

Record the Interview

Record the interview. To make sure the recording is legal, tell the reporter. You say, as you turn on the recorder in plain view, "You don't mind if I record this, do you?" You can do the same thing in a telephone interview.

This tells the reporter you have a complete transcript of what you said. There will be no your-word-against-mine dispute.

(See **SKILLS/Defending Yourself** and **INSIDE THE MEDIA/ Libel** for elements of truth, news media risks & defenses)

You Need to Complain

It may be that you do everything right, and you're still misquoted. Or the story is so distorted, you wonder if you and the reporter attended the same event.

You need to complain. Set the record straight.

Not a nasty, angry complaint. A careful, straightforward telephone call or letter to the reporter and the editor, showing what was reported and what you really said. Or what really happened.

In most cases, you won't ask for a retraction or correction. But if you don't file your complaint, the flawed story goes into the newsroom library. In the future, every reporter who writes about you or the same subject matter will pull that inaccurate story from the library and repeat the inaccuracy.

Once it's on the air or in the newspaper three times, it becomes fact.

(See **STRATEGY/Fighting Back** for more detail on how to file your complaint, when, and with whom; pros and cons of corrections)

Good Reporters Sweat

Believe it or not, an inaccurate story is extremely painful for good reporters. They take immense pride in their ability to get it right. The story goes on the air, or in the newspaper, and they suddenly realize there's one other angle they didn't check that could change the accuracy or fairness of the story.

They sweat and there's a knot in the bottom of their stomachs until they check that neglected angle to make sure it doesn't change the story.

Good reporters also have the grace to admit they were wrong, and make it right.

How To Speak TV, Print & Radio

SKILLS

DEFENDING YOURSELF

Ambush Interviews
And Other Traps

It may be a bright spring morning. You will have no warning, no inclination to be cautious. As you leave your house and unlock the car in the driveway, you probably will not notice the van parked halfway up the block. Even if you are wary, you will not see the hidden camera videotaping everything you do. As you come out of the driveway, the van starts up and pulls away from the curb. It stays a discreet half-block behind as you drive to your office.

You Will Not Suspect

You drive to your usual parking spot, a block from your building. Again, you do not notice the same van, double-parked just ahead. As you walk past, two men jump out the rear door. You do not see them. One is a photographer, carrying a videotape camera on his shoulder. The other is a reporter who thinks of himself as an understudy for Mike Wallace, complete with trenchcoat. They come at a trot, approaching from behind. You never hear them.

The reporter steps out in front of you, blocking the sidewalk. At that instant, the cameraman bursts ahead. With a start, you see them for the first time. The reporter says, "Good morning, I'm Mike Wallet from Channel Seven. I'd like to talk to you about your company's financial problems."

A Difficult Time—

It is a difficult time, no matter how cool you are. The surprise of the ambush is a jolt. You look frightened. Your pulse is racing.

Your breathing is short and hard. You have only a fraction of a second to decide what to do. You may not make a conscious decision. You may act reflexively.

Some of your options:

1. Punch out the reporter, swing your briefcase at the camera, and run like crazy to get away from them.

2. Keep walking, but duck your head and put your hand in front of the camera lens. The photographer will stick with you, the reporter firing non-stop questions, into the lobby, all the way up the elevator, into the reception area of your office. Somewhere along the way, you will probably utter a "No comment" as you grit your teeth and stare straight ahead.

3. Stop dead in your tracks. "I have no idea what you're talking about. Now if you'll excuse me, I have to get to work."

4. Say: "Good morning, Mike. Gee, if you want to talk to me, come on up and I'll see when I can squeeze you in today. If you'd called, I would have been glad to give you an appointment." In this scenario, the reporter will still keep the camera rolling, and fire questions all the way to the office. He is afraid you will renege on the appointment.

5. Say: "I'll be very glad to give you an interview, but let's talk first, off camera. If you're sincere in wanting to talk to me—in doing a fair, accurate story—and not trying to make me look like some kind of criminal, turn off the camera and come on up. I'll get us a cup of coffee."

They Win, You Lose

The ambush technique has been used, and abused, throughout the history of investigative reporting on television. Radio and print reporters ambush their targets, too. Remember, we can't see the fear and pain on your face in those media. The reporters tell us, in their own words, how frightened and guilty you looked, then give us your response.

Reporters know they can usually count on the ambush to make the target of their story look bad. At the same time, they're carrying out their obligation to get your side of the issue. It's heads they win, tails you lose.

Some veteran reporters who have ambushed their targets for years now question the fairness of the technique. Mike Wallace of "60 Minutes" says he will use the ambush technique only if the target refuses to give him an interview.

The audience has become more sophisticated. Part of the re-thinking involves their not wanting to look like a TV bully picking on a defenseless little guy. The audience believes television has enormous power. If reporters and camera crews abuse that power—if it appears they don't fight fair—the audience will side with the little guy.

They Will Persist

Television is words and pictures—mostly pictures. If they are to write words about you, they must have your picture. Good investigative reporters take great pride in their persistence. If they truly want your picture, they will get it. Unless you lock yourself in a fallout shelter for the next year. Even then, there are ways to get to you, or smoke you out. So the only question is, what do you say when they catch up with you?

Let's go back and examine your options in an ambush.

1. Punch out the reporter. This makes great video. You can be sure every moment will be played on the air. At least three or four times. You will enhance your reputation as a hoodlum. Few people will side with you. They will decide you are guilty, as charged. If there is another side to the story, it won't be told. The reporter can have you arrested for assault and battery. There are excellent grounds for a civil suit. The proof for either criminal or civil action is all on videotape. You will boost the reporter's career immeasurably.

2. Refuse to talk, keep walking. In most cases, this will also make you look like a nasty guy with something to hide. Remember—television, like politics, is often a matter of impressions, not exact words.

3. "Excuse me, I have to get to work." Here, you've said something. The audience knows you're human. But you're still cold, elusive, probably guilty. This option has many modifications. If you don't want to give a full interview or answer questions, you can take this opportunity to get at least a brief statement on the air. "No comment" is like taking the Fifth Amendment. Many people will assume you're guilty. Otherwise, why not talk to the reporter? You need to explain. (See **STRATEGY/Ten Commandments**)

His question has suggested there are financial problems in your company. You can say something like, "We've become concerned about a cash flow problem in the last week or so, and we're working on it. I'm confident the company is not in danger. We're negotiating now with some new investors, and I'm sure we'll work it out. But that is a delicate thing. I really can't say very much about it. If you'll give me your name and phone number, I'll be glad to call you when we come to an agreement."

This answer will guarantee a string of questions, that you can politely refuse to answer, repeating your reason for declining. You may want to answer some of them.

4. Make an interview appointment. If you're polite, the reporter tends to return the courtesy. In making the appointment, try to find out as much as you can about the story. You may have to do some research to answer some of the questions. Delaying the interview for several hours will give you time to be better prepared. (See **SKILLS/Interviews-General**)

5. "Let's talk first, off-camera or off-the-record." This is usually the best choice if you're concerned about getting a fair shake from the reporter. News people work a lot on instinct. From experience, they tend to be suspicious. Anything you do that appears to evade, to delay, to deceive or cover up will feed their suspicion and probably will be reflected in their copy. (See **SKILLS/Off-the-Record**)

Lay It All Out

During that off-camera or off-the-record talk, if you're not guilty, lay all your cards on the table. That may be the end of the interview, and the story. The off-camera interview gives you a better opportunity to fully explain your side of the issue. The reporter may not have all the facts from the other side. Collect documents and bring in staff, if that's necessary for a full presentation.

Libel Suit Strategy

There is another element of self-defense that you should keep in mind. If you are a public person you cannot collect in a libel suit unless the media publish or broadcast something false about you with malice. The U. S. Supreme Court says you must show they had "reckless disregard for truth."

You must not only prove it was false—you must prove the reporter did a sloppy job; had information showing the story was false, but ignored it. If you meet with reporters or editors to refute the story they're working on, make sure you can prove what you told them. Tape record the meeting. Have your attorney or some other reliable witness present. Get a signed receipt for any documents you provide.

Keeping Reporters Honest

If you are concerned about the integrity of the reporter who asks for an interview, it might be a good idea to take the same precautions. Have a staff member sit in on the interview. Keep track of the records you provide. Make your own audio or video recording of the entire interview. Let the reporter know you're recording it.

Reporters who know you have the tape are much more careful in quoting you. With a transcript of the entire interview, you can make a major dent in the reporter's career if the story is not fair and accurate. Editors are very concerned these days about reporters who can't write truthfully. They are a $20 million libel suit, looking for a story. (See **INSIDE THE MEDIA**/**Libel** and **STRATEGY**/**Fighting Back**)

If, in asking for the off-camera or off-the-record conversation, you say you'll talk later on camera, or for quotes, don't back out. If you'll lie about giving an interview, surely you'll lie about more important things. Reporters are always afraid to delay on-camera and on-the-record interviews. Too many people change their minds.

The Lie Will Never Die

Remember: Reporters and cameras are excellent lie detectors. Like the polygraph, the camera can sometimes be fooled. But if you're caught in a tape-recorded lie, television and radio will never forget. It will be played over and over again. You can't say you were misquoted. The lie is there, on tape, to haunt you forever.

The audience is also smart enough to know when you're evading a question. In most cases, it's probably better to say you can't answer than to evade the question.

A good reporter, like a good courtroom lawyer, usually knows the answer before the question is asked. Police investigators go to school to learn how to decipher body English so they'll know when suspects are lying, or when they have guilty knowledge of a crime. Reporters learn the same skills through experience.

The Human Polygraph

Almost unconsciously, they constantly monitor your fidgets and eye-blinks; what you're doing with your hands; whether your breathing is relaxed or strained; whether you're sweating more than the temperature calls for; how tightly your legs are crossed; whether you avoid looking them in the eye.

One of the real problems for television interviews is the fear of the camera. Stage fright gives the same physical symptoms as guilt and deception. You may be signalling that you are Public Enemy Number One, when you've really just got a bad case of stage fright.

The Camera Monster

Interestingly, most people are not as afraid of a newspaper reporter with a shorthand pad. The camera is the monster they fear. The fear can be misplaced.

Newspapers do much more investigative reporting than television. Their investigative teams spend months—sometimes years—on one story. Newspaper investigations are much more tenacious and persistent than those in radio and TV.

The wire services pick up the stories. They go all over the world. Congressional committee chairmen and federal prosecutors read them and begin major investigations.

Take More Control

I urge clients to take more control of the interview—print or broadcast. If the room is hot and you're sweating, suggest that you take a break, turn off the TV lights, and let the air conditioner catch up. If you realize you made a mistake in something you said several sentences back, tell the reporter. "You know, I told you we're planning to spend $54 million on that project next year. My memory was bad. Ask me that question again and I'll give you the correct figure."

Or "I told you we are planning to spend $54 million on that project next year. I'm not sure of that figure. Let's stop a minute while I check the numbers."

Or "You know, my answer to that question about next year's budget was awfully wordy and convoluted. If you ask me that question again, I think I can give you a better answer."

Deciding whether to talk to an investigative reporter is very complex unless the charges are absolutely false. If the reporter has been misled—if an understandably false conclusion has been drawn from the evidence—then you should definitely talk.

Not Guilty: A True Story

A real-life example:

An anonymous caller once told me I should investigate why the Urban Renewal Agency paid the city attorney twice as much for his house as it paid the owners of other identical houses on the same block. I went to property records at the courthouse and discovered the tip was accurate. The lots on the block were all the same size. The houses were all similar, built at the same time, and had been carried on the tax assessor's rolls at virtually the same value. Yet, when the Urban Renewal Agency bought the entire block, it paid the city attorney, with good political connections, twice as much as anybody else. Apparently an open-and-shut case.

The Target's Response

I went to the city attorney to get his response—the last step before broadcasting the story.

"Yeah, they paid me twice as much," the city attorney said. "But I didn't get the money. You see, I had leased the house to a color photo processing company. The lease said if they ever had to move for any reason during the term of the lease, I would have to pay for their relocation and build them another processing plant. I've got a copy of the lease in my file, if you'd like to read it."

Oh. I see. Three days of research down the tubes. No story.

When You've Goofed

If the story the reporter is pursuing involves your making an honest mistake, it's probably in your best interest to say so. (See **STRATEGY/Ten Commandments of Media Relations**)

Past the point of admitting an honest mistake, the decision on whether to be interviewed for quotes or on camera gets stickier. It depends on how serious the accusation, and your involvement in it. In a sense, you are on trial. The reporter will present the charges, and the evidence against you, to the audience/jury. If the defense decides to rest with no evidence, no witnesses, we have been conditioned to believe that is a concession of guilt.

Conning the Reporter

Looking guilty by refusing to talk to a reporter may be better than taking the stand and convincing the audience you're not only guilty, you're a liar as well. Career con men often amazed me by agreeing to a sit-down interview. It is a heady challenge, to see if they can out-smart, out-talk the reporter. They rarely win.

If there are people and documents that support your side of the controversy, the reporter may not know about them unless you disclose them. Refusing to talk will almost always insure a one-sided story.

What Are You Hiding?

It's hard to draw lines for every situation. But generally, reporters believe people have something to hide if they try to keep them out of offices, or meetings, or records. The more open you can be with reporters, the more open and fair they tend to be with you. (See **STRATEGY/Ten Commandments of Media Relations**)

Remember—whatever the reporter does that is sneaky, or belligerent—behavior that might raise eyebrows—will never be broadcast or written. Anything you do that is less than flattering will be preserved for all the world to see. We will see it, hear it, read about it many, many times.

There are other kinds of surprises reporters spring. They call and ask permission to shoot videotape in your business or office. "Just general footage to go with a story we're doing." Or the print reporters who say they need a general briefing on a benign subject. Once inside, you discover they have quite another mission, and have entered by subterfuge.

Questions from Nowhere

In the middle of what you thought would be a friendly interview, the reporter gets nasty. Springs a completely different subject on you. A sort of verbal ambush. The sandbag question.

"Didn't your corporation fire four women in 1975 simply because they were pregnant?" the reporter snarls. You may not have the foggiest idea.

Too often, people who don't know the answer to a surprise question answer it anyhow, saying what they assume or hope is true. Later, when it turns out they're wrong, it looks like they were lying or trying to cover up. If you don't know, say so. And tell the reporter you'll get the answer.

Become More Aggressive

If the reporter's question is a complete fishing expedition that unfairly or inaccurately impugns your character or motives, you should become very aggressive and adamant in your response.

If you're not insulted by a false, damaging suggestion, the reporter will believe the allegation is true. Controlled anger is the key here. A seething resentment that the reporter would stoop so low. And a clear, positive statement, delivered with great intensity—

"This company is not a racist company, and I defy you to find a single shred of evidence that would even suggest such a thing."

Or—"I have never beaten my wife. I have never abused my wife, either physically or mentally, and I resent your throwing that kind of question into this interview. You are completely off-base, and I'm sure your viewers/readers/listeners will come to the same conclusion if you report such a scurrilous question— and have the integrity to include my answer."

How Are Things Going?

If a reporter asks you how things are going in your company or department, be careful. The landscape is littered with the carcasses of executives who said proudly they had solved the problem, not knowing the reporter had proof the problem was even worse than before.

Typical of this kind of mousetrap was a TV interview with a hospital administrator, bragging that his institution ran a model program to deal with contaminated waste. He gave a lengthy lecture, saying the waste was carefully controlled within the hospital until it was incinerated at another site. The temperatures there, he said, would destroy AIDS or any other infectious virus or bacteria. Nobody could be harmed, even accidentally.

The TV reporter had asked him to do the interview on the loading dock outside the receiving department because the light was better there. As the administrator was talking, he was unaware that the camera was zooming over his shoulder to a red bag of bloody waste, lying untended on the loading dock.

They Could Be Better

If the question is general about how things are going, the best answer is, "Pretty good, but I'm always trying to make them better. Do you have any specific area in mind?" That will make the reporter who knows something you don't re-phrase the question, getting closer to the real issue.

If a reporter surprises you with an allegation about your organization, your answer should be something like:

I'd Like to Know

"I'm not aware of that, but if that were true, I'd be very concerned about it. I'd like to know anything you have so I can do something about it."

If you knew about the problem and have been quietly working on it, this is the time to unload everything you've done. There aren't any secrets now, so you might as well look impressive as a manager or executive who makes things right.

Accuracy Can Hurt, Too

If you say you're working on it, but don't say how, the reporter will suspect you're lying to cover up. An accurate statement of your position can be written that telegraphs the reporter's suspicion:

"The chief said he has been investigating the allegation for two months, but refused to say who is conducting the probe; how they're doing it, or what they've found."

You may want to make a deal with the reporter, to keep things quiet a little longer. This will involve a confidential agreement, in which you persuade the reporter to delay the story. To do this, you'll have to trade something. The price will usually be information that would not be available without this special agreement. (See **SKILLS/Off-the-Record**)

Beat Them to the Punch

Once you know you have an internal problem, you may be able to solve it before the story is published or broadcast. The story is not nearly as damaging if the problem has already been solved.

Call the reporter and announce what you've done, with thanks for bringing the problem to your attention.

If you really want to zap the reporter, hold a news conference and give the entire story—problem and solution—to the competition before the investigative report can be printed or aired. (See **SKILLS/News Conferences**)

Air Your Own Dirty Linen

You will almost always look better announcing internal problems before the media find them.

If they find them, they tend to make the story bigger and more sensational. It's a way to pat themselves on the back. If you announce it, the story is usually smaller. They downplay it because they should have found it themselves. It makes them look slow or incompetent.

Responding Under Fire

When there is an allegation that is damaging to you or your organization, here is a generic response that can be modified to fit almost any situation. You need to tell the media:

Your concern about the allegation. You try to run a first-class operation here. Any complaint or allegation is a major concern.

What you're going to do about it. Here, I suggest you give as much detail as possible. If you are launching an immediate investigation, tell us how many people will be involved. How will they conduct their investigation? Will outside investigators be brought in?

A general timetable. If you can't be sure how long the investigation will take, make it clear that this is only an estimate. You may find more to investigate than you expect. If you see you won't make the timetable, tell the news media well in advance, with a clear explanation of why it's taking longer than you expected.

Your personal investment in finding the truth. Here, your reputation for being open and fair with the media are critical if you are to be credible.

A reminder that the allegation may be false. Unfortunately, the reporting of allegations in the media are often heard and read as a conviction. The reputations and lives of innocent people can be destroyed.

You will disclose the truth when you find it. Investigations are meaningless if the public never knows what you found.

You will see that justice is done; any problems corrected. If the allegation is false, the suspended employee will be reinstated. If it is true, you will personally help the prosecutor.

You will review procedure and training. Sometimes the system is at fault, not the people in it. Sometimes they have not been trained to handle a crisis, and shouldn't be blamed.

SKILLS

INTERVIEWS-BROADCAST

Talk to the Camera, But Think of Joe Sixpack

Listening to one end of a telephone conversation, you can often tell who's on the other end. If it's long distance, most people tend to talk louder. Subconsciously, they think they have to speak up to be heard clearly a thousand miles away. We slow down if we sense that the person at the other end of the line is old, or has a thick accent. We change the tone of our voice if we're talking to a child, or a lover.

The same kind of subtle changes take place when people talk to cameras and microphones.

An Audience of One or Two

If they know they're being taped, many people reflexively talk as if they're making a speech at a civic club. There may be half a million—perhaps a million—people out there listening. With a crowd that large, you want to make sure the people in the back row hear what you have to say.

But they're not all in one place.

The broadcast audience is one or two people. It is Joe Sixpack and Aunt Millie, sitting in the living room or kitchen, six or eight feet away from the TV set. The radio listener is even closer. Probably in a car. One of the secrets of broadcast interviews is to keep that audience in mind.

Radio and television are very intimate media. The zoom lens on a camera invades your zone of privacy, moving even closer than a person would, to focus on a drop of sweat, the flared nostrils, the gritted teeth. Radio's microphone lets us eavesdrop on the conversation at the next table. When it is best, the people we're hearing do not seem to realize they're not alone.

How To Speak TV, Print & Radio

Think of the Living Room

Part of your preparation for a radio or TV interview ought to be changing your mind-set so you're talking to that small, intimate audience. It may help you to think of a real living room, and real people. Think of the camera or microphone as a specific person, and that may help. Your spouse, a neighbor, the cashier at the restaurant where you have lunch, the bartender who knows you well enough that you no longer have to order.

Remember, the camera or microphone is not one of your professional colleagues. It's somebody you just met at a dinner party, who knows absolutely nothing about your job and won't understand its jargon.

You're not making a speech, or a statement. You're having a conversation.

The Camera Spots Phonies

The camera detects phonies. Bring to that conversation the real person inside you, not a front. Let your emotions show, if they're real. You can be angry, or sad, pleased with yourself or your organization, shocked or dismayed at what you've just learned.

Changing your mind-set will change your body language. A candidate holds up his arms and flashes a big grin to communicate warmth in the noise and confusion of a political rally. He uses a very different kind of smile and body language if he's trying to charm a beautiful woman sitting across the table in a quiet restaurant.

For the broadcast interview, create in your mind the living room, the intimate atmosphere, and the people you'll be talking to.

The radio or TV reporter does not want many facts or figures when you are being taped.

There is not enough time. You probably don't have the skill to boil down the facts extemporaneously. Even experienced reporters have trouble doing that. To condense them to 20 or 30 seconds may require a half-hour at the typewriter, eliminating a word, rewriting a phrase to save another three or four seconds.

H. L. Mencken once wrote, "I'm writing you a long letter because I didn't have time to write a short one."

The Sony Sandwich

If your interview is taped in the field, it is probably going to be the meat in a Sony Sandwich. What you have to say will be sandwiched between a reporter's introduction and the reporter's summary or conclusion.

The purpose of the interview is to add the personal, human perspective. In virtually every interview, the reporter at some point will ask you how you feel about the issue or event. How you are coping. (See list of feeling words in **SKILLS/Interviews-General**)

The Story Comes Alive

In that first section of the Sony Sandwich, the reporter quickly sketches the scenario. It is like a line drawing, stark and two-dimensional. It is a stick drawing of a human figure, but we cannot tell whether the person is old or young, tall or short, happy or sad, proud or afraid. The interview gives the stick figure warmth and personality, emotion and flavor, color and dimension. The story comes alive.

The reporter may edit a series of interviews together— different people giving their reactions to, or perspectives on, the same incident. Or the interviews may pit one point of view against another. A tenant says the landlord refuses to fix the plumbing. Without a pause, the landlord angrily says he's spent $5,000 in the last month on repairs, but the kids in the building tear it up faster than he can fix it.

Editing Distills Conflict

When sound "bites" are edited against each other, the conflict is distilled quickly and effectively. Instead of watching a ten-round boxing match—mostly dancing, feinting and clinches—we get to see and hear just the knockdowns.

Occasionally, if the sound bite is very strong, it will be placed at the beginning of the reporter's story. In this position, it is usually very short. Then a longer portion of the interview, expanding that opening bite, goes in the middle of the story.

Job Conditioning

People in certain professions are interviewed more often than others. The ones who get the hang of it find reporters coming back to them on future stories. They make the reporter's job so much easier. Unfortunately, the experience and training for some careers tend to make some people poor interviewees.

Doctors, lawyers and accountants are often terrible on camera. They're accustomed to dry, lengthy, logical, step-by-step reasoning, with lots of footnotes. The subject matter is complicated. The simplest question takes three minutes to answer. This kind of conversation is a horror to edit. They call the next day and complain that they were quoted out of context. (See **INSIDE THE MEDIA/Editing**)

Human Synthesizers

On-camera police and military officers often become voice synthesizers spouting official reports. The cop who just caught two armed robbers after a shoot-out speaks very normally until the camera comes. Then he says something like:

"My unit was dispatched to 4481 Ocean Street at nineteen hundred hours. As I approached, Code Three, I observed two white males rapidly exiting the dispatched location in an easterly direction with weapons drawn. When the perpetrators observed my vehicle, they commenced firing. One projectile impacted my vehicle. I then returned the fire."

Unusable.

What Did He Say?

What did he say? I think he said:

"As I rolled up, these two guys with guns were running out of the jewelry store. They saw the patrol car and started shooting. When the first bullet hit the windshield, I jumped out and shot back."

Which leads to the reporter's question:
"You ever been shot at before?"
"Nope."
"How did it feel?"
"Scared the hell out of me."

Guess which section of the interview is certain to be included in the Sony Sandwich.

Police officers and doctors have been conditioned to talk that way not only by writing reports, but by testifying in court. On the witness stand, you are not allowed to express how you feel. Just the facts, please.

What Are We Afraid Of?

Some surveys show stage fright is America's biggest fear. Bigger than war, cancer, or dying in a plane crash. What are we so afraid of?

People in front of a camera often talk non-conversation because they're afraid they'll make a mistake and look stupid. They're not sure the boss will like the idea of their talking to a TV camera. So they cram and memorize, to avoid mistakes. To look like walking encyclopedias.

Instead, they look like robots. They look stupid. The one thing they most fear.

Other people deal with the stress by drawing themselves into tight little knots, making their voices small and flat, and saying every word very carefully. They pause a lot. On TV or radio, they are deadly. More than five seconds, and everybody in the audience will be snoring.

We expect leaders to be patient with the people they lead. If you lose your temper on camera—particularly with an employee, or a young reporter—the audience may not forgive you.

What Does It All Mean?

The closing section of the Sony Sandwich is also formularized. The reporter sums up the story. Perhaps tells us what to expect next.

"What does it all mean? Only time will tell. I'm Tom Trite, Channel Four, Action News."

Understanding the story formula will help you craft a quote for broadcast news that will be used exactly as you said it, without editing.

If you can learn to do this, you'll seldom be misquoted or taken out of context. You'll find your interviews go very quickly.

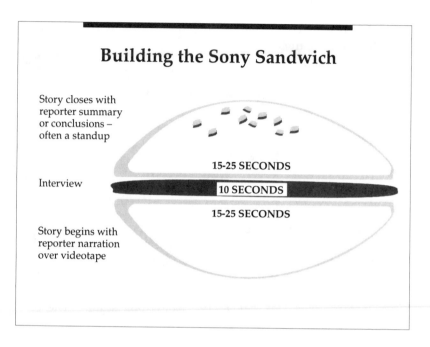

Building the Sony Sandwich

Story closes with
reporter summary
or conclusions –
often a standup

15-25 SECONDS

Interview

10 SECONDS

15-25 SECONDS

Story begins with
reporter narration
over videotape

As soon as the reporter hears the magic, formula quote, it's time to pack the gear and move on to the next assignment.

The FACE Formula

I invented the FACE FORMULA to help you remember what the reporter is looking for when you're being interviewed for television. If we're going to see your face, you need to keep these factors in mind:

Feelings.

Analysis

Compelling C's.

Energy.

Reporters are going to ask you how you feel in 80 per cent of all interviews. In the other 20 per cent, they'll ask you to analyze something that is very complicated. They come to you because you're the expert. You may discover that analysis for rank amateurs is even more difficult than expressing your feelings.

F— Feelings. Let the audience know what you're feeling. Go back from time to time and review the Sony Sandwich story formula to help you reflexively craft quotes that begin with how you feel.

A— Analysis. Give them your assessment of the situation. In one phrase or sentence, tell them what the bottom line is. The audience wants your opinion on the subject. That's why the reporter is talking to you. The expert must be able to translate into understandable English. Educators, computer programmers and engineers are typical professionals who speak strange languages. After the reporter has said there seems to be no danger from the accident within the nuclear power plant, a recognized expert says on camera:

"We've put the effluent through exhaustive electron microscopy plus radiofluorocarbon laser analysis and we come up with a count of point four, seven, zero micro mini roentgens." Or:

"You'd get more radiation sitting in front of a television set for two hours than you would if you took a bath in the water that leaked out."

C—The Compelling C's. Most news stories revolve around at least one of these basic elements:

- **Catastrophe**—"I'm afraid we're facing a national disaster if we don't change the way we dispose of toxic waste."
- **Crisis**—"They're crazy not to evacuate. The tidal surge will sweep across the highway and cut off their escape route if they don't leave now."
- **Conflict**—"I hate him. I'll fight him to my last breath.
- **Change**—"I'm confident things are going to be different around here when we control the statehouse."
- **Crime and Corruption**—"I grieve for the victims of this horrible crime. And I'm resolved to find who did it."
- **Color**—(We used to call it human interest.) "I'm really amused. Anyone who believes that also believes thunder curdles milk."

E— Energy. There is one major difference in talking for television and talking to your friends in their living room. To be effective on camera, your conversation must project energy. Like a salesperson who must believe in the product, you must show that you truly believe what you're saying. Since so many stories for television news involve conflict and imminent danger, you must convince us, through the energy you invest in what you're saying, that we ought to be concerned, too.

Executive Cool = Dull

Some executives in high-pressure jobs adopt a cool, clinical personality that says to their employees, "I know exactly what I'm doing. If the building were on fire, I could lead you to safety." That deliberate, slow, calculating style can appear, on TV or radio, to be boredom, disinterest, or a mask for insecurity.

Forget About Memorizing

Don't memorize, or write out what you intend to say when the camera or recorder is rolling. It makes the interview seem staged and rehearsed. Sections of statements read at live presidential press conferences are about the only prepared statements that make the air.

The first thought that comes to your mind is usually the best, the brightest, and the most sincere. You may want to go over in your mind the main points you'd like to make. No more than three. If you're afraid the stress of the interview will make you forget, write yourself a cheat sheet, the same way students cheat on exams.

Using a Cheat Sheet

The cheat sheet should be just three words—one for each point. Cues that will refresh your memory if your mind goes blank. Put the cheat sheet where you can glance down at it if you need to.

For television, the trick is to suddenly look thoughtful, pause and glance down as if you're thinking deeply, then look back at the reporter to finish the thought. This is a natural head movement in normal conversation. Nobody will know you cheated if you do it carefully. For radio, you don't even need to hide the cheat sheet.

Writing the three points helps you remember. Having the cheat sheet handy is an assuring psychological prop. If it's there, you probably won't need it.

Remember—unless it's a 30-minute talk show in the studio, you have to *condense, condense, condense.* In public speaking courses, the instructor gives you a subject and forces you to make an immediate, five-minute extemporaneous talk. The exercise teaches you to think and talk on your feet.

Some Training Exercises

To train yourself for broadcast interviews, try to say how you feel about a difficult subject—and three reasons why—in 12 seconds or less. Then pad it out to make 20 or 30 seconds.

Pick tough, complicated subjects and practice with a tape recorder or video camera. In one sentence, say how you feel—and why—about difficult subjects like:

- Abortion
- Gun control
- Capital punishment
- Prayer in schools
- The welfare system.

There is no quick miracle drug, no magic diet, no futuristic exercise machine that will make you an instant success. It takes regular, conscientious mental calisthenics if you want to be truly good at it. This exercise, practiced regularly, will develop your mental agility for condensing what you know and feel about complicated subjects.

Congressional Pros

The real pros of TV interviewing are congressional leaders who have been interviewed several times a day for the last 20 years. They develop stopwatches in their heads. Before the camera rolls, they discuss the story with the reporter. They get some idea of how their quotes will be used, and how long they'll be allowed to speak.

"How much time do you need?" the congressman says, clearing his throat and brushing his hair aside.

"About 12 seconds," the reporter tells him.

"OK. Ready?"

"Rolling."

The congressman speaks for 12 seconds. Perhaps 11. Sometimes, 13. And then he stops. He has learned the language, and the game. He edits himself. There can be no distortion. He is rarely quoted out of context.

You Can Do It, Too

Most of those who've learned to speak Television and Radio did it the hard way, through trial and error. For many, it became a self-defense tactic. The news media are kinder to some people than others. One person's slip is never aired. Another, similar stumble becomes the comedy element in tonight's news.

Watch and listen to TV and radio news. Make notes on the people who are effective in their interviews. Learn from the mistakes and blunders of other people.

Watch The Process

If you're in a position where you expect to be interviewed regularly, ask for a guided tour of the local newsroom and editing facilities. If you can, spend a day with a TV camera crew or radio reporter. Watch them shoot, write, and edit a story. The more familiar you become with the entire process, the easier it will be to adapt your speaking style to the medium.

Learning to speak Broadcast requires some concentration, and some hard work. But it's a lot easier than Spanish or German.

You can do it.

Antagonistic interviews are covered in **SKILLS/Defending Yourself.** For now, let's assume the reporter is friendly, or at least objective—neither warm nor cold. Most radio interviews will be done by telephone. There are special hazards there. (See **SKILLS/Interviews-General**)

Do TV Interviews Early

If you make an appointment for a TV interview, try to make it at least four hours before the newscast. The closer to air time, the more harried the crew. They'll do a better job of lighting, shooting, interviewing and editing if they're not pressed against their deadline.

Choose Your Turf

Choose a place that's comfortable for you. If possible, one that fits the story. If you're a doctor, and you'll be talking about a new surgical technique, do the interview with a backdrop that says *medicine*. If you're a computer programmer, let us see a VDT behind you. It's a real advantage if viewers who turn on their sets in the middle of the interview know at a glance this story has something to do with doctors or computers.

If you're more comfortable standing while you talk, suggest that to the TV crew. Some people find it much easier to invest energy in what they're saying if they're standing. When they sit down, it appears—on camera—as if they've let the air out. They go flat. Their entire speech pattern changes. You'll have to watch yourself on videotape to see if this happens to you.

Don't Cram

For the interview, you don't need to do any cramming. If you, the expert, can't remember, how do you expect viewers to retain what you say? The reporter doesn't want statistics on camera. Go over the numbers before, or after, the interview. Most people can't absorb spoken statistics. They *do* remember analogies. "The money we spend treating this disease would buy everybody in the state a new Cadillac this year."

Provide Graphs & Charts

If the audience is to retain numbers, the story will have to be told with graphs and charts that put them in perspective. Seeing the numbers on the screen helps most people remember them. Most reporters in major cities would not think of printing or broadcasting a news release exactly as you wrote it. But they will often use your graphs or charts with no editing whatever. Your providing graphics saves them a lot of time and effort, and helps their story immensely.

The Pecking Order

You should know there is a rigid pecking order within a TV news crew. In most places, the photographer works under the direction of the reporter. The sound technician or grip (rapidly disappearing with the advent of lighter, more compact equipment) is considered the photographer's assistant.

For a network interview, the story producer will often accompany the correspondent. Or the producer may come ahead of the correspondent to gather information, scout interviews and shooting locations.

The correspondent makes more money and technically has more authority than the producer. But the producer often does more work on the story than the correspondent. For many stories, the producer does some of the on-camera interviews. The producer and correspondent then work jointly later, editing it all together.

If the reporter doesn't introduce the other crew members to you, introduce yourself. Remember, the photographer is the one with the power to make the shot flattering, or downright ugly. It never hurts to be on good terms.

Help—Don't Push

You can suggest a place for the interview, but leave the final decision up to the crew. There may be some technical problem with the background of the spot you've chosen. It will take about 15 minutes to set up the equipment.

It will help if you know where the electrical panel is, in case their lights overload a circuit.

If the crew is using a small "peanut" mike that clips to your clothing, try to hide the cord. Run the wire inside your shirt or blouse to the waist, then inside your waistband to one side. (See **SKILLS/Talk Shows** for more ideas and illustrations)

There's always a clumsy moment when a male crew member tries to clip the mike to a woman's silk blouse. Help him, so he doesn't feel like he's invading your privacy; and so the alligator clip on the mike doesn't damage your clothes.

Forget the Mike

If they're using a hand-held mike, the tendency is to lean down, or toward the mike. You don't have to do that. It makes you look stoop-shouldered. Forget about the mike. Picking up good sound is their job. If you're not speaking loudly enough, they'll move the mike, or tell you to speak louder.

Talk to the Reporter

During the interview, talk to the reporter, not the camera. The camera is there, listening to the conversation, but it doesn't ask questions. If you answer into the camera, the audience re-acts. The reporter asked the question—why are you giving *me* the answer?

Another fine point—look at the reporter's eye that is closest to the camera. In normal conversation, we switch back and forth between the eyes of the person we talk to. If the camera zooms in very tightly, we will see your eyes darting back and forth. Shifty-eyed.

So stay with the reporter's eye nearest the camera. In this way, we will see more of your face, but you won't be looking at the camera.

Try not to blink too much. That can also be interpreted as a sign of stress or deception.

The Swivel Chair Hazard

Swivel chairs are a real hazard. You want to rock in them. Stress makes you twist back and forth while you rock. They squeak. The viewer gets seasick as you bob up and down on the tube. Avoid couches and overstuffed chairs where you sink so deeply your arms on the arms of the chair are at shoulder level. Looks like you're hanging from parallel bars.

Sit Up and Lean Forward

Don't lean back in the chair, whether it's hard or soft. Lean-ing back changes your body English. You tell us, without words, that you're not very enthusiastic about what you're saying. Re-member the E in the FACE formula. To convey a sense of energy and interest, lean slightly forward.

There's No Hurry

Take your time. If you start a sentence that gets tangled and confusing, start again. That's what editing is for.

If you don't understand the question, say so.

If you're nervous and your mouth is dry, stop for a drink of water. Keep thinking of the living room and the friend or neigh-bor you're talking to. That will relieve the nervousness. If the lights heat up the room and you begin to sweat, take time to wipe your face. Suggest that you take a break to let the air conditioner catch up. Once the camera is rolling, most people give up all control of their lives to the TV crew. Don't do that. Take more control. Like:

"You know, I gave you an answer several minutes ago that took me much too long to get to the point. If you'll ask me that same question again, I think I can give you a better, shorter answer."

Short and Simple

Try to talk in short, simple sentences. Corporate lawyers and judges have a tendency to speak in outlined, organized form—firstly, secondly, thirdly—or to label their points A, B and C. Suppose the reporter is only interested in your third point, and you've run the words together, so they can't edit out "thirdly." They may have to throw away the entire section.

Another common phrase: "As I said earlier." There's not enough time in a news story to let you say it twice. If you drop the "as I said earlier" in the middle of a sentence, the entire sentence will have to be dumped.

Talk to the Jury

Some of the best on-camera interviews are with trial lawyers who have spent their entire careers summing up complicated cases for jurors. They keep it short, and simple, conversational and colorful. They're good at one-sentence conclusions jurors will remember and repeat to each other in the jury room. For the main point, they let their feelings show.

Jurors are very much like those people sitting in front of the television set after a hard day's work. They're easily bored. They want it simple. They want it interesting. They want to know what it was really like. How did it feel?

Eliminate Parentheticals

Any kind of parenthetical thought can make a sentence too long for radio and television.

Example: "I've come to believe, *as most of my constituents do, who've had any experience with firearms,* that every person in this country has the God-given right to own a gun."

It will edit better if the senator says, "I believe every person in this country has the God-given right to own a gun. I'm sure

most of my constituents who've had any experience with firearms feel the same way." With this version, the reporter can use
either sentence, or both.

Anticipate a Why

Another technique that can help the editing process:
QUESTION: Then you will not vote, Senator, to outlaw Sat-
urday Night Specials?
ANSWER: No.
QUESTION: Why?
ANSWER: The Saturday Night Special is a phony issue.
QUESTION: Why do you say that?
ANSWER: Most policemen, and most store clerks are killed
with expensive weapons. Why should the poor homeowner be
denied a weapon he can afford to protect himself and his family?
If you give a "Yes" or "No" answer, it will almost always be
followed by "Why?" Anticipate the Why. And if you repeat the
question as part of your answer, it saves valuable response time
between questions and answers. This answer will enable the reporter to cram the entire response into about two-thirds as much
time:
QUESTION: Then you will not vote, Senator, to outlaw Saturday Night Specials?
ANSWER: I will never vote to outlaw Saturday Night Specials. They're a phony issue. Most policemen . . . etc.
Incorporating the question into your answer allows the reporter to drop the sound bite into the story without having to set
up what you were asked.

It May Not Be Today

Try not to date what you're saying, particularly if the interview will not be used today. If you talk about something that
happened "today," it won't be accurate if the story runs next
week.

Show Me While You Tell Me

What the audience *sees*, if you're genuine, may communicate
more than what they *hear.*

How To Speak TV, Print & Radio

Years ago, advertising agencies learned how to use visual signals in print. A lot can be said in a picture that doesn't require words. Because of television's time limitations, that technique has almost become a science.

Soft drink commercials aimed at teenagers use crowds of tanned, beautiful bodies having fun at the beach. One glance tells the target audience, "Kids who are good-looking, athletic, bright, popular—kids who have enough money to play in the surf with their boats or dune buggies—drink Fizzy Cola." All that in half a second, without speaking a single word.

Visual Shorthand

Politicians are learning to use visual symbolism that will carry over from their advertising to television news stories. When there is a flood or earthquake, it has become a tribal ritual for the governor—dressed in fatigues and combat boots—to survey the damage from a National Guard helicopter.

Is that really necessary? Can't governors get reports from experts who are better equipped to assess the damage? Yes, but we've come to expect it. If we don't see the governor, the President or the Vice President at the scene of the disaster, we think they don't care.

The Great Communicator

Ronald Reagan's popularity was helped immeasurably by his understanding of the camera and the need to be seen doing something rather than talking about it. Do you think he really liked to chop wood on his ranch in California? More likely, his media managers decided it would convey other, unspoken messages about him if he were photographed, early in his first term, clearing brush and chopping firewood. They frequently arranged for him to be photographed on horseback. The John Wayne image never hurt a politician.

The Clothes You Wear

The clothes you wear are part of the visual shorthand. Jimmy Carter liked to be interviewed in a plaid shirt and sweater. To enhance his "just plain folks" image, Carter always tried to carry a piece of luggage when he was embarking from a plane or helicopter even though a small army of aides and Secret Service agents were empty-handed.

Richard Nixon wanted to suggest a more regal kind of presidency. You sometimes wondered if he slept in a coat and tie.

In Early TV, Blue Was White

In the early days of television news, men were told to wear blue shirts. That's because they were shooting black-and-white film. A white shirt glowed in the harsh light and high-contrast film. A blue shirt *looked* white when the film was broadcast. With color cameras, white looks white, and blue looks blue.

Generally, your clothes for television should be subdued. Stay away from stripes and checks and bold prints. Don't over-dress. A business suit for an interview in your living room will seem as out-of-place as a tuxedo at Burger King. Your choice of what to wear will succeed if we can't remember what you were wearing.

Don't Get a Haircut

If you know the camera is coming, don't go to the beauty salon or the barber shop. We will probably be able to tell that you spruced up for the interview. This is a spontaneous, unrehearsed conversation, not a portrait gallery.

Flashy Jewelry Distracts

The goal: Don't let anything about your appearance distract from what you're saying. Large, flashy jewelry is so distracting we may not remember anything you said.

Wear Your Eyeglasses

If you normally wear glasses, wear them for the interview. Without them, your eyes will have to work harder, and you may look very strange.

But don't wear dark glasses for TV interviews. In this culture, you're supposed to look people in the eye when you talk to them. The stereotyped movie hoodlum wears dark glasses during conversations—perhaps to hide the evil thoughts his eyes would reveal if we could see them.

How To Speak TV, Print & Radio

Prescription glasses that darken in sunlight may also turn dark in TV lights. If you have that kind of glasses and know you'll be talking to a camera often, you should buy another pair with regular lenses.

Squinting in Sunlight

If you're being interviewed in bright sunlight, it is almost impossible not to squint. Try this:

Just before the camera starts rolling, close your eyes and look up at the sun. The bright light, coming through your closed eyelids, will contract your pupils. When the camera is rolling, bring your head back down and open your eyes. The pupils will stay contracted for a short time, and you won't sense the glare as much. If you have to talk very long, though, you'll start squinting again.

Suntans vs. Sunburns

A suntan makes you look healthier and younger. A sunburn makes your skin shiny and puffy.

In-Studio Makeup

For field interviews, men don't normally use makeup. Women should use the same makeup they'd wear to work. But in the harsh lights of a TV studio, you'll look strange without special attention to makeup. (See **SKILLS/Talk Shows**)

In the TV Studio

Interviews in the studio use many of the same techniques as field interviews, but are different in many ways. You need to understand the differences. Some field interview techniques used in a talk show will make you look like a wind-up toy. (For a preview of what the TV studio is going to feel like and the difference in techniques, see **SKILLS/Talk Shows**)

Live Remotes

The most difficult of all TV interviews is the live remote. Most local stations now have the ability to beam back to the studio audio and video that can be broadcast live during the newscast. Microwave systems were the first "Live Eye" employed by local stations in the 1970s. In this kind of system, a standard portable videotape camera is plugged into a microwave transmitter system, usually carried in a van. There is a collapsible antenna that telescopes 50 feet in the air from the roof of the van.

Microwave Problems

The microwave signal must then be aimed at the station's receiving antenna. Mountains and buildings can block the signal and make it impossible to transmit from some spots. The antenna sending the microwave beam must be on a line of sight with the receiving antenna. Back at the station, the microwave signal is converted to the broadcast frequency and re-broadcast with no time delay.

Satellites Do It Better

In the mid-1980s, satellite technology became a much better way for stations to beam video and audio back to the station. New portable transmitters became small enough to mount on a van. The stations rent time on satellites in space that can relay back to the station from anywhere in the world what their camera is shooting.

Until this technology was available, the networks were the only source of instant video from international points. As more stations invest in satellite equipment for live shots, they send local reporters to other countries for the local angle on stories. In effect, they are competing with the networks. In the past, networks provided news coverage the local stations couldn't reach for broadcast the same day. Now that they can get it themselves, the role of network news is being re-assessed. (See **INSIDE THE MEDIA/Networks**)

The Toughest Interview

The toughest form of live interview involves your having a conversation with an anchor back in the studio. In this format, you talk to the camera lens and it looks like you're talking to the anchor.

You'll have to wear an earphone to hear the anchor. Television reporters have their earphones custom-molded, like a hearing aid, to improve the quality of the sound.

A Better Ear Bug

But they'll give you a clumsy ear "bug" with a bent wire that hangs it loosely over your ear. It will be hard to hear what the anchor is saying. You often see live shots where the person on the street has one hand pressing an ear, head tilted. Pushing the earphone tighter, struggling to hear.

If you know you're going to be interviewed regularly in live shots, it's a good investment to have a custom earphone made. Call a local news director and ask where reporters get theirs, and any special technical requirements.

The earphone has other uses. I have an adapter so I can use mine on long flights to listen to music or the in-flight movie audio. It's much more comfortable than the earphones the airlines give you. It can also be adapted to listen to a portable audio or video tape recorder.

Quickly, Quickly!

If your interview is a live shot, the pressure to condense is greater than in any other interview form. Remember, everything you say is broadcast instantly. There's no chance to edit, and very little opportunity to use cutaways and other video techniques that can keep viewers visually interested while you talk. Many TV news producers believe there is absolutely nothing more boring than a "talking head." If you're not quick, they'll cut you off.

It takes practice to be good at it.

SKILLS

INTERVIEWS-GENERAL

Quotable Quotes That Won't Be Misquoted

When reporters want an interview, the most basic rule is: **Give Yourself Time to Think Before You Talk**. The quotes that people regret are usually said reflexively, in the heat of anger or the shock that follows a rude surprise or sudden loss. If you can stall for even five minutes, you'll do a better job of speaking for yourself or your organization.

If Your Pulse Races, Pause

The rule is especially critical if the reporter's first question makes your adrenaline or pulse rate jump. You don't think well when you're in the fight or flee mode. You need a little time to get back to normal—to get your thoughts together.

If the reporter shows up unexpectedly, find an excuse to delay for a few minutes. (See **SKILLS/Defending Yourself** for ambush interview tactics) If the reporter calls on the phone, say you'll call back in five or 10 minutes. From that initial contact with the reporter, you'll have some idea of what the story is about. Find out as much as you can, then spend a few minutes getting ready.

One Sentence, No Breath

Use the time to decide what you really want to say. Boil it down to one sentence you can speak without taking a breath. That one sentence will then become the base of the interview. Other thoughts will branch out from it. You'll want to keep coming back to it. Explaining it. Expanding it.

You may also need some time to check with staffers. "A reporter just called. The lead they're pursuing caught me completely by surprise. Is there something I should know?" The delay rule isn't necessary if the reporter's request is for simple information that poses no threat. But if you react viscerally, buy some time.

Telephone Interviews

Most of your routine interviews will probably be done on the telephone. Reporters save a lot of time by gathering quotes and information this way. Be careful. A reporter on the telephone is less threatening than in person. Many people are less cautious when they can't see the reporter. They get sloppy. They say things they later regret.

If the interview is critical to you or your organization, *do it in person.* It's much easier for you to get a handle on the reporter and the story angle if you're face-to-face.

If you don't recognize the name or voice of the reporter on the phone and the story is sensitive, use the delay tactic. When you return the call, use the newspaper or broadcast station's general number. The number the reporter left is probably a straight line bypassing the switchboard. Ask the switchboard operator for the reporter by name to make sure the call was legitimate. Private eyes, insurance investigators, and your competitors sometimes pose as journalists.

Are You Being Taped?

You should know whether the reporter is recording the interview at the other end of the phone line. In some states, you don't have to tell the other party you're recording. If your state has more restrictive laws, you commit a crime if you don't notify the other person. (See **INSIDE THE MEDIA/Privacy**)

Ambushes on Radio

Radio talk show hosts delight in calling people—particularly public officials—for an instant, live interview. FCC regulations require them to tell you you're on the air. Which means instant stress. It's radio's version of the ambush interview. Review the ambush interview portion of **SKILLS/Defending Yourself.** The suggestions for dealing with a TV ambush can easily be adapted for radio.

Once you begin a telephone or face-to-face interview, where you've had time to think about what you want to say, the next rule is: **Conduct a Pre-Interview-Interview.**

What's This Story About?

From the first contact, where you arranged to delay the interview for a few minutes, you know generally what the story is about. Expand that inquiry. Weave it into the social chat that begins most conversations. While a television photographer is setting up the lights and camera, talk to the reporter about the story at hand. I call it the pre-interview-interview.

If you understand what the reporter is after, you can save a lot of time and anxiety. You need to find out as much as you can about the reporter's:

- Intelligence.
- Experience.
- Knowledge of the subject.
- Preconceptions about the story.
- Other sources.
- Deadline.
- Scheduled publication date or broadcast time.

Are They Here To Hurt You?

Is the reporter here to gut you, or does the story need your quotes to give it authority and credibility? If you discover the reporter knows very little about the subject matter, the way you structure the pre-interview-interview will strongly influence the questions when the real interview begins.

The room will sound like an echo chamber. The reporter will ask you questions that let you repeat what you said before the note-taking or recording began. That's all the reporter knows to ask.

Pre-interview Ethics

It is considered unethical for a reporter to tell you exactly what the questions will be. The interview is supposed to be a spontaneous conversation. To rehearse either questions or answers is staging. But there is a fine line here. Most reporters consider it proper to tell you the subject they're covering and broad areas they want to explore in the interview.

Remember, the reporter will also be sizing you up. And the impression you give in those first few minutes will be critical to the slant on the story. (See **SKILLS/Media Morality** for personality traits reporters love and despise)

The pre-interview-interview is the time for names, addresses and statistics.

Have Your Staff Handy

For stories that involve a lot of numbers or complicated, technical details, it's a good idea to have your staff experts sit in. They can hand you documents when you grope for the right number. You can ask them to fetch something the reporter needs for the story. Having someone friendly in your corner may also make you feel more at ease and less threatened.

The Perennial Question

In the Foreword of this book, I estimated that about 35,000 people are interviewed by the news media in America every day.

This is hard to believe, but I already know exactly what the reporters are going to ask in about 80 per cent of those interviews. It doesn't matter where the interview takes place. Doesn't matter who the reporter is—who is being interviewed—doesn't even matter what the story is about. I know the key question they're going to ask you.

How Does It Feel?

How does it feel?

The perennial question was institutionalized by a television news story formula—the Sony Sandwich. (See diagram in **SKILLS/Interviews-Broadcast**) It has now spread to all news media. The meat in the Sony Sandwich is the interview in the middle. It gives the story flavor, substance, emotion, humanity. It is sandwiched between the facts the reporter gives at the beginning, and the conclusion the reporter draws at the end.

The Sony Sandwich

The reporters sets up the basic facts for the reader, the viewer, the listener. Then we go to the central figure in the story.
How does it feel to be told you have terminal cancer?
(On election night) How does it feel to lose after 24 years in the Senate?
How does it feel to win the New York lottery?

The Top on the Sandwich

Then the reporter puts the top on the sandwich by drawing the conclusion, telling us where the story goes from here.

Print reporters once laughed and made fun of broadcast reporters who always asked, "How do you feel?" But you'll hear newspaper and magazine reporters asking it now, too.

Television has changed the format for all news media. Newspaper stories today are much shorter. They use more pictures and graphics. To compress their stories—just as broadcasters do—they've adapted the Sony Sandwich to print. If you can learn how to speak media language, and give a formula response to the formula question, you almost guarantee they'll use what you said, exactly as you said it. No editing or taking out of context. It is the best self-defense technique to avoid being misquoted.

Disguising the Question

Reporters are so aware of their trite question, they try to disguise it. But it is still the same search for that magic quote that will give the story warmth and emotion—the human perspective.

Tell me what you were thinking when the section of the airplane just ahead of you blew out? When the officer walked in the door with your baby in his arms, what was it like? How does it feel to do what you did . . . see what you saw . . . hear what you heard?

What Was It Like?

Someday, I may be in that same place, going through that same dramatic experience.

How To Speak TV, Print & Radio

More than anything else the reporter can tell us, we want to know what it was like to be there. That has always been the essence of story-telling. If a ghost story is told skillfully, I shudder and look over my shoulder in the dark. Tell me the story of a blind child who can see for the first time, and I get a lump in my throat. When she tells me what she's feeling, I may cry.

Few people outside the news media understand this basic purpose for the interview.

Verbal Shorthand

Words that express feeling tell us a lot very quickly. They are verbal shorthand—headline words that communicate like no others in our language.

When the reporter asks how you feel about something, he is asking, "What do you think about this?—What is your reaction to the situation?—What is your opinion?" But we will understand your reaction—your opinion—your conclusion—much more clearly if you tell us how you FEEL. There are lots of words that express feeling in our language. A sample—

Words That Say How You Feel

Abandoned	Abused
Aggravated	Afraid
Alienated	Alone
Amazed	Ambushed
Amused	Angry
Anxious	Ashamed
Astonished	Astounded
Besieged	Betrayed
Bored	Burned out
Caught in the middle	Certain
Chagrined	Cheated
Confident	Confused
Cozy	Crazy
Dazzled	Deceived
Delighted	Deserted
Disappointed	Dismayed
Disorganized	Elated

More Words To Convey Feeling

Embarrassed
Energized
Envious
Exhausted
Fearful
Frantic
Frightened
Grateful
Grief-stricken
Happy
Hate (I hate it!)
High
Hopeful
Horrendous
Hounded
Humiliated
Impatient
Ineffective
Inspired
Invaded
Jaded
Joyful
Justified
Lonely
Loser (Like a loser)
Mad
Mortified
Naked
Offended
Optimistic
Outgunned
Outraged
Overwhelmed
Parental
Pessimistic
Powerful
Prepared
Proud
Put out
Ready

Encouraged
Enthusiastic
Excited
Exposed
Fed up
Friendly
Glad
Great!
Guilty
Harried
Helpless
Homicidal
Hopeless
Horrible
Humble
Hurt
Impotent
Insecure
Intrigued
Isolated
Jealous
Jubilant
Livid
Love (I love it!)
Lucky
Marvelous
Mystified
Nauseated
On top of the world
Out of touch
Outnumbered
Overjoyed
Paranoid
Peeved
Pleased
Powerless
Protected
Put down
Puzzled
Regret

Tell Me How You Feel

Rejoice	Rejuvenated
Relieved	Resentful
Responsive	Rested
Sad	Satisfied
Scared	Secure
Sick	Skeptical
Stupid	Supportive
Sure	Surprised
Surrounded	Sympathetic
Terrible	Terrific
Terrified	Tired
Torn	Uncertain
Under control	Undone
Unjustly accused	Unwanted
Unworthy	Used
Victimized	Victorious
Vulnerable	Warm
Weak	Weary
Weepy	Winner (Like a winner)
Wonderful	Worried
Worn out	Wounded

Condition Words

Some of the feeling words in the list above are not real feelings. Rather, they are conditions that convey several emotions or strong feelings. When you say, "I feel betrayed," you tell us—with just one word—you feel angry, deceived, abandoned, vulnerable.

When you say, "I feel disorganized," you tell us you are feeling out of control, insecure, pressured to put things in order.

Interviews add flavor and spice to a story. Once the conflict, the catastrophe, the crisis are established, we want to hear the participants. We want to know how they feel about it.

Quotes They'll Use for Sure:

• "I'm embarrassed. The mayor has made a terrible mistake, and we're all going to suffer for it." Or:

- "I'm serious about this. When I'm President, every animal in the country will be wearing clothes to hide his nudity. You'll see." Or:
  - "It's frightening. This guy is completely bonkers."
  - "I wasn't afraid. I was terribly sad. Just before we hit the water, all I could think about was that I'd never see my son again."
  - "I feel like a kid again. You know, like I've got a whole new life ahead of me."

A Word of Caution:

There are a few rare times when showing too much emotion on camera can be hazardous to your career. We don't expect a homicide detective to break down at a murder scene. Unless the victim is his partner, or his own child.

Edmund Muskie may have lost his campaign for the Democratic presidential nomination in 1972 when he cried in the snow in New Hampshire as he talked about a newspaper editorial that had defamed his wife. That might be acceptable for some professions, but we expected the President in those days to be tougher than that.

The Rules are Changing

Society's expectations are changing. During the 1988 presidential debates, Gov. Michael Dukakis—an opponent of capital punishment—was asked how he would feel on that issue if his wife was a rape or murder victim.

Dukakis showed no emotion. His answer was academic, distant, unfeeling. People in the audience said to themselves, What sort of man is this, who doesn't react to the idea of his wife being violated or killed? One of his nicknames in the campaign was "Zorba the accountant." In that same campaign, George Bush's media experts asked focus groups what kind of President they wanted. One of their top priorities was a sensitive, caring President.

Bush, the Caring Candidate

In television interviews, Bush began to talk about his family as sensitive, caring people. The Bushes, he said, show what they feel. Sometimes they cry in public. His saying that drew a sharp contrast between himself and Dukakis.

At a church service hours before his inauguration in 1993, a TV close-up showed tears running down the cheeks of President Bill Clinton.

Schwarzkopf's Tears

The most dramatic demonstration of how the rules are changing came during Barbara Walters' interview in Arabia with Gen. Norman Schwarzkopf shortly after the Persian Gulf War ended in 1991. "Stormin' Norman" talked about how much he missed his family, half a world away, and the tears welled in his eyes. When Walters asked about his dead father, who had also been a general, the tears came again. "I'm sure he'd be proud of me," Schwarzkopf said, his lower lip trembling.

There was a long pause in the interview. "You know," Walters said, "The old picture of generals—is that generals don't cry."

"Sure they do," Schwarzkopf shot back, listing names and places. Ulysses Grant after the battle of Shiloh. William Tecumseh Sherman. "And these were the tough old guys. Lee cried at the loss of human life, the pressures that were brought to bear. Lincoln cried. And frankly, any man that doesn't cry scares me a little bit. I don't think I would like a man who was incapable of enough emotion to get tears in his eyes every now and then. That's not a human being."

Women are caught in a cross-fire as the culture shifts. Cry at the office and the men in power are likely to invoke the old standards that said showing emotion was a sign of weakness. "Just like a woman," they mutter under their breath.

Quotes Without Misquotes

My goal for you is to craft quotes that will be used, and used exactly as you spoke them.

The formula that reporters use is so predictable, I make a bet with my seminar groups: Send me a transcript of your next media interview. Print, radio, TV. Doesn't matter. I'll bet you a steak dinner I can pick the quote the reporter uses.

Reporters are constantly looking for that quote that will tell us how you feel about the issue.

SKILLS

INTERVIEWS-PRINT

No, You Can't Talk To My Psychiatrist

Compared to broadcasting, print interviews can be a very lengthy process. To compete with broadcasting's immediacy, newspapers and magazines go overboard with detail. Minute trivia is showcased. It's common for print stories to tell us what brand of cigaret the interviewee smokes and just how the smoke is inhaled. The brand of tires on the car. The designer of the dress. How many centimeters from the victim's hand the gun was lying.

The Luxury of Time

Print reporters have a luxury that few broadcast reporters ever have—the luxury of time. Lots of time to research and write the story. Writers at newspapers like *The Wall Street Journal* and *Washington Post* may work on one feature story for weeks. Investigative projects can take more than a year.

Another reason for this kind of trivia is an effort to draw a picture with words. Many newspaper editors are still not interested in pictures. They are word people. They simply don't understand the impact of pictures. When they have good photos, they don't know how to display them to their best advantage.

In television, the reporter and photographer work closely as a team. Without pictures, the reporter has no story. Every word the TV reporter writes must have a picture to go with it. The reporter and photographer map out ahead just what they'll need to illustrate the story. Pictures tell us more than the words.

Separate Words, Pictures

In newspapers, reporter and photographer generally work separately. Even at a breaking news story like a plane crash or building collapse, they go to the scene in separate cars and have little contact with each other. They bring their work to an editor independently. It is the editor's task to merge the words and pictures.

Print reporters' obsession with trivia can be a real pain. They may want to just hang around and watch everything you do for several days. They'll want to talk to your spouse, your children, your boss, your employees, your parents and your psychiatrist.

Drawing the Boundaries

You may have to decide just how much time and privacy you're willing to give up. Early in your contact with the reporter, you may want to diplomatically draw some boundaries. Celebrities often do this to protect their families.

Remember that barring a door often whets the appetite of a reporter to get inside. (See **STRATEGY/Ten Commandments of Media Relations**) But knowing very early how the reporter views the assignment—the talent and experience the reporter brings to the story—can help you make that decision. (See pre-interview-interviews in **SKILLS/Interviews-General**)

Print Is More Tenacious

Print reporters are often much more tenacious than broadcast reporters. The luxury of time permits them to doggedly stick with a rumor, trying to prove it's true. Broadcast reporters will usually be pulled off and sent to another story if they don't find what they're looking for quickly.

In the mid-1980s, everyone wanted to buy a TV station and be a media mogul. Many were bought at ludicrously high prices. The owners are now having a hard time making the mortgage payments and reaping the profits they thought they'd make when they acquired the stations. So there's a real emphasis on pushing every employee to be as productive as possible. That often rules out any serious investigative reporting at those stations.

Experts With a Specialty

Reporters at the larger newspapers are generally better educated and more experienced than their broadcast competition.

They are experts who develop a specialty. Police reporters do nothing but crime and law enforcement stories. Reporters on the school beat may know more about schools than members of the School Board. The school beat is a full-time job. School Board members may serve part-time.

When you know a print reporter will be interviewing you as part of a major assignment, it saves time if you can supply written material before the interview. Collect data that will educate the reporter. Supply history and statistics. Arrange other interviews with staff who are technicians. When the reporter is ready to do your interview, it will save a lot of time.

Charming and Disarming

Good reporters—both print and broadcast—know how to be very charming and disarming. With the luxury of time, newspaper and magazine reporters will begin to seem like old friends. They'll hang around a lot. Have meals, drinks and coffee with you. Their goal may be to get your guard down. Don't get defensive. Just be aware. That's their job.

In a confrontation with a newspaper or magazine, a written statement can be effective. If we don't see you on TV or hear you on radio, it seems like you're hiding. Quotes from a written statement in print don't telegraph that same message. Even if the story points it out, few readers will care that you issued a written statement rather than be interviewed.

Questions in Writing

If you refuse to be interviewed, you can offer to answer written questions in writing. This can avoid a slip of the tongue in a touchy situation.

You may want to grant an interview with certain restrictions. Remember, the ground rules must be agreed on by both parties in advance. You can't talk to a reporter, then ask that part of what you said be forgotten. (See **SKILLS/Off-the-Record**)

Newspapers keep mug shots in their libraries. Often they're old and unflattering. If you don't like the picture they dig out of the library, send a new, more flattering one. The cover letter should say the old shot is out of date, and you're offering an updated one. During an interview, if the reporter doesn't ask about shooting your picture to go with the story, you may want to offer a picture. Portrait photography is not what they're interested in. The picture you offer will have a much better chance of being used if it's more candid and informal.

The same may be true of an old report on your company or department. Send the latest one, just to keep in their files.

While most daily newspapers won't print news releases verbatim, they'll often reproduce graphic material you hand out. To emphasize your points in an interview, give the reporter copies of graphs and charts that illustrate your point. (See **STRATEGY/ Selling Your Story**)

SKILLS

MEDIA MORALITY

Saints and Sinners
As the Media See Them

I often tell my audiences I teach human relations more than news media relations. How you deal with a reporter in the first few minutes will have enormous impact on the story. Reporters claim to be unbiased and objective. But no matter how hard they try to meet that goal, they are inevitably affected by their personal experience and their first impressions.

Media Morality

The news media have developed their own morality. Good Guys and Bad Guys. Your action, your body language, the words you choose lead them to quickly stereotype you. It is an instinct developed over years of experience. They take pride in being able to size you up in a few moments.

The story may not say outright that you are a Saint or Sinner. But the trivia that is noted, in words or pictures, will make the point very clearly. A lot is written between the lines in media coverage.

Of course, they're sometimes wrong. But that first impression will be passed on to their readers, viewers and listeners. Once the perception is transmitted to the public, it is very, very hard to change.

Perception Becomes Reality

In a mass communications society, the perception becomes the reality.

In the cowboy movies of the 30s and 40s, Good Guys wore white hats; Bad Guys, black hats. There were no shades of gray.

Good Guys did not smoke, drink or swear. They were chivalrous, brave, honest, idealistic, clean-shaven, and fresh-scrubbed.

How To Speak TV, Print & Radio

No matter how dusty the trail, their rhinestone-studded outfits looked like they just came from the cleaners.

Bad Guys smoked foul cigars, slugged down rot-guy whisky and muttered oaths behind scowling eyebrows. They slapped women around, were bullies and cowards (it always took two or three to duke it out with one Good Guy), cheated and stole from their partners and their mothers.

You could tell immediately, with just a glance, whether they were Good Guys or Bad Guys. The news media have set up a very similar morality play.

THE MEDIA MORALITY SCALE

GOOD GUYS	BAD GUYS
Caring. Sensitive to human values, quality of life.	Lust after money and power. Insensitive to human needs.
David vs. Goliath. Underdogs willing to Fight City Hall.	Bullies. Enjoy taking advantage of little people.
Risk-takers, particularly with their jobs or financial security. Unconcerned about social status.	Unwilling to take risks if they will jeopardize their job, financial security or social status.
Rugged individualists, to the point of eccentricity.	Conformists who worship rules and red tape. Intellectually limited.
Idealists who do what is morally right in their view.	No conscience. Will follow the party line or boss's orders.
Candid. Open. Willing to admit mistakes.	Secretive. Evasive. Unable to admit fault.
Fierce competitors who expect to win against all odds.	Wimps who think of themselves as losers and give up easily.

Let's look now at seven perceptions that can make you a Good Guy or a Bad Guy in those first few moments with a reporter:

1—Sensitive and Caring

Good Guys care about people. They forget costs when human pain and suffering are involved. They are sensitive to human needs and place them above profits or career.

Bad Guys love money and power. When was the last time an American movie or novel portrayed the corporate president as a warm, loving, sensitive individual who cares about children, puppies, clean air and water? American mythology says insensitive executives care only about themselves and their money/company/power/career. They never had time to invest in their children or their spouses.

They got to the top by stabbing their colleagues in the back, and climbing up the pyramid of dead bodies to the executive suite. They do not care about pain, or poverty, death or destruction—so long as it is not theirs. That is one of the myths that can be easily reinforced by how you appear in the media.

The Exxon PR Disaster

The most devastating public relations disaster after the 1989 oil spill in Alaska was Exxon executives who seemed insensitive to the damage spreading along the coastline.

In their immaculate coats and ties, they suggested it was a minor thing, a drop in the ocean. Seconds later, we were shown the oil-covered bodies of birds and animals; the fear and anguish of oil-soaked fishermen who would not be able to pay their mortgages next month. The insensitive Exxon executives stoked our sense of outrage. They fit precisely the old corporate executive stereotype.

Reporters Side With Victims

Reporters identify with society's victims. The victims are news. Victims of natural disasters, medical malpractice, corporate policy, governmental incompetence are news. They generally are open to reporters, because they know the story may help them.

How To Speak TV, Print & Radio

Reporters spend time with them and get to know them as human beings.

The people who run large organizations often make themselves inaccessible to the media. Most reporters have never spent even half a day with a corporate president, a general, a governor, the director of the Central Intelligence Agency. They are distant, two-dimensional figures. Because reporters do not know about their human side, they make easy targets. Nothing happens to displace society's myths about them.

2—Courageous Underdogs

The David vs. Goliath story appeals to most Americans. That was the theme of the "Rocky" movies. We admire the town marshal who will go out alone to face the outlaw gang in the street. We love the housewife who fights City Hall. The kids who defy the zoning department with their lemonade stand. The dark horse who wins the derby or the political campaign.

Bad Guys are bullies. They take advantage of little people. They abuse their power and get great pleasure out of it. They boast about their position and wealth. If the boast is not verbal, their possessions and corporate perks speak louder than words. Too much money, too much power are never enough.

Ralph Nader—Media Saint

Ralph Nader is probably our most revered media saint. Nader, the poor, young, bright, eccentric writes a book—"Unsafe at Any Speed"—that attacks General Motors. The book contends that GM produces cars with deadly design flaws; that the company is more interested in shaving costs than saving lives (Moral # 1). He is David, choosing the stones for his slingshot while Goliath GM sets out to destroy him and discredit his book. With help from the news media, Nader hits GM between the eyes. The corporate giant is staggered. Corvairs go out of production. Seat belts and head rests become standard equipment.

The bigger they are, the harder they fall.

3—Risk-Takers

Good Guys are risk-takers. Adventurers. They live on the edge. They thumb their nose at the boss, or company policy, if it feels good. They're not afraid to fail. They know they can find another job if they lose this one.

Bad Guys are afraid of losing their jobs. The job is more important than almost anything. They will sit silently and watch terrible atrocities take place, if it means risking their position in the organization. This is a side effect of Moral # 1. Bad Guys are security-centered. Cowards.

Fire Me, I Don't Care

Newspaper reporters are paid so little they have absolutely no fear of losing their jobs. They become fiercely independent. They have great contempt for the executive who puts his job above his convictions, whether in government or the private sector. Looking forward to retirement is not in their value system. Those who do, in their thinking, are burned out or incompetent.

In TV, Firing is No Disgrace

Television news is one of the few professions where being fired is not a disgrace. It comes with the territory. When ratings begin to slip, management shuffles people, looking for a winning combination. The shuffling is constant. Television people, unlike those in newspapers, work on a short-term contract. Some of television's brightest, most successful stars were fired from TV jobs early in their careers.

4—Rugged Individualists

Good Guys are rugged individualists who do things their way. They are rebels with glorious causes. They hate red tape, and will find ingenious ways to short-circuit the system to get things done. They love to tweak the nose of pompous authority.

Eccentrics who run for public office or keep trying to patent the Original Perpetual Motion Machine often get warm, amused, but-you-have-to-admire-them coverage because they display this trait.

Reporters identify with it because good reporting requires a certain amount of individualism. Reporters in the field have very little close supervision. Good reporters are self-starters. Those who are innovative, willing to try anything, often get the story. They leave their habit-bound competitors in the dust.

How To Speak TV, Print & Radio

Bad Guys Are Conformists

This is a side effect of Numbers 1 and 3. Bad Guys do things by the rules, no matter what the cost in human terms. They believe that one broken rule can lead to the breakdown of the entire system.

Bad Guys wallow in red tape. This part of Russian life was frequently reported as a way to laugh at Russian society during the Cold War. It is still popular in reporting about new, inexperienced officials in Third World countries. Journalists sneer at this value system. They have a snobbish belief that those who follow it are corporate drones, cannon fodder, bumbling bureaucrats, not the brightest people in the world. Bad Guys slavishly follow the rules because they are not bright enough to function without a manual that guides them, step-by-step.

This journalistic prejudice often appears between the lines in stories dealing with religious zealots, union organizers, and military officers.

5—Idealists

Good Guys are idealists who sight on a personal star and never waver. They are persistent. Dedicated.

Bad Guys have no real conscience or moral value. They do whatever the job, the boss, the party require.

6—Candid and Open

Good Guys are candid and open. They have nothing to hide. Their lives and their organizations are an open book. One of the most disarming tactics you can take with a reporter who seems antagonistic is to offer access to everything. It confuses the media morality radar.

Good Guys sometimes make mistakes, but they're big enough to take responsibility for the mistake and put it right.

Bad Guys are secretive and evasive. People who are guilty skulk in the shadows. They do not want their pictures taken. They growl at the sight of a reporter or photographer. They run. They refuse to disclose information about themselves or their employer. They sic their bodyguards or attack dogs on representatives of the media. To truly be memorialized as a Bad Guy, put your hand over the camera lens and throw the photographer out of your office.

Bad Guys try to cover their mistakes.

7—Expect to Win

Good Guys are fierce competitors, even when they're at a severe disadvantage. They pick themselves up and charge once more against enormous odds. They expect to win. They never give up.

Bad Guys see themselves as losers. They're wimps. They're burned out. They don't even try any more.

Reporters believe it is their duty to put losers out of their misery. It's a dirty job, but somebody has to do it.

They also feel some responsibility to encourage winners. The story will have much more human interest appeal if the underdog wins through sheer force of will.

Most reporters are fierce competitors themselves. The business is so competitive, they don't last very long if winning is not a priority.

My analysis of Media Morality fits closely with **STRATEGY/ Ten Commandments of Media Relations.**

SKILLS

NEWS CONFERENCES

Productions That Sing and Dance

News conferences are a necessary evil. Good reporters don't like them. Everybody will come away with the same story. Most reporters need to win. To beat the competition. Stand out from the pack. But news conferences are efficient. It would take all day to give individual interviews to four television stations, a dozen radio stations, and two newspapers. So you do them all at once at a news conference.

Use Media Competition

News conferences are also a way for you to take advantage of the fierce competition between the media. If the story is marginal, they may all use it to prevent their competitors from having a story they don't have.

When the reporter returns from a news conference, the producer or city editor wants to know, "Who was there?"

"Everybody," the reporter says.

The producer or city editor had been lukewarm on this story. Competition changes that. "Maybe this is a better story than I think. To be on the safe side, I'll run it."

Neat, Convenient Packages

News conferences offer some real advantages. You can provide several people, in one place, that reporters need to talk to. Properly produced, a news conference provides for a reporter all the elements needed for a story in one neat, convenient package.

Suppose you had to choose between a story that will take a lot of legwork and one that's easy. Both of them are fairly equal in news value. On most days, if you're the assignment editor or city editor, you'll take the easy one.

Now, the Disadvantages

News conferences also have some disadvantages. They're much less intimate.

If you call a specific reporter to suggest a story, you get to pick the reporter. At a news conference, you never know who they'll send.

In a news conference crowd, you can't give reporters you trust confidential background material. If you're under attack, and the mob of reporters and photographers smell blood, you can lose control.

You should think of a news conference as a stage production. It needs a script, a cast, a director, a theater, props, and an audience.

First, a Script

Decide what you want to say. Outline it. Write the outline in the same form used for plays and TV. What the characters say is in the right-hand column of the page. What the audience will be seeing while the characters speak is opposite the spoken words, on the left-hand side of the page. (See sample script in **INSIDE THE MEDIA/Newscast**)

Choose a Cast

Movies, plays and TV shows have a cast of characters. Each is necessary to tell the audience what the author wants them to hear and understand. To move the plot along. Each member of the cast is chosen very carefully. Talent, experience, and audience appeal all play a part.

The Director's Role

Good news conferences need a director. A stage manager who supervises the production. The director is often the public relations director or public information officer. The director's job includes: notifying the media, preparing the room, distributing the handouts, establishing the ground rules, introducing the cast, and closing the news conference when a pre-set time is reached, or when questions taper off. (See **STRATEGY/PIOS**)

Good Props Are Vital

Trial lawyers have learned that juries are more convinced by evidence than by witnesses. Witnesses have faulty memories. With sharp cross-examination, witnesses can become confused. If two witnesses contradict each other, who's telling the truth?

But hard evidence—documents, pictures, the murder weapon—can be touched and studied by the jurors. Evidence can be carried back into the jury room during deliberations.

Reporters Are Like Jurors

If you're under attack, the group of reporters at a news conference is very much like the jury at a trial. They've already heard the plaintiff's or prosecutor's side. Now they're ready to hear your side. Persuade them with the right witnesses AND ESPECIALLY THE RIGHT EVIDENCE.

You need to use props all through the news conference. Refer to the charts and graphs. Hold up the broken part that caused the crash so all the world can see it.

A Cure for Broken Hearts

Suppose your company is announcing a major medical breakthrough. You have perfected a small pump that can replace an ailing human heart.

Show us the new artificial heart. A device so small it fits in the patient's chest and runs for a year on an inexpensive battery. Let reporters handle it.

Bring the frisky German shepherd in whom the prototype was implanted three years ago. Let the media photograph and play with him.

Make sure the cast includes the inventor who toiled in a garage for 20 years. Let us hear about the failures and disappointment, until the night the inventor woke out of a sound sleep, knowing immediately how to solve the critical problem.

The new idea was tried. It worked. Guaranteed question:

"How did you feel at that moment?"
The answer is a guaranteed quote and sound bite.
Here are some suggested guidelines—

What Deserves a Conference?

News conferences should be called only for stories that all media will consider important. BEWARE false alarms. If you call news conferences for stories that don't merit them, you'll seem like the boy who cried, "Wolf." Next time you call a news conference to announce a cure for cancer, nobody will come. They've been burned before.

Alerting the News Media

If possible, alert the **CITY EDITOR** at the newspaper and the **ASSIGNMENT EDITOR** at radio and TV stations, in writing a day or two in advance. Just a simple note. We will hold a news conference at a certain time and place to discuss a certain topic. Say who will be there to answer reporters' questions.

Don't be vague or mysterious. You need to sell the idea to the editor. There may not be enough staff to gamble on an unsure story idea. If your note clearly explains why this is a good story, they'll be there.

Call the assignment and city editors the day of the news conference, to remind and update them.

If there's not enough time for a written announcement, do it by phone. If you've got a hot topic, they'll be there.

The Earlier, the Better

If you want the story to break on the noon news and in the afternoon newspaper, call your conference no later than 10 a.m. Nine or 9:30 is better.

If you want the story to break on the evening news and in tomorrow morning's newspaper, call your conference no later than 3 p.m. One-thirty or 2 p.m. is better.

Let's look at the timetable—If you begin at three, the television crew may not be able to break down their gear and get away before four. A 30-minute drive back to the station gets the writing started at 4:30. Script finished and approved by 5:15 means only 45 minutes to edit, during the worst traffic jam of the day in the editing booths. If other stories are breaking late that day, your news conference may have a tough time competing.

In a crunch, a daily, 90-second news story can be slapped together in 15 minutes. But it looks like it. Since a news conference can be called at any time, the earlier you set it, the more care and attention the story will have.

Choose The Right Place

Where you hold the press conference is also important. Most of them are set in big, bare rooms. It's sort of like eating at McDonald's. You've seen one, you've seen them all.

Think about the way television reporters shoot their standups. If the story involves a trial, we see the courthouse over the reporter's shoulder. Network correspondents who cover the President do their standups on the lawn of the White House. At space shots or political conventions, we see the launch pad or the banners in the background.

It is a kind of visual shorthand that television has developed. It says the reporter was actually there. It suggests that being there makes you a real authority.

Place Gives You Credibility

With a news conference, you can sometimes do the same thing. If you're an officer in the longshoremen's union, hold your news conference on the docks, so we can see the ships docked at the wharf behind you. If you're a military officer, have the tools of your trade in the background—a tank, a fighter plane, a submarine.

If you're a cop, talking about street crime, go to the most violent neighborhood in your community and talk about the problem on the street, where it happens. It tells viewers you know what you're talking about. You've been there.

That kind of field location is not always possible. A television camera is a magnet for kids, who swarm to get in front of the lens. Grinning, jumping, waving, yelling "Hi, Mom," and "Am I on TV?."

Indoors, Special Needs

If it's indoors, the room needs to be big enough to hold everyone you invite, and all their equipment. It needs electrical outlets with circuit breakers that can withstand the heavy loads of TV lights. The crowd and the lights produce a lot of heat. The room needs an air conditioning system that can keep the room cool.

If the topic is truly hot, reporters will need telephones as soon as you've finished.

Who Should Speak?

In most organizations, protocol requires that certain people be featured at news conferences. They'll get their feelings hurt if they're not invited. If they're good spokespeople, that's great. But they may not be. It's embarrassing when the boss doesn't know the answer, fakes it, and someone on staff has to correct the error.

Generally, the boss needs to be there to speak about policy. But bosses often don't know much about the nuts and bolts. You need someone there who is personally familiar with the equipment or procedure.

The Boss Can't Tell

If you're talking about a major event, where someone has made a breakthrough in research or saved a life, that person should be there to tell the world how it felt at the moment of triumph. The boss can't tell us how it felt.

For most news conferences, use two or three people, if possible. More than three can get clumsy. One of them should be able to speak about policy. One should be the person closest to the event. You may want some other expert, like a lawyer, or accountant, or engineer, to explain technical details.

One Plays Relief Catcher

When one of the participants gets overwhelmed by questions, one of the others can step in for the rescue. "Let me answer that question," the relief catcher says. That gives the first person a break. Time to catch your breath and organize your thoughts before the next assault.

Many news conferences are a major technical problem for broadcasters. A common setup puts five or six people at a long table, facing the reporters and cameras.

That format was created for press conferences—the printed press--before radio and television were invented. It just doesn't work for the electronic media.

Avoiding Musical Chairs

Where do you put the mikes? If all the mikes are at the center of the table, we won't hear what the people at each end are saying. Unless they get up and trade chairs with the person at the center, where the mikes are.

And that almost guarantees the next question will be for the person who just moved from the center, who will have to move back now in this endless game of musical chairs. Unless you're in front of a mike, radio and TV will not be able to record what you say. It's also difficult to swing the camera from one end of the table to the other and refocus when someone else speaks.

The sound problem can be overcome, if each person participating has a microphone that feeds into a central sound system, and each broadcaster can plug into that system.

Do It Standing Up

If you don't have a sophisticated sound system, do your news conference standing up, with a podium for the microphones. Those participating in the conference stand close to the podium. Reporters can ask questions of specific people, and they can easily move to the mikes to answer, then step back.

Most people who don't have a lot of experience (and many who do) are much more effective standing than sitting. They invest more energy in what they're saying.

If you're expecting 100 reporters and photographers, you may need a sound system to be heard at the back of the room. And, as we said earlier, make sure there are enough electrical outlets, air conditioning, and telephones.

Avoid Stupid Questions

One of the most frustrating things about news conferences is stupid questions that are often repeated by several reporters. That's because many reporters at your news conference will have no background or experience in the subject matter.

Hand out written material that educates them before the news conference begins. It shouldn't be very long—just a fact sheet or background sheet that brings them up to speed on the subject. Include in that sheet the names and titles of those who'll be taking questions.

If the subject matter involves complicated numbers or statistics, include them in your handouts. Give reporters time to digest the written material before you begin, so they can ask intelligent questions. If you're proving a point, include in the handout material copies of documents and records that help make your case.

Openings We'll Never Hear

Somewhere in Media Class 101, they told you that all news conferences should begin with the boss reading a statement. Dull. Deadly dull. Presidents do this, but their news conferences are carried live and the audience HAS to sit through the entire statement. Or switch to the movie channel.

Forget about prepared statements for news conferences. Reading them makes everybody snore. You may want to distribute a statement as part of your handout material. Newspaper reporters don't need to hear you read it. If there are one or two sentences in the statement that summarize your position, you might read them for the benefit of television and radio. But it would be a lot better if you made that summary without looking at a script.

The electronic media will summarize the gist of the news conference and then look for two or three ten-second quotes. They'll almost always be your off-the-cuff answers to questions.

Pictures, Charts, Graphs

Bring to your news conference posterboard-sized visuals that help tell your story. Graphs. Charts. Diagrams. Outlines. Lists of problems, goals, or accomplishments. You can also do this with slides or videotape.

If you're telling us what you're doing to solve a problem, include a poster that lists each step you've taken, or plan to take. This kind of board serves as a cue card when you're speaking. Have the board near the podium and the microphones. Go down the list, pointing to each item as you discuss it.

The TV cameras will shoot you at the board. Even if they don't have time to list all the items you discussed, some of us at home will be able to read them. We'll know you've got a lot of solutions to the problem. We'll be impressed.

A Visual Gimmick

It is a visual gimmick, and it works. Newspaper photographers will also shoot you at the board. If you're the editor who chooses between two pictures, which would you choose—someone standing at a microphone, or someone pointing to the chart? If they have a choice, newspapers avoid talking heads, too.

If your poster is a chart or graph, try to have it reproduced in a smaller size as part of your handout. You'll find that many newspapers and TV stations will run your chart exactly as you created it. Again, you're making it easy for them to do a good job, reporting what you said.

In America, if you don't show me, I don't believe it. What you show me speaks so loudly I can't hear what you say.

Backup People and Material

Have backup people there who can, hopefully, rush out and get material you may have overlooked, and supply it to the reporters before you adjourn. If you can't get it in time, tell the reporters how they can get the information later in the day.

Keeping It Under Control

Like dogs and horses, groups of reporters can smell fear and sense when you're losing control. Once it happens, the mob mentality takes over. The first drop of blood puts sharks into a feeding frenzy.

It's *your* news conference. They're there at your invitation, and they need to understand what the rules are IN ADVANCE.

If you try to change the rules, or close the conference in midstream, you look like a coward who couldn't take the heat.

Time Limits Let You Out

If you expect a stormy session, have a staffer announce in advance that you can only give the reporters X minutes. That staffer should then be the timekeeper who announces the time is up and gets you to your next appointment.

At that point, you can always be the good guy, if you choose. "Let me take just one more question." You can take one more question all afternoon. You're in control.

If you're briefing reporters in the middle of a breaking disaster, you may want to announce at the beginning that you will not answer questions. You should also say when you'll come back with more details and take questions.

One Question At A Time

When half a dozen reporters all ask questions at the same time, you need to be firm in saying you can only deal with one question at a time. If that happens, ask reporters to hold up their hands and be recognized before they ask a question.

Careful With the Names

In a one-on-one interview, it's usually a good idea to use the reporter's name in your answers. "I'm doing this, Sally, because I think the school system is a disaster."

In a news conference, your recognizing one television reporter by name may prevent the competing stations from using your answer. That's how competitive they are.

Don't Leave Too Soon

Good reporters who know a lot about the subject of the news conference may want to interview you privately after you finish. They don't want to disclose their exclusive by asking key questions that would tip their competitors.

The reporter with an exclusive angle will want to get you aside, where others can't hear, to get your response on that angle. It may be so hush-hush the reporter will arrange to meet you somewhere else for a private interview.

So don't leave too soon, before those more knowledgeable reporters have a chance to buttonhole you, one-on-one.

SKILLS

NEWS RELEASES

Save the Trees
Stop PR Junk Mail

America would have more trees if public relations firms would stop cranking out so many news releases. Editors consider them an insidious form of junk mail. Most go straight to the trash can. PR people blanket the nation with news releases to justify their jobs or their fees. Look what I did, they tell the boss or the client. I've been churning them out, but those editors are really stupid. They wouldn't know a story if it hit them in the face.

The boss's name is in the release, probably in the first sentence. And the boss is attached to some quotes the PR firm wrote. Good stuff, the boss thinks. The PR people are right. We have a truly dense group of local editors.

Historical Artifacts

For most news coverage, the written news release *in news story form* is obsolete.

The news release was invented to cater to lazy newspaper people. Since it was written in newspaper style, a sluggish editor or reporter could simply re-type it, word-for-word, and put it in the paper.

In the bad old days, some sleazy reporters would even put their own by-lines on the story. Public relations people loved it. They could not only plant stories, they could actually write them exactly as they appeared in print. It was better than free lunch in the old-time saloon.

Times have changed.

News Release Ethics

Most daily newspapers today consider it unethical to run an unedited news release. Some weeklies, however—short on staff and budget—will run them just the way you send them.

The moral for people trying to get publicity:

If you can still get away with it, do it.

But if they don't run them the way you mail them, you need to re-think the whole process of writing and sending news releases.

The news release written in news story form takes a lot more time and paper than just a straightforward, quick summary telling an editor about a possible story.

Television news doesn't write a script until it shoots the videotape first. The script has to fit the pictures. If it has actualities, radio will write the script around them. So your effort to write a script for broadcasting can be a waste of time.

Advance Notice for TV

What all editors—print and broadcast—*DO* need is advance notice in writing or by phone, so they can have a reporter and/or camera there. Simple, one-paragraph letters will do, addressed to the city editor (print) or assignment editor (TV and radio).

"Mike Megawatt will speak to the Chum and Chowder Society next Tuesday at 12:30 p.m. in the Anthracite Hotel. He'll talk about the company's requested rate increase and the Power Company's petition to burn coal in the Smoky Hollow plant. We hope to have copies of the speech available for your reporter shortly before the meeting begins." (See **STRATEGY/Selling Your Story**)

Fact Sheets

If you're opening a new plant, send both print and broadcast editors a fact sheet, not a flowery news story. Something like:

The Wee Widget Company will open its new plant Monday. The new assembly line will be the most automated of its kind in the world. Robots will perform many of the jobs formerly done by workers. Production will increase by at least 30 per cent. Brief opening ceremonies begin at 9:00 a.m. A special tour for the news media begins at 9:30 a.m.

Plant construction cost—$ 46.3 million.
Building Contractor—Saw and Hammer Corp.
Construction time—21 months.
Square feet—92,500, all air-conditioned.
Special features—Employees' cafeteria, child care center, swimming pool, gymnasium, solar panels to heat water and generate electricity.
Expected production capacity—6.6 million widgets per year; retail value, $134 million, to be sold east of the Mississippi and in Central and Latin America.

Better Questions

If the editor decides to cover the opening, the fact sheet will go to the reporter who's assigned the story. It will result in better questions, and give some idea of what's available for photographs.

Fact sheets are especially helpful if you have a news conference. I've covered news conferences where the only handout was a release in news story form that ran several pages. The facts, names and numbers I needed were hidden far down in the copy. Or simply weren't there. (See **SKILLS/News Conferences**)

Obsolete Forms

News releases churned out by government agencies often follow the rigid form J. Edgar Hoover perfected in the 1940s. Every press release began: "FBI Director J. Edgar Hoover announced in Washington today. . . ."

The opening sentence changed for several years in the early 1960s when Bobby Kennedy was U. S. attorney general and, technically, Hoover's boss. They did not like each other, and were involved in a constant power struggle.

During those years, the releases began: "U. S. Attorney General Robert F. Kennedy announced in Washington today. . . ."

Bureaucrats love the format, because their name is right up front. And those kinds of releases usually include some stiff, wooden quotes from the boss that no respectable newspaper, radio or TV station would run.

Nobody seems to notice that the releases are not published or broadcast. It's done that way because that's the way it's always been done. It creates work for someone in the public affairs section.

TV Is Pictures and Sound

Television is pictures, and sound. Radio needs actualities. Some major corporations are beginning to catch on. There is even a glimmer of understanding in a few government agencies. The modern news release for television is a broadcast-quality videocassette, sometimes produced by a professional studio.

The print version of the release is high-quality still pictures with cutlines taped to the print. In some situations, the newspaper or magazine will prefer color slides. You need to be aware of their technical requirements and preferences.

The Photo as News Release

Automobile crashes videotaped and photographed in laboratory safety tests are a good example of this kind of release. The tests take place over months, or years. Knowing that someday you may want news coverage, you photograph the tests as you go along.

When you're ready for publicity, you don't try to produce a television news story or a magazine photo layout. You supply videotape copies and still photographs of the crash tests, along with a fact sheet on the tests and what the pictures show. Perhaps some technical detail on how they were shot.

Your fact sheet notifies editors you'll have copies of the photographs for them. Laboratory officials and engineers will be available for interviews. The reporter puts the story together, incorporating some of the crash pictures. On TV, the videotape can be used to cover part of the interviews with the technicians.

When a new airliner makes its inaugural flight, the manufacturer supplies videotape and pictures of engineers at the drawing board, wind-tunnel tests, the assembly line, the cockpit instruments, the plane's interior, and finally, the plane in flight, outlined against a spectacular sunrise, with the company name prominent on the tail section. Hard to produce a story without using some of those pictures.

Video and Photo Libraries

The Pentagon has extensive photo and videotape libraries showing weapons systems, ships, planes, and troops in war maneuvers. When a reporter does a story that needs pictures, the public affairs office is happy to supply them. They make their people and their equipment look good.

Corporations and government agencies need to build similar libraries.

Staff Photographers

Many police and fire departments now have broadcast-quality equipment and talented photographers who get to major disaster, fire and crime scenes before the news media do. They move in close, shoot pictures news photographers may not be able to shoot, then make them available to the media.

If the public is going to know who you are, and see you doing what you do best, it must be on film or videotape.

Medical Research

Major medical research facilities do the same thing. In some kinds of pioneering surgery, the risk to the patient is too great to invite a news camera. So the hospital photographs and videotapes the entire procedure. Once the procedure becomes less risky and is publicly announced, the tape is part of the announcement.

Sometimes, still pictures released are shots from the video monitor. The quality is poor. Newspaper editors don't like to use them. It shows that TV had a higher priority.

If at all possible, shoot both still pictures and videotape.

Don't tell me. Show me.

Videotaped Interviews

True story—

In a major city, two cars loaded with teenagers collide head-on at 2 a.m. A 16-year-old boy receives massive head injuries. The paramedics rush him to the nearest hospital. The hospital refuses to treat him. The emergency room does not have a neuro-surgeon on duty.

After a heated argument, the paramedics take the boy to another hospital, where he dies. The first hospital's failure to treat the youngster is leaked to a reporter and becomes a major news story. Day after day, the ethics of refusing medical treatment are debated in the media. You can smell the lawsuit coming.

Sure enough, a prominent attorney calls a news conference to announce that he represents the parents of the dead boy, and has just filed a multi-million-dollar suit against the hospital.

Control Over What is Said

He explains the basis of the suit and how he plans to pursue it. In closing, he says, "I know you would like to interview my clients, the parents. But they have been through so much pain and suffering, I just couldn't put them through that ordeal.

"But—knowing you would want to hear their story—I video-taped an interview with them. I have copies here, for each of you."

In this real case, every local TV station used portions of the taped interview. By making his own videotape, the lawyer was able to completely control what his clients said publicly, while he shielded them from questions he wanted to avoid.

A Brand New Technique

This is a brand new technique. It will be used a lot in the future.

Isn't this just like the old written press release that editors feel uneasy using? Well, sorta.

If the videotape is good stuff, however, they'll use it every time. They'll probably warn the audience that they didn't shoot it. Make clear where it came from. But they'll use it.

You don't have to own expensive video equipment to do this. With the proliferation of home video cameras, TV news is using more amateur video all the time.

The quality of home video cameras is very good today. If you're in the right place at the right time, both local and network television will quickly grab your videotape and broadcast it. Just as newspapers and magazines have bought amateur photographers' work since the camera was invented.

The Rodney King Video

In the late 1980s, CNN began asking viewers to contact the network if they shot videotape that might be newsworthy.

Amateur news video came into its own shortly after midnight on March 3, 1991, when George Holliday heard a commotion outside his apartment in Los Angeles.

He had a new video camera in his hand as he stepped onto his balcony. Down below and across the street, Rodney King had just emerged from his car after a high-speed police chase.

The novice photographer turned on his camera and videotaped the entire incident as police shot King with an electric stun gun, then beat and kicked him repeatedly.

Powerful Pictures

Purchased by TV news and broadcast incessantly all over the world, the tape was seen by virtually every person who has access to television.

It made King's name a household word; led to the indictment and trial of the officers involved; the resignation of the police chief; and was instrumental in focusing the anger of the black community. That anger would explode in massive, deadly riots when the officers were later acquitted.

The King tape was shot at night, under very poor lighting conditions, but dramatically demonstrated what amateur equipment can do.

Radio Actualities

Local radio news is becoming a rarity as station owners discover the profits to be made in completely automated stations. Those that still have local news staffs are cutting back to be competitive. (See **INSIDE THE MEDIA/Technology**)

They're hungry for anything that can make their news seem more enterprising. This provides marvelous opportunities for taped interview quotes when you're trying to get coverage for your issue. Fed by telephone, this is the audio tape version of a broadcast news release.

In a rural community with no daily newspaper, radio is an especially powerful medium. The audience is very loyal. This is their only source of daily, local news.

The news staff at those stations is usually one person. And because the community is small, news is frequently hard to find.

Recording a Radio Feed

Suppose you run the state bartenders association. There is a proposal in the legislature to require bartenders to have Ph.D.s in philosophy. Your association is violently opposed to the bill.

With a cassette recorder, interview your president or executive director. Ask for a reaction to the proposal.

"How do you feel about Sen. Fogbound's proposal?"

"I'm outraged. Next thing we know, they'll want cows to wear caps and gowns while they give milk. Maybe we should require legislators to have degrees in common sense."

Dubbing the Feed Tape

Cue the tape to the quote you want to give radio. Then connect that recorder to a second recorder, with a wire you can buy at any electronics store. You dub (copy) onto a second cassette just that quote.

If you get fancy, you'll give the station a packaged feed. On the second cassette, you record an introduction to the sound bite with a countdown. Something like:

"The legislature is considering a proposal that would require all bartenders to have a doctoral degree in philosophy. The State Bartenders Association is violently opposed to the bill. The following is a quote from State Bartenders Association President Harvey Wallbanger. Three—Two—One—I'm outraged. Next thing we know . . ." etc.

Counting Down the Quote

The countdown helps them copy your quote onto their final, recorded version of the story. It marks the beginning of your quote precisely, just as the countdown at a rocket launch is used to time the exact moment of ignition and liftoff.

Now you're ready to feed the tape to every radio station in the state. If the story is big enough, to every radio station in the country.

Connecting to a Phone

Go to a local radio station news department and they'll show you how to wire your tape recorder into a phone line. With the old Western Electric phones, you could unscrew the mouthpiece. This exposed two metal tabs.

A special connecting wire plugged into your tape recorder at one end. Two small alligator clips at the other end made the connection to the two metal tabs inside the mouthpiece.

You called the station, told them what you had, then made your connections, ran the tape, disconnected the wires, screwed the mouthpiece back on, and talked to the station to make sure they got everything OK.

Newer, Better Ways to Feed

Many newer phones can't be taken apart so easily. There are simpler connections from your tape recorder directly into a phone jack. In effect, the tape recorder becomes an extension phone that can transmit to the radio station.

If you're going to make radio feeds on a regular basis, invest in a machine that does all this automatically. For less than $500, the machine is a sort of audio fax machine.

You store the phone numbers of stations you call on a regular basis. You dial them automatically. Once they're on the line with their recorder rolling, your machine feeds your cassette into the recorder at the radio station.

Charts and Graphs

For television and print, charts and graphs that make numbers meaningful are critical if you expect the public to understand your operation, your problems, or your solutions.

Newspapers, magazines and television love them. They have staff artists who spend all their time creating graphics. *USA Today* started a revolution in newspaper design. Color graphics are a major component in the new look of American newspapers.

You can create multi-colored graphics as part of your news release and save them the trouble.

Big-city newspapers won't run the copy from your written news release. But they'll run your charts and graphs exactly the way you make them. This is a modern-day, disguised version of the old news release I talked about earlier in this section.

Use Computer Graphics

You don't even need an artist. Create your graphs and charts with your computer graphics program. Put the graphic on the monitor screen in a dark room and shoot the screen with a single-lens reflex camera.

With a high-resolution computer monitor, you'll get excellent results. The darkened room is necessary to avoid reflections on the monitor screen. The slides can be printed at a photo lab if you need both slide and print versions.

Higher Quality Graphics

In most cities there are graphics designers who will work with you to create computerized graphics and then copy them electronically for slides or prints. The equipment they use will give you much higher quality than shooting off a monitor. The price of half a dozen graphics created this way will buy a sophisticated camera if you want to do it yourself.

For many uses, the do-it-yourself version is completely adequate. You'll need to experiment with it so you'll know what you can produce.

TV crews can copy the print version onto videotape in the field. Back at the studio, they can make an even better videotape copy from a slide.

Include copies of your graphics in the media package when you hold a news conference, make an important speech, or testify at a public hearing. (See **SKILLS/News Conferences** and **Speeches**)

SKILLS

OFF-THE-RECORD

Leaking So Plumbers Can't Find the Source

A crucial skill for the media game is knowing how to successfully leak information. It happens every day in politics, government, and the corporate world. Suppose your competitor has a major skeleton in the closet. If the media wrote about the skeleton, the competitor would be embarrassed or eliminated. The only way the media will find out is through a tip.

Confidential agreements have other uses:

- To brief reporters in advance, so they can produce better stories.
- To negotiate for the delay of a story.
- To correct a wrong when the system seems powerless or disinterested.
- To bring reporters into an investigation, so they'll feel more personally invested and put more effort into their coverage.
- To bring an outsider in as an observer when you feel vulnerable and overpowered.

When I begin to talk about off-the-record skills, occasionally on officer in one of my law enforcement seminars frowns at that idea. "I'd never do that," the officer says. "I'm not a snitch."

Cops consider informers a necessary evil. They do not respect them. Informers are usually the kind of people who should be in jail. But to catch bigger fish, you have to give the informer a "walk." If the gang member will testify against his partners, he goes free, or gets a much lighter sentence.

Snitch = Traitor

Law enforcement thinks of informers as traitors who turn against people who trusted them. They'll sell their mothers if the price is right.

Information from a law enforcement informer is always suspect. It is being sold—bartered—and the informer frequently enlarges the truth to improve the bargaining position.

Media Sources Different

Confidential sources who leak to reporters, however, are very different kinds of people, with very different motives.

As an investigative reporter, I made off-the-record agreements with dope smugglers, gamblers, con men, bagmen, prostitutes and murderers. But they were the exception.

My most frequent source of confidential information was a conscientious law enforcement officer, doctor, lawyer or government official who became completely frustrated with injustice or incompetence and the system's inability to cope with it.

Setting the Agenda

They went outside the system, and their leak of information to me often brought about sudden changes in the system. Prosecutors who had been blind to certain types of activity suddenly began personal crusades.

One of my most successful series involved the Original Sleazy Lawyer, who had lied, cheated and bilked his clients in two states for 40 years. Officials at several levels had tried to put him out of business. They failed. He had an uncanny ability to weasel out of it—or a corrupt connection somewhere in the system.

So one of those frustrated officials secretly came to me with a confidential file—the transcript of four days of secret, federal testimony. Using that as my springboard, I found the lawyer's victims. I interviewed them on camera, and gathered the documents that supported their accusations.

Amazing Things Happen

Suddenly, amazing things began to happen. A federal agency that had seemed impotent announced a hearing on The Original Sleazy Lawyer's qualifications to practice. A federal prosecutor indicted him for encouraging a client to commit perjury. He was convicted, and went to prison.

Interestingly, all of the details about the client who had lied were in the original information leaked to me. It was available to the prosecution all along. But nobody did anything about it until my stories turned up the heat—moved the topic to the top of the agenda.

Honest Insiders Leak

In working stories on law enforcement corruption and medical malpractice, my usual confidential sources were other officers or doctors anxious to clean up their own profession.

I have met people in unusual places at all hours of the day and night, with signals that would tip us to each other's presence and all sorts of games to make sure neither of us was followed or bugged.

I have been brought into corruption investigations, to do my own work, because the officers doing the investigation knew that in a corrupt system, the honest investigators quickly become the targets of a dishonest prosecutor leading a grand jury.

Outsiders Keep it Honest

They brought me in as an outside, objective observer, who would know the truth from the inside when the case finally surfaced.

I have accepted information in confidence from people who would be killed if certain people knew they had talked to me.

But most leaks are not nearly that cloak-and-daggerish. The most frequent reason to leak to the media is to give them advance notice, so they can gather better information and produce a better story, when the time comes.

Sometimes, in the real world, you will leak to the media to counter your opposition's leaks. A well-timed leak can mean millions of dollars in corporate America. It can decoy attention away from what you need to do quietly. It can change the course of a political campaign, or a corporate takeover. Without "Deep Throat," the Watergate scandal might never have been uncovered.

Plumbers Stop Leaks

In many cases, there is risk for the source who leaks. Government agencies—as the Nixon White House did during Watergate—appoint groups of "plumbers" to stop leaks—perhaps fire and prosecute the leakers.

I cannot give you guidelines for your conscience, in terms of deciding to talk to reporters in confidence. But if you decide to become a confidential source, I can help you do it successfully, with minimum risk.

Off the Record = ?

You can no longer be sure what "off-the-record" means. The Washington press corps has created half a dozen gradations for talking to the news media in confidence. They accept information for "background only." Or "deep background." Or quotes for "non-attribution."

Few people outside the Washington bureaucracy know what they're talking about. Even the insiders are sometimes confused.

Before you tell something to a reporter in confidence, be sure you both understand the terms on which you give—and the reporter receives—the information.

A Clear Contract

There should be a clear verbal contract before you stick your neck out. That contract is terribly important. If it's broken, you could lose your job, your reputation, or your life. The reporter's career could be destroyed.

Talking to a reporter, and then adding, "Now, that's off the record" won't work. The contract must be made before the information is given. You can't spill the beans and then ask a reporter not to tell.

Most good reporters won't accept information if they have to pledge they'll never use it. Their job is to gather, publish and broadcast information, not store it in their heads. They may already know what you're about to tell them. Promising you they will never tell would prevent them from using it.

"In Confidence"

Your approach to a reporter should be, "I'd like to tell you something in confidence." If the reporter is not experienced enough to explore exactly what you mean, you should spell it out. Variations of the contract:

1. You may use the information I'm about to give you in any way you choose, so long as you are very careful not to quote me directly, or to even hint where it came from. This kind of information is often attributed to a "confidential source" or a "highly reliable source."

2. You can indicate my organization or group. The story's credibility is increased if the source is less vague. "A confidential source in the police department." Or "a highly-placed executive in a major oil company."

3. You must agree to hold the story until a later time. "I want you to be aware of this," you say, "Because I know you'll need some advance work to write a better story when it breaks." Lengthy police investigations are often leaked in advance to the media on this basis. Television, particularly, needs extra time to look for file tape, to collect pictures of people, to shoot "real estate" (buildings or places where parts of the story took place), to produce charts or diagrams that will help explain complicated figures or relationships.

If the information is leaked for later use, be sure to discuss with the reporter the care that must be taken in gathering background material to avoid tipping your hand. Stories like the retirement or appointment of a key executive; the introduction of a new model or product; the filing of a lawsuit; a revolutionary medical technique.

There is always a risk to the reporter in accepting information and agreeing to hold it until later. The competition may find out about it, and get a beat on the story. Some contracts provide for that. The reporter agrees to hold what you've told him until the agreed time *unless the competition is about to break the story.* If that is imminent, then the reporter may go with it. This will involve your being able to trust the reporter to be honest with you about any competitive threat. You also have an obligation under this kind of contract to tip the reporter if a competitor approaches you, asking questions about the story.

4. "You may use this information if you can confirm it with another source." This, also, involves trust on your part. It is usually used if you think very few people know about it, and the story would immediately point the finger at you as the source. The information may be more widespread then you realize. If the reporter can find it somewhere else, you will not be as suspect.

5. Backgrounding. "I want you to be aware of some things that are happening. In the next few days or weeks, a story will break, and then you'll understand the importance of what I'm about to tell you. You must not do anything that would ever suggest you received this briefing from me."

6. No quotes. "You may use everything I'm about to tell you, and use my name, so long as you don't quote me directly. You must paraphrase what I say." This is a protection for the source, in case there is bad public reaction to a trial balloon. You can always come back with, "Let me clarify my position on this."

7. "You may never attribute anything to me unless I specifically say, 'You can quote me.' " This is a time-saving device if you have a continuing confidential source relationship with a reporter. You understand that there is a continuing contract that is in operation every time you talk, unless you make an exception.

Here are five broad rules that you should review when you make a confidential source agreement with a reporter:

1. **Know the reporter.**
2. **Do you have authority to sign the contract?**
3. **How many others will know the information or the source?**
4. **How far will you go to protect me?**
5. **What are the exact words you will use in referring to your source?**

Let's go over each rule.

Know the Reporter

I call this a contract, but it is a contract you will not be able to enforce. If you are a secret source, and want to remain invisible, how can you publicly accuse the reporter of violating a section of the contract?

Some reporters can be trusted more than others. All those who call themselves reporters do not live up to the generally recognized ethics of journalism. (See **STRATEGY/Ethics**)

As a general rule, reporters for major publications and broadcast outlets will be more reliable to deal with in confidential relationships. The ethical standards at *The New York Times* should be higher than the *Podunk Tattler*. But not always.

Older May Be Better

Another general rule: older, established reporters may be more reliable in this kind of agreement. Younger reporters' primary motive is *getting the story to prove they can*. Older reporters, with an established reputation for getting the story, will let a story die rather than taint their reputation for integrity in dealing with sources.

If you don't know the reporter, call friends in your field and ask what they know. Your call, however, can be a tip to those friends. Once the story breaks, they will guess that you were the leak in your organization.

References

When I left my job as Washington correspondent for *The Miami Herald*, I moved under deep cover to investigate political and law enforcement corruption for WHAS-TV in Louisville, Kentucky. I knew nobody in law enforcement there. I would be working alone. To protect my cover, nobody except the station owner, manager, and news director was aware of my assignment. For the eight months I was under cover, I never went to the TV station. To avoid a paper trail that corrupt officials could follow, I was not even on the payroll. The news director brought my salary and expense money to my home every Friday night.

To succeed, I needed confidential sources.

So I called law enforcement officers I had worked closely with all over the country. I asked them if they knew anyone in the Louisville area that might be helpful. Several did.

You Can Trust Him

They called ahead. You will be approached by a reporter named Clarence Jones, they said. He is a reporter who can be trusted. You can talk to him and be sure he will not disclose you as a source.

With those kinds of recommendations, I could immediately begin confidential relationships with federal, state and local law enforcement officers who were willing to help me investigate the corruption.

Complaining

If you feel a reporter has violated a confidence with you, in most cases the immediate superior will know you are the confidential source. You should complain about the violation in much the same way I suggest that you complain about inaccuracies in **STRATEGY/Fighting Back.** This time, though, *you should be very angry from the beginning.* Violating a confidence is one of the most serious sins a reporter can commit. (See **STRATEGY/Ethics**)

Do You Have Authority?

Does the reporter have authority to promise you confidence? In some news organizations, only a supervisor can give that pledge.

There are atrocity stories of reporters who pledge sources confidence, then run to the newsroom to tell the editor what they've learned. "Hell of a story," the editor says. "We'll lead the front page with it tomorrow morning."

"Wait a minute, boss," the reporters says, in panic. "I told my source we'd hold this until next Friday."

"You did, but I didn't," the unethical editor says, with a smirk. He shafts both the source and his own reporter.

If you have any question about the reporter's ability to pledge confidence, bring the editor into the conversation before you make your agreement.

Who Else Will Know?

How many others in the news operation will be aware that you are the source?

Secrecy is often broken by accident, not intentionally. The more who know, the greater the chance of a leak.

When Janet Cooke wrote her story about a child heroin addict, she did not tell her editors at *The Washington Post* how she found the boy, or where he lived. She said she was doing it to protect the confidential agreement that led her to the boy. She won the Pulitzer Prize before the story was unmasked as fiction. Embarrassed, the newspaper had to admit the hoax and return the prize. Because of that danger, most newsrooms now require editors or company attorneys to know the identity of sources for stories that hinge on confidential information.

How Far Will You Go?

You should ask how far the reporter is willing to go to protect your confidence. Would the reporter go to jail rather than disclose you as the source?

Shield Laws

Some states have shield laws that give reporters legal protection for confidential information. They cannot be forced by the judicial, legislative or executive branches of government to disclose their confidential sources.

Most states shield ministers, lawyers and accountants from being forced to disclose information given them in confidence. There was an assumption that reporters had that same kind of shield under the First Amendment until the 1970s, when the U.S. Supreme Court ruled otherwise.

If a state wants to give reporters that protection, it may, the Supreme Court said. But if the state does not, then a judge may decide whether the public good is more important than the reporter's claim of First Amendment rights. The judge can order the reporter to disclose the source. And if the reporter refuses, the reporter can be held in contempt of court and jailed until the court order is obeyed.

The Exact Words

One risk you might not think about is the way in which the reporter will refer to the source. This part of the contract may be especially critical. Confidential sources often ignore it, leaving it to the reporter to disguise the source.

The problem here is that the reporter can unintentionally identify you. "A veteran executive in the power company's research and planning division" may tell everybody in the company you are the source, since nobody else in the division has been there more than two years.

Your leak will be a lot safer if you discuss with the reporter *the exact words* to be used in referring to the source.

Confidentiality and Libel

Confidential sources raise major problems in libel litigation. To win libel suits, the media must prove the story is true (or, in the case of a public person, that they broadcast the story, believing it was true).

If it is based on confidential sources, they have no way to prove truth without disclosing the source. In some states, their refusal to answer questions during the pre-trial discovery process will result in an automatic judgment against them. The only question then for the jury is how much in damages to award the libel victim.

Affidavits & Escape Clauses

One way to cover that possibility is to give the reporter a sworn affidavit, with a written agreement that your identity will be kept confidential unless it is needed to defend a lawsuit.

If that happens, you agree that the reporter can disclose your identity, and the contents of your sworn statement. This technique is invaluable if the story is extremely sensitive.

I worked as producer and editor for a series of investigative reports after a group of doctors at a major hospital became concerned about several staff members. They said heart specialists were performing experimental, unnecessary surgery on elderly patients so they could publish their findings in medical journals. The death rate in those procedures was very high.

The Doctor Was Not In

Some anesthesiologists at the same hospital were not even present during major surgery, their colleagues told us. They substituted interns, but the patient was billed as though the more experienced anesthesiologist had been there the entire time.

A number of more ethical doctors on the staff were alarmed about what they knew, but were reluctant to go public with their accusations.

They leaked internal hospital records to us, and gave us sworn affidavits about what they had seen and heard in the hospital. On the back of each affidavit, we gave the doctors a written agreement never to disclose the doctor's identity unless the statement was needed to defend a lawsuit.

In our script, we said, "We have sworn affidavits from a dozen doctors who say they have seen. . . ." There was never even a suggestion of a lawsuit from either the doctors or the hospital. They knew we had the evidence that would convince a jury the story was true.

Plain Brown Wrappers

An anonymous telephone call to a reporter is sometimes all it takes to get the story out. Or copies of documents, mailed to the reporter in a plain envelope. The reporter is protected in that way, too. If the source ever becomes the focus of a grand jury investigation, the reporter can honestly say, "I don't know who sent those papers to me."

Another technique for leaking information is to write a detailed internal memo and circulate it widely. If a copy winds up in a reporter's hands, or in the mail, it could have been leaked by lots of people.

Partial Shield Laws

Some states have partial shield laws. The reporter cannot be forced to reveal the source, but any physical evidence provided by a confidential source can be obtained through a court process.

This happened to me once in Kentucky, which had a partial shield law. I had broadcast a tape recording of a police official carefully explaining the payoff system to a man who wanted to open an illegal gambling joint.

The tape had been made as the officer drove the ambitious gambler around in his squad car. You could hear the police radio in the background.

How Was the Tape Made?

I was hauled into court and asked how I obtained the tape. I refused to say, and the judge upheld my right to remain silent. But the prosecutor was able to obtain the audio cassette. It was put through extensive laboratory testing, in an effort to determine how it was made, and who made it.

They were looking for evidence to prosecute the source who gave me the tape for violating the eavesdropping law. They never found out how the tape was made.

Fingerprints & Copies

The moral here is: Wipe fingerprints from anything you mail a reporter anonymously. If you are sending copies of restricted documents, make the copies at a public copying machine, or one that is used by dozens of people. With microscopic analysis, some copies can be traced back to the machine that made them. Use rubber gloves in handling the copies and the envelope you mail them in.

Another favorite trick for leaking information is to simply leave it out on your desk, as the assistant U. S. attorney did in the movie, "Absence of Malice."

After a corruption investigation in Miami, I tried to obtain the list of people who were being notified that their conversations with the corrupter had been intercepted. The list contained dozens of public officials.

Disclosure a Federal Crime

But it was a federal crime to disclose the list. I checked my mailbox each day, looking for the Plain Brown Wrapper. No luck.

One afternoon, I received a call from someone I knew. "Can you come over to the boss's office right away?" he asked. "He needs to talk to you about something important."

I dropped what I was doing and ran over. When I arrived, the man who had called me was sitting in the outer office, alone. The receptionist was gone. The boss' office was empty.

I Must Look Stupid

"The boss is down in the men's room," my contact told me. "Go on into his office. He'll be back in a minute."

I thought it was strange to be ushered into the inner sanctum with the boss absent. Then it became stranger. My contact left me in the office alone, and closed the door.

On a table in plain sight was the list of people intercepted on the wiretap. Beside it was a blank legal pad. I know I look dumb, but that day I must have looked truly stupid. My contact in the outer office rolled a pencil under the door.

SKILLS

SPEECHES

Waking Up the Photographers

It is a major speech. You know the media will be there. You want them to be there because the audience you need to reach is the entire community, far beyond the civic club or union hall. And so you spend a lot of time writing the speech. Polishing phrases. Trying them out on your co-workers.

The big day comes. Sure enough, there are three television cameras with their legs spread wide, standing directly in front of the platform. The bright lights come on as you're introduced, and you begin, with all the cameras rolling.

But the beginning is jokes and fluff. By the time you reach the heart of the speech, the lights are dark and the cameras dead. The photographers are back at their seats, eating their pie. Or dozing.

Where's the Good Stuff?

Speeches are like white water rafting. Hard to tell where the exciting stuff is. You coast on smooth water, so quiet you can hear birds in overhanging trees. Then, quite suddenly, there is a rush of sound ahead. You come around the bend into rapids and the roar of white water.

When you get to that point in your speech, the reporter will nudge the photographer. Wake up! Get the camera rolling! But by the time the camera is fired up, you may be back into calm water. The photographer shrugs his shoulders and goes back to the pie.

You may interrupt dessert several times. The real message may never reach the television audience.

Don't let it happen next time. Here's how to make sure the photographer will be awake and rolling at the critical moment:

How To Speak TV, Print & Radio

Release Advance Copies

Give copies of the speech in advance to every reporter there. This gives them an opportunity to read through and pick the sections they want to videotape.

Since they will only have air time to report your major thrust—perhaps one side issue—they will mark those sections, and tell the photographer to shoot them.

Back at the station, this saves editing time. They know exactly what they have on tape. It doesn't have to be logged, and they don't have to roll back and forth through long sections of dull tape, searching for a usable bite.

Radio Will Like It, Too

Radio will usually record the entire speech. A transcript helps them, too, find what they want on the audio tape. If you're in a room where the speaker system is feeding into a source for the news media, radio can save tape and editing time by only recording what they've marked in the script.

Print reporters won't have to take notes. They will follow along, marking the spots where you deviated from the prepared text. You'll find the quotes on tomorrow's front page are much more accurate this way.

Leak Part of It

Leak portions of the speech to the morning newspaper the day before. This will work only if what you're saying is truly newsworthy. If it is, the morning paper will have a story:

"In a speech prepared for delivery at today's meeting of the Chum and Chowder Society, Power Company President Mike Megawatt says electric bills will rise much higher if his company is not allowed to burn coal in its Smokey Hollow plant."

The advance story in the newspaper convinces radio and television assignment editors they should have reporters there to cover it. Radio news, based on the advance story, will advertise the speech all through the morning.

The newspaper will be there, also, to see what else happens. You might say something in the question-and-answer session following the speech. Or the audience might lynch you.

Two for One

Leaking the speech gives you two newspaper stories for one speech; the newspaper alerts readers to watch for the story on television tonight; it convinces the TV assignment editor the speech is worth covering, and the advance stories in both print and radio will probably turn out a bigger, more responsive audience.

IMPORTANT: Don't leak everything to the newspaper in advance. Save the best quotes. That way, your audience won't feel like they're hearing a second-hand speech. And there will be fresh material for radio this afternoon, TV tonight.

Signals for the Good Stuff

Many of the best, most newsworthy speeches are not written in advance. They are spontaneous and unrehearsed. So you need to develop signals that tell the TV photographers and radio reporters you're approaching something worth taping.

You're moving along, and you know the exciting stuff is just around the corner. You look over and see the cameras are idle. To wake up the photographers, give them a warning. Something like:

Listen Up, Now

- "Now, if you don't hear anything else I say today, I want you to hear this. This is important." Or:
- "What I'm about to say is going to make a lot of people angry. It's going to cause a lot of hard feelings."

You can hear the cameras and tape recorders clicking on.

- "Before I came here today, I gave a lot of thought to what I'm about to say. Nobody else has been willing to say this in public. I think it's time we talked about it."

That kind of tease not only wakes up the photographer, it whets the appetite of your audience. It makes them sit up and pay attention, too.

Tell 'em What You Told 'em

You may discover that the summary is the perfect form for the time limitations of broadcasting. After every important section of a speech, either prepared or off-the-cuff, summarize.

The summary will often be the bite broadcasters use in their stories.

You should never again make a speech at the Kiwanis Club or a stockholder's meeting without drawings, pictures, graphics, charts—something visual.

Show While You Tell

You must show me something while you are telling me something. Otherwise, I won't remember. Television has conditioned an entire generation of Americans who listen, learn and remember only if the message is both sound and pictures.

Often the pictures will be the stronger element in their memory and response to what you say. You can do it with a wide variety of gadgets that range from poster boards and flip charts to new devices that project onto a wall-size screen the words and pictures contained on the disk of a laptop computer.

(See **SKILLS/News Conferences**)

Try Not to Read It

Try not to read your speech. A speech read to a live audience seems much more lively if you're there. On TV and radio, unless you're an accomplished reader and actor, it puts you to sleep very quickly.

There are typewriters with large type, and word processing programs that support large type on computer printers. Rather than type the entire speech, have a simple outline of your main points.

This way, you talk extemporaneously about each point. You'll be more convincing, both to your live audience and your broadcast listeners.

Speech TelePrompTers

If the speech is especially sensitive and you can't trust yourself to deliver it extemporaneously, you can rent a TelePrompTer that works just like those the anchors use in TV studios. (See **INSIDE THE MEDIA/NEWSCAST**)

You may have noticed little panes of glass on each side of the podium at national political conventions or presidential speeches. The first time I saw them, I thought they were bullet-proof glass to protect the President.

They're actually glass reflectors for a small, closed-circuit TV set. The set is lower, where you can't see it. On the TV screen, the speech scrolls by. The glass reflects the words and the speaker reads them. The speed of the scrolling is controlled by an operator who keeps pace with the speaker.

Reagan's Speech Reading

Ronald Reagan was very good at using the TelePrompTer when he delivered speeches. He would read a sentence or two from the prompter to his left, then switch to the prompter at his right. It looked like he was simply making eye contact with the entire audience.

If you didn't know how major speeches are choreographed, you were not aware he was reading. Occasionally, he would give it away by lapsing into a steady rhythm, swinging back and forth between prompters. One sentence to the left, turn, one sentence to the right, turn, one sentence to the left, turn again.

The Contact Lens Trick

Suppose you're far-sighted, wear contact lenses, and need glasses to read. Some people who work hard at their speech technique have one contact lens made with a reading prescription; the other their normal prescription.

If they're reading from a prepared text, they read with one eye. When they look up and make eye contact with people in the audience, they use the other eye. It takes concentration, practice, and a strong stomach. Looking at the audience with your reading lens can make you instantly seasick.

Wireless Microphones

One of the neatest gadgets to free you from the podium and let you be more animated is a wireless microphone. They're widely available now in electronics stores for less than $100.

The microphone is a peanut type, clipped to your tie or lapel. A wire runs to a transmitter clipped to your belt. The transmitter is battery-powered, about the size of a telephone message beeper.

The mike transmits to a small radio receiver, which plugs into the room's loudspeaker system.

Freedom to Wander

When I finish speaking and take questions from the audience, my wireless mike allows me to walk into the crowd and have a close-up conversation with those who ask questions. The mike picks up their voices, as well as mine, and amplifies them through the speaker system.

The people who ask questions feel they get a much more personal response this way.

During breaks, remember to turn the mike off. Otherwise, everything you say in the hall or restroom will be amplified through the speaker system.

When the speech is over, don't leave too soon. Stay long enough to let reporters covering the speech talk to you. In this way, they can make their stories unique. They may need more background. The story about your speech will often get better play if it doesn't look like a carbon copy of the competition.

SKILLS

TALK SHOWS

Learning to Be Acceptably Rude

When you walk into the TV studio, it will seem like a big, cold cavern. The ceiling will be a jumble of black, oddly-shaped stalactites, wires and booms, catwalks and stage lights. Over in one corner, there will be a cozy little set—perhaps a cardboard bookcase or fireplace, some potted palms—and two chairs, where you and the moderator will talk.

Or it may be a panel show, where you sit facing a group of reporters who fire questions at you. There may be other guests there to debate your point of view.

It's Cold in There

The air conditioning is set low in television studios to counteract the heat of the lights. When they're all turned on, they raise the temperature in the entire studio. If it weren't that cold before the show, you'd sweat and be uncomfortable before the show ended. The thermostat is usually set for men who wear coats and ties. Women wearing thin, short-sleeved dresses sometimes turn blue and have to fight to keep from shivering. Long sleeves will help you cope with the cold.

Wear clothes and jewelry we won't remember. Unless you're trying to tell us something about clothes or jewelry. (See **SKILLS/Interviews-Broadcast**)

Arrive Early

It's a good idea to arrive about a half hour before the show is scheduled. Producers have nightmares about guests arriving late, or missing the show entirely. Being on time is just as critical for a taped show as a live one. At most stations and networks, the studio and crew time are scheduled solidly for months in advance. If you miss today's taping time, there may not be another opening. Getting there early gives you time to get acquainted with the moderator and the other guests.

Time for Makeup

You'll need some extra time to apply makeup. For field interviews, women should wear the same makeup they'd wear to work. But in a TV studio, the light will be much brighter and harsher. You'll need heavier makeup. Eye shadow and cheek blush should be a tone darker than usual.

Outside the studio, men don't normally use makeup. In the studio, to look normal, you need to wipe pancake makeup across your beard area and the shiny places. The floor crew will have makeup and a communal sponge. You may want to bring your own. It's available in most drug stores, in different shades to match skin tone. To apply, wet a small sponge, rub it on the hard cake of makeup, and then wipe it on your face.

The Object—Look Normal

It doesn't smell, and will wash off easily when the interview is over. Receding hairlines and noses are particularly shiny in bright studio lights. And even if they shave just before they go to the TV station, some men with very dark beards look like they live on skid row.

The idea is to apply just enough makeup to look normal through a studio camera. If it's done right, you can walk out of the studio and nobody will know you're wearing it.

The Choice Place to Sit

By arriving early, you'll have a better idea of the ground the moderator intends to cover. You can become accustomed to the strange surroundings. If there are more than two people on the show—and you have a choice—take a seat on the end, rather than the middle. From the end seat, you can look at the other guests without moving your head back and forth. In the middle, it's like a tennis match as the conversation bounces back and forth.

Hiding the Mike Cord

Clip your mike so we won't see the cord. This may take some effort, but it's worth it. If the mike is clipped to a tie, run the cord inside a buttoned shirt to the waist band, then inside the waist band to one side. The only cord we'll see will be at the mike.

Clipped to a coat lapel, the cord can run from the lapel under the coat to your waistband at the side.

With a pullover, short-sleeved top, you may have to run the cord inside the shirt or a sleeve, then out at the neck.

Another route is up your back, then under a collar to the front where it's clipped.

You Can Take More Control

In some ways, in-studio interviews are very different from field interviews. Most of these shows will not be edited. They're broadcast live, or videotaped for later broadcast just as they were shot. You have more control over subject matter.

Through your answers, you can lead the discussion from one area to another. Your answers can be a little longer. But if you begin to ramble, a good moderator will cut you off, try to force you to answer the question, or move on to the next subject before you make your point.

Careful About Repeating

In a taped interview, you can make your point repeatedly. They'll edit and use just one. You must be much more clever on a talk show. To repeat the same thought, you must state it very differently. Otherwise we think you're getting forgetful, and can't remember that you've already said that. Or that you've been programmed by a speech writer and can't hold a conversation without a script.

Late in the 1988 presidential campaign, Michael Dukakis appeared on ABC's "Nightline" with Ted Koppel. No matter what Koppel asked, Dukakis reverted back to his canned campaign material, repeating it several times. He looked like a wind-up toy.

Quick and Snappy

When the moderator asks a question, the best standard answer is usually a concise, one-sentence statement of your feeling or opinion, followed by your explanation of why. If you begin to talk too long, and get cut off, you'll still make your point.

Compared to other forms of radio and television, talk shows are boring. They normally feature "talking heads." No visuals for TV, no natural sound for radio. No interviews to insert, and change the pace. Just talk.

Talk shows work best when there is quick, snappy dialogue between guest and moderator. The quicker the. exchanges, the more interesting the conversation seems to listeners and viewers.

Yell and I'll Believe You

The person who is the loudest and most aggressive is usually the most believable for those in the audience. Particularly if the obnoxious person goes unchallenged. That's why so many talk show hosts are so aggressive and insulting. It also keeps the audience awake.

A talk show on radio or TV will often have more than one guest. Sometimes they have very different points of view. There's only so much time. And there are no rules to give each guest an equal share of that time.

The assertive guest will get more time than the others. So you have to learn how to be what I call "acceptably rude."

Learn to Be Acceptably Rude

For television and radio, you'll find that you're much too polite. You wait until others have finished their thought. You're patient while they ramble, trying to find their point.

When they make a mistake, or say something that is obviously untrue, you've been conditioned to sit quietly until it's your turn.

DON'T DO THAT. As soon as the moderator or another guest says something that's inaccurate, interrupt.

"Wait a minute!" you say loudly. "That's not true, and you know it's not true. Why would you say something so obviously phony?"

No Interruption—It's True

If you don't interrupt, the thought or statistic will be lodged as truth in the minds of viewers and listeners. It's much harder to dislodge it several minutes later. Interrupting also gives you an opportunity to take center stage.

And if the guest or moderator you've interrupted comes right back, then the show becomes more interesting.

I remember hosting a talk show on capital punishment. The proponent was the state attorney general. The opponent was an American Civil Liberties Union lawyer. Both had done this before. They knew how to mix it up to make it interesting.

All I had to do as moderator was introduce them and get them apart for commercial breaks. The half-hour went by incredibly quickly. As I passed through the control room on my way back to the newsroom, a technician who'd watched the taping said, "Boy, that was good television. I'd watch that!"

Conflict Makes Us Listen

Sharp conflict is a major element for intellectual debate and spectator sports. We like contests where the two opponents are evenly matched and eager to do battle. Team sports with lopsided scores—boxing matches where the fighters only dance and clinch—make us go to the bedroom, the bathroom, the kitchen, or another channel.

Knowing how far you can go without being obnoxious or rude is very difficult unless you've seen or heard yourself on tape. In my media training for the talk show format, I push people to be more rude and assertive.

I goad them until they feel they're out of bounds. Then they look at the tape. In playback, you are not nearly as rude or assertive as you thought you were. Audio and videotape tend to tone down the conflict. It takes some practice to position yourself with just the right amount of aggression.

If you overdo it, you'll be shrill. You turn us off. Or you can overpower another guest and make us feel like you're a bully. We will side with the underdog.

Take Along Your Visuals

If you have videotape, film, still pictures or slides that will help tell your story, let the producer of the TV talk show know several days in advance. The producer needs to look at them and decide whether to use them.

Your visuals may have to be converted to fit the station's technical equipment. You and the producer work out in advance how you'll cue the pictures. You can do it like a sportscaster—"OK, let's go to the videotape." This accomplishes several things for you—

- By pre-planning the use of the pictures, you get to have a hand in structuring what you'll be talking about.
- Switching off you as a "talking head" makes it possible for you to continue much longer than the usual 10 or 15 seconds. If the video is good and captures our attention, you can talk as long as the video runs.
- If you're in a debate format, your pictures will be much more compelling to sell your side of the issue. And they may also enable you to have more time than your opponent.

Bring the Book or Product

If you're there to talk about a book or a product, bring it along so the studio cameras can show it while you're discussing it. If you're dealing with a very technical subject, or one that involves a lot of numbers, the producer may want to sit down with you well in advance so the station's artists can sketch or diagram what you're talking about to make it more understandable. (See **SKILLS/News Conferences** for other visual ideas)

Avoid the Monitor

In the TV studio, there will be monitors that show what the audience is seeing. After the show begins, avoid the enormous temptation to watch the monitors. It's very difficult not to sneak a look at yourself on TV, but the camera may catch you. Very amateurish.

Pay attention to what other people are saying. Look at them. Remember, the director will be constantly switching to cutaway shots to make the video more interesting. Don't get caught picking your nose or yawning when someone else is talking.

Bring an Assistant

In **SKILLS/Interviews-General,** I suggest having a staff member present for an interview, to help you retrieve information you can't remember. When you participate in TV or radio talk shows, the assistant is even more vital. The assistant should bring a briefcase with pertinent documents, a legal pad and a Magic Marker. The aide sits in the studio, where you can see the cues, but the camera can't. During radio talk shows, the assistant can sit across the desk, in plain view. If you forget a point or a number, the staffer writes it on the legal pad and holds it up like a cue card.

Between Rounds

If you're in a debate format, the assistant can run over during commercial breaks to whisper in your ear, or hand you a document to use during the next block. Just like the assistants who help boxers between rounds, your staffer can patch up your cuts, tell you what seems to be working, and which strategy to abandon. The aide will have a much better feel for how well you're doing than you will.

Pace Yourself for Time

Once the show begins, you need to pace yourself, and be aware of time. If the conversation is lively, 30 minutes goes very quickly. You may discover that you never got to the main point you wanted to make. If it looks like the moderator is not going to reach that area, look for some way to take the conversation there yourself.

"You know, we've danced around this entire subject without getting to what I believe should be our main concern." Then tell us what it is.

Time Signals

There are some strategies that can be played with time segments of the broadcast, particularly if you're debating with another guest. A 30-minute show usually has two or three commercial breaks. The floor crew holds up signs that tell the moderator when to break for a commercial. A big "2" means two minutes. A "30," thirty seconds before the break.

The signal that tells the moderator to hurry is both hands rolling—the same signal a football referee uses to restart the clock. In television, that means speed it up. If they need to slow down and fill time, the floor manager gives a signal that looks like stretching taffy—"Stretch it out." Waving at the moderator means, "End the show. Tell everybody goodbye." And a finger drawn across the throat means, "Cut it NOW. RIGHT NOW."

If you're aware of those signals, it helps you form an answer that will fit before a break. The moderator won't have to interrupt you in mid-thought.

Time Strategy

If you want to drop your big bomb so the camera can catch your opponent's surprise and fluster, make sure there's enough time before a break. You'll lose the effect if you drop the bomb and the moderator says, "We'll be right back to get the other side's response." That will also give your opponent about two minutes to hide the shock and come up with a good alibi.

Or, you may decide that it's to your advantage to dump your most scandalous accusation just before a break, so the audience has a chance to digest it and let it sink in before your opponent can deny it.

Surprise!

There are few surprise witnesses or shocking new evidence in criminal trials these days. Unlike the Perry Mason show, most rules of court procedure now give each side an opportunity before the trial to take depositions from every witness who will testify. They get to examine every shred of evidence long before the trial begins.

One of the attractions of live television debates is the chance that we'll see the gladiators use a surprise attack. We want to see them speared to the wall, writhing in mortal agony. There's no better place to drop new documentary evidence than in front of a live television camera.

The scenario can go something like this:

SENATOR BACKWATER: Nobody has a better voting record than mine when it comes to civil rights issues. I have spent my entire life fighting for justice and quality, regardless of race, creed or color.

CHALLENGER UPSTART: (reaching into a briefcase) Funny you would say that, Senator. I just happen to have a picture here of you, at age 21, leading a Ku Klux Klan parade down the main street of the little town where you went to college. I'll hold it up so the cameras can see it.

SENATOR BACKWATER: (flustered) That's a damned lie. Whatever trash you have there is a phony, cheap counterfeit.

CHALLENGER UPSTART: I thought you might say something like that, Senator, so I did some more research and came up with this column which you wrote for the college newspaper. Let me refresh your memory. In it, you say that blacks—I guess I should quote you directly—you say "niggers" are genetically inferior and should never be allowed to enter the campus because they would not be able to understand abstract thought or civilized behavior. And I have here a sworn affidavit from the editor of that newspaper, certifying that you are the same Phineas Backwater who led Ku Klux Klan rallies and wrote this essay. I'll make all of this material available to the reporters here in the studio just as soon as this debate is over.

ZAP!

No other forum can match the impact of live, juicy exposure on television. But you must be sure the information is absolutely true. If it's not, you'll be accused of dirty tricks. If you hit below the belt, or take cheap shots, you'll look shady and sleazy. In the end, you'll be damaged more than your opponent.

Try Not To Evade

If you're on the receiving end of a tough question, radio and television make an evasive answer much more obvious. Pauses and stumbling for the right word are amplified. It's probably best to answer the question as directly as you can, put your position in its best light, and move on. Use the question that points to your weakness as a springboard to reach your strength.

OTTO MAKER: Yes, we fought the recall of that model because there has not been a single critical injury as the result of a failure of that part. Not one. On the other hand, we voluntarily recalled the 1986 model when we realized we had a problem with a bolt in the rear suspension system. Nobody had to force us to spend 80 million dollars for that recall. We did it voluntarily, once we were able to confirm there was a problem. And while we're talking about accidents, let's look at the difference in fatal accident frequency for domestic cars versus imports. I just happen to have the latest study here with me, charted so the camera can pick it up.

Take the Tough Ones First

For best overall effect, get the troublesome questions out of the way early. Then you have the rest of the show to counter with a brighter side. Television producers format their news shows that way. Put all the bad news at the beginning of the newscast. Close the show with a light, funny feature story—a "kicker" that leaves the audience smiling or feeling that maybe everything's not so bad after all.

Some radio talk show hosts are so insulting you have to be a masochist to accept an invitation. You'll feel flattered when the producer calls you. If you're not familiar with the show and the host, ask around. It may not be in your best interest to accept.

On the show, you'll get some wacko calls. Laughter is sometimes the best defense for stupid or insulting questions. The callers to these shows also tend to be at the far ends of the opinion spectrum. You're not going to change their minds. State your point, and if the host doesn't cut them off, move on with something like a chuckle and "It's very clear to me that I'm not going to change your mind and you're not going to change mine. But I respect your right to that opinion."

Remember to invest a lot of energy when you're on a talk show. After it's filtered through the process, you'll always sound and look more boring than you do in real life. (See **SKILLS/Interviews-Broadcast**)

Part 2
STRATEGY

STRATEGY

ETHICS

Do They Make Up Rules As They Go Along?

When I mentioned journalistic ethics in a seminar, a middle-aged police chief interrupted. "Reporters have no ethics," he said. "They'll do whatever it takes to get a story. They have no conscience. They make up the rules as they go along." Sometimes, I conceded, that's true. But in most cases, the media live by a very rigid code of ethics—some of it written and spoken—some of it understood. That's what makes it seem so mysterious and strange to outsiders.

The ethics for many professions are established in state and federal law. Many people who deal with the news media believe, "There oughta be a law against reporters who . . ." You can fill in your own complaint.

But the First Amendment keeps popping up. "Congress shall make no law abridging . . ."

Cleaning Up Their Act

If reporters and editors seem to make up the rules as they go along, it's because they keep making those rules more strict. Journalists in America have cleaned up their act considerably in the last 25 years, as a result of public embarrassment and criticism.

People who live in glass houses, the old saying goes, shouldn't throw stones. Media people are the stone-throwers in this society. And they work in corporations that are increasingly brittle and transparent. Hypocrisy is a cardinal sin, for both journalists and the people they write about.

The rules they live by are widely recognized and understood within the profession. And when they break their own rules, there are some things you can do about it.

How To Speak TV, Print & Radio

The Out-Take Ethic

For outsiders, there is no ethic more baffling than editors and reporters who refuse to give up out-takes. Out-takes are pictures, audio tape or videotape that were never published or broadcast. In the editing process, they were taken out. Editors decided to use other pictures or tape, or none at all.

The out-take issue took on national significance in the summer of 1968, after the street demonstrations during the Democratic National Convention in Chicago. Those demonstrations were some of the first major protests, involving thousands of people, against the Vietnam War. Both federal and state prosecutors decided it was time to treat protestors more harshly.

Chicago—the 1968 Riots

They went to newspapers and television stations with subpoenas, demanding all film (videotape was not used by TV news crews yet) and still pictures taken during the demonstrations. From those pictures, they planned to prosecute anyone they could identify.

Many editors and news directors had never dealt with the issue before. Some quickly handed over their out-takes, without a fight. Others refused, saying they would destroy the pictures, if necessary, and risk contempt of court.

People outside the media could not understand why reporters, photographers and editors thought themselves immune to subpoenas and court orders. The police were using pictures already printed and broadcast to round up protestors. What was the difference between those and out-takes?

First Amendment Theory

The argument against giving up out-takes uses a First Amendment theory. "If I give you these pictures," the news media argue, "And you use them to prosecute people, then my photographers have become police agents. The public will know that. At the next demonstration, the crowd will attack the photographers to prevent their gathering evidence for the police. We will not be able to cover the demonstration, because we will be perceived as policemen. Therefore, the government subpoena violates the First Amendment—Congress (*government*) shall make no law (*subpoena or court order*) abridging freedom of the press."

We'll Never Give Up

After the 1968 hassle, many news organizations adopted a broad policy that says, "We will never give up out-takes to any governmental agency. We will destroy the pictures or hide them and risk contempt of court rather than handicap ourselves in future news gathering."

Case-by-Case Approach

Other news organizations take a case-by-case approach. "In some instances," they say, "We can give up out-takes without jeopardizing future freedom to gather news."

The hard-liners say, "If you do it once, you set up a precedent that will make it harder to refuse out-takes next time."

It is a tough question.

Suppose, for instance, that a television reporter is shooting a standup in a downtown park. The reporter flubs several times. The sun goes in and out behind the clouds. The photographer is unhappy with the light, so they do it once more. An airplane passes over and the sound is ruined, so they do it again. They use one of the standups in a story for the six o'clock news. The six flawed standups become out-takes.

Well, Almost Never

The next morning, a police detective shows up at the newsroom. "I understand you were shooting videotape in Downtown Park yesterday about two o'clock," the officer says. "I'd like to look at that tape. There was an armed robbery in a jewelry store across the street from the park at 2:05. A clerk, in the store alone, was killed. Your camera may have unknowingly photographed the killer entering or leaving the store. Right now, we have no other leads."

Is there now a reasonable argument to deny the police access to the out-takes? Some organizations will give them up in a narrow circumstance like this. There is a loophole for the station with the "no out-takes" policy. They could look at the videotape, and if it does show someone going in or out of the jewelry store, they could run it on the news tonight. Great follow-up to the murder story. Once on the air, it would no longer be an out-take, and the station could honor a subpoena without violating its policy.

Reporters as Police Agents

Twenty-five years ago, there was little concern about reporters becoming police agents. Police officers and reporters often collaborated. The police gave reporters story leads, and the reporters passed information to the police. A two-way street. It is still common in some cities for reporters to pursue an investigative story until they reach a dead-end, then turn it over to a prosecutor who can use the police and subpoena power to get information the reporter can't reach. They agree that the results of the search will be leaked to the reporter.

And if the prosecutor makes a criminal case, the reporter who supplied the tip gets an exclusive when it's time to make arrests.

Reporters Can Be Too Cozy

Some people in the news business now question that kind of coziness between the media and the police. It is not the media's job to make criminal cases, they say. That is a function of the criminal justice system. To become a police informant, they say, compromises a reporter's independence; there should be a more arm's-length relationship between reporters and the governmental agencies they cover.

In some news operations, one reporter is assigned the police beat. That reporter, for many intents and purposes, becomes a closet cop. The longer on the beat, the more the reporter is trusted. The reporter and officers do favors for each other. If there is a critical story about the department, another reporter does it. And those assigned to investigate police misconduct or corruption are careful not to do any favors—or accept any—from the police.

Reporters As Witnesses

Some news organizations have severe misgivings about their employees testifying in a criminal trial, or before a grand jury. In the early 1970s, three reporters in separate incidents refused to even go inside grand jury rooms. They had been subpoenaed to testify about illegal activities they had witnessed and written about.

They said they arranged to watch those activities by promising that they would never disclose the names of the people involved. If they went into a secret grand jury session, they argued, and their sources were later arrested, the sources would believe the reporters had betrayed them inside the grand jury room.

The Supreme Court's View

The U. S. Supreme Court combined the three incidents because they were so similar. In one decision, the court ruled that reporters have no First Amendment immunity from grand jury subpoenas. The justices said a reporter might refuse to testify about certain things once in the witness chair, and that refusal might have to be argued in court; but there are many other subjects a reporter is obligated to talk about, just as any other citizen.

Deception Through Staging

Television coverage of civil rights and war protest demonstrations made "staging" a major issue in the 1960s. TV was new. It was still exploring the power of the picture. If the camera got there after the rocks were thrown, a photographer would ask the demonstrators to throw some more rocks, with the camera rolling.

The FCC established severe penalties for stations who broadcast scenes that appeared to be spontaneous and unrehearsed when—in fact—the event had been staged for television. At some stations, rules were written that instructed staff: "You may arrive at the scene of a demonstration, and nothing is happening. When the camera is ready, the demonstration begins. It's clear they were just waiting for the camera to arrive. Leave without filming anything if you determine the demonstration was staged purely for television."

This is a slippery concept.

Photo Opportunities

Politicians and celebrities quickly learned to create "photo opportunities" for both TV and print. The politician or movie star is in the news, but impossible to reach. Then a publicist announces the politician will go to the scene of a chemical spill for a personal inspection.

Is that staging? Yes. It is an event created purely for the media.

Enhanced Media Events

An event can be greatly enhanced through staging. During presidential campaigns, where the candidate is in a motorcade driving across the city, it is not unusual for campaign workers to recruit people to enlarge the crowd. If there are stationary cameras along the way, large crowds will be arranged in the vicinity of those cameras. There may be blocks without a single person to wave at the candidate. But the crowds near the cameras give the perception that multitudes were hysterically enthusiastic along the motorcade route.

It is staged. It is deceptive. Sometimes the media tell us about the staging. Sometimes, if it makes good video, we are not told.

Dramatizations

In 1989, the use of dramatizations became popular in TV news. Actors re-enact an event that was not videotaped when it actually happened. This is a story-telling technique that has been used without question in movies and on the stage. On television, the agreed-upon ethic decreed that if dramatizations are used, the audience must be told very clearly that this is not the real event.

ABC, in a story about an alleged espionage case, videotaped a re-enactment of a State Department employee handing over national security secrets to a Russian agent.

In broadcasting the story, it was not made clear to viewers that this was a re-enactment. The videotape had been shot amateurishly, as though it were authentic counterspy surveillance. The story caused such an uproar, many TV news organizations outlawed all re-enactments and dramatizations by their news departments. Newspapers were particularly holier-than-thou in their coverage of the controversy.

Print Holier-Than-Thou

But virtually every newspaper in the nation publishes pictures of people accepting awards. If you've been at the award ceremony, you know the still photographers line the people up, position them, tell them to hold still, and then hold still for "one more."

Newspaper photographers regularly pose people involved in news and feature stories. They arrange the pose so the shot will be artistic, or another element will be in the background. It is not a candid shot. Is that staging? Yes. And print reporters, to tell us about an event they did not witness, collect witnesses and information, then write a story that—in effect—is a re-enactment.

The difference here may be the power of the picture. Television has conditioned Americans to expect video of major events, as they happened. If we see it, it must be so. Not necessarily.

Junkets and Freebies

A hundred years ago, P. T. Barnum—or one of his proteges—learned how to get free advertising when the circus came to town. First, you hired schoolboys to paste circus posters on the side of every barn within 20 miles. They'd do it for nothing if you gave them free circus tickets.

Newspaper reporters were the same way. All it took was a batch of free tickets, and a reporter would write a glowing story about that wondrous extravaganza of excitement, that colossal collection of color and courage, that stunning display of spine-tingling skill waiting for you under the Big Top.

It still works.

See the World—On Us

Until the early 1970s, it was not unusual for reporters to accept all sorts of freebies. Travel writers took elaborate trips, with an airline or a resort picking up the tab. Political writers traveled with a candidate in planes the candidate or the party paid for.

Press rooms were provided in public buildings for free. Critics received free tickets to the events they reviewed, and sportswriters almost universally accepted batches of season tickets for every conceivable event that was related in any way to sports within a hundred miles.

The Free Ticket Furor

An investigative story in a magazine caused a major furor. It told how sportswriters at major newspapers accepted large numbers of valuable season tickets, which they could sell or pass out to ingratiate themselves with other people. Embarrassed newspapers began announcing they would no longer accept free tickets to sports or cultural events.

Many news organizations drew up—some for the first time— a code of ethics for their staffs. Most now forbid accepting gifts or anything of value from any person or organization a reporter might expect to cover. Some are so strict, they won't even let their employees accept a drink or free lunch. They pay their pro rata share of transportation costs when they travel with candidates, and they even pay rent for the use of press rooms in public buildings.

Massive Freebies

But there are still freebies on a massive scale. Tourist attractions fly reporters, photographers and their families in for a weekend—everything on the house—when they open a new section or celebrate an anniversary. Many accept the invitation. Media people know a phone call will always get them as many free tickets as they want at some attractions.

Airlines invite the media along for first-class service when they open a new route to an exotic destination. Hollywood and the TV entertainment business have huge, week-long, expense-paid parties for the media to unveil their new season's shows. Some entertainment writers accept the freebie, others pay their own way.

Those policies are still evolving as news organizations become more sensitive to their own conflicts of interest. Those who refuse freebies argue that if they constantly search for conflicts of interest among public officials and corporate executives, they have to keep their own skirts clean.

A Duty to Get Both Sides

Reporters have an obligation to be fair. To get both sides of the story. To interview you, and give you a chance to answer the allegations against you. The story should be balanced and objective, unless it is clearly labeled as the journalist's personal opinion or commentary.

Truth and Accuracy

Media stories should be accurate and true. Reporters have an obligation to go beyond the obvious in search of the truth—particularly if the story will damage someone.

Promises to Keep

Reporters who accept information with strings attached are obligated to honor that contract, which is often a verbal agreement. (See **SKILLS/Off-the-Record**)

Reporters and editors must live by the same laws that other citizens do. The Constitution does not give them special dispensation to trespass, or break and enter, or wiretap your telephone.

Breaking the Law

In practice, reporters break minor laws in order to expose a problem. As an investigative reporter, I bought illegal numbers tickets and bet on horses in illegal bookie joints to show law enforcement's failure and corruption. But I did it knowing I could be prosecuted. The reasoning my editors and I used was that the public service to be gained outweighed the minor illegality.

Do journalists play God? Of course they do. Deciding just how many angels can dance on the head of their pins is tricky business.

Undercover Reporting

Undercover work to obtain a story is hotly debated within the news media. No national consensus has been reached. Some say reporters should never pose as anything but reporters. They should interview other people to obtain inside information, rather than go inside themselves in disguise.

I took the opposite position. If truth and fairness were my ethical goals, I wanted to see and hear—record and photograph—what was going on. I wanted it to be a first-hand account. If you're doing a story on a home improvement scam, do you go to the construction company office with a press card in your hat? "Hi, I'm Clark Kent of the Daily Planet and I want to know whether you've been bilking little old ladies."

The Entrapment Issue

Some journalists argue that inviting the aluminum siding salesperson into your home for the sales pitch is entrapment. Entrapment is a legal term. It is a part of the criminal law that protects innocent people from being framed by police and prosecutors. The law says defendants cannot be persuaded or coerced into breaking the law by the government, and then prosecuted by the government.

Those who endorse reporters working undercover say reporters—very much like narcotics agents who pose as dope dealers—must be very careful in what they do and say so the swindler will push the scam without any suggestions or encouragement.

Where a hidden camera is used, the audience can judge for itself whether the swindler was improperly coerced or persuaded. In states with strict laws forbidding secret recordings, hidden microphones cannot legally be used by reporters. (See **INSIDE THE MEDIA/Privacy**)

"Sneaky" Reporters

"Sneaky" is the word often used to criticize stories and pictures obtained by reporters posing as potential victims or fellow thieves. Yeah, as an investigative reporter I learned to be sneaky. I maintain that some stories and some criminal cases can never be accomplished any other way. How many of the congressmen in the Abscam investigation would have been successfully prosecuted if they had not been secretly videotaped stuffing payoff cash in their pockets and negotiating the bribes they demanded?

Within the news media, the jury is still out on ethics rules for journalists who go undercover.

Public Service Responsibility

Media people often polish their public service halos. This is a catch-all ethic. The public's need to know. Sometimes this ethic can be warped by the desire to break the big story first. If the public had waited another week before it knew, would any great harm have been done? This is the never-ending debate when the news media disclose an undercover police investigation before the case is finished. Or disclose that the highway authority is secretly planning to buy land for a new road, to keep the price down.

The same debate rages over how much the public should know about a criminal case before it goes to trial. Does the public's right to know outweigh the defendant's right to a fair trial? Those issues are still evolving.

Checkbook Journalism

Checkbook journalism became a nasty term in the middle 1970s after CBS paid H. R. Haldeman $25,000 for a lengthy interview. Haldeman had been Richard Nixon's White House chief of staff. Throughout the Watergate investigation, Haldeman had said nothing to the news media. The CBS interview was a coup that backfired.

Paying an interviewee raises the same questions that come up when a paid informer testifies at a criminal trial. Can you really believe someone who's been paid to talk? Was he paid to say that? Was there an agreement to avoid certain subjects? Would he have talked about them if the price had been high enough?

Because the Haldeman interview received so much adverse publicity, it became extremely rare for a news organization to pay cash for an interview. Other forms of payment took place, however. A newspaper or television station would charter a jet to help a crime victim confront the defendant; pay for the transportation to reunite a family; fly a critically ill child to a well-known medical center. The transportation arrangements insured exclusive coverage for the news outlet that paid the bill.

In my seminars on media ethics, newspaper editors often say, self-righteously, that they would never pay someone for an interview. That would be unethical.

Cash vs. Transportation

But as I move the hypothetical along, they say they would not hesitate to provide an airline ticket to a key witness if that meant they could get an exclusive interview. They have a very hard time explaining why paying cash is different from providing transportation or hotel accommodations.

Before the Haldeman flap, newspapers and magazines had paid people for their first-person accounts after major news events. Life magazine signed a lucrative contract with the original group of astronauts for their exclusive, personal stories. That was checkbook journalism, but there were few protests.

I suspect that the code of ethics in some editors' minds is there because it has been the custom—not because it has been carefully thought out.

Tabloid Journalism

Tabloids in the 1970s and 1980s never let the ethics banning checkbook journalism get in the way of a juicy story. Their correspondents were often in bidding wars for exclusive access to people or information. Conventional journalists looked down their noses at their trashy brethren.

In the early 1990s, the enormous success of TV shows like "Hard Copy" and "A Current Affair" diluted considerably some of the old journalistic ethics.

The TV shows were called "Tabloid TV" or "Trash TV" because their choice of stories—and the way they slanted them— were very similar to the print tabloids. Sex, crime, aliens from outer space, celebrities, money, family violence, scandal and schmaltz became standard ingredients.

William Kennedy Smith's Case

When Sen. Ted Kennedy's nephew was charged with rape in Palm Beach, the case filled every tabloid reporter's wildest fantasies. There, wrapped in one story, were all the elements that drive their coverage.

There was a bidding frenzy for exclusive interviews with witnesses and friends. In the heat of combat for new tidbits of information, both NBC News and *The New York Times* disclosed the identity of the alleged rape victim. That had always been considered unethical. There was a great deal of pontificating to justify their breaking the old code.

Tabloid journalism's influence on news worldwide continues to grow. Once the tabloids exploit stories of sex, scandal and violence—particularly involving celebrities—the conventional media join the pack. Examples:

- During the 1992 presidential campaign, Gennifer Flowers' allegations that she had an extended affair with Bill Clinton.
- In 1992 and 1993, stories about estrangement and marital infidelity among members of the British royal family.
- The Amy Fisher story. In early 1993, all three networks produced documentaries or docu-dramas after the New York teen-ager was convicted of shooting the wife of her lover.

The ethical concepts of what journalists should pay for, and how personally intrusive they should be, is constantly changing. Many of those changes are driven by competition, profit, and the media's relative immunity from lawsuits when they write about public people (See **INSIDE THE MEDIA** chapters on **Libel** and **Privacy**).

Previewing Stories

Interviewees often ask if they can see a story before it is published, or goes on the air. That's considered a no-no. If you saw it, and didn't like what the reporter wrote, or the way it was presented, you'd say so. The reporter might be influenced, and lose independence. In effect, you would become an editor for a story about yourself. You're not very objective about something you're personally involved in. So don't ask.

Use Everything or Nothing

If you're doing battle with a news organization, you may not trust their editing of what you say. Many people in this situation say they'll submit to an interview only if the reporter agrees to print or broadcast what they say, unedited.

This kind of offer is almost always refused. Newspaper and magazine editors don't like to be told what they can print. As a part of their FCC licensing, broadcasters accept responsibility for everything they put on the air. In effect, they would be handing that responsibility to someone else. They can be sued if you use their station to libel someone. You might be irresponsible in other ways, like using four-letter words the FCC frowns on.

There's a way around the problem. Draw up a letter of agreement in which they say they will print or broadcast everything you say—or nothing at all. That leaves them complete editorial control of what goes in their story.

If you expect them to use what you say under that agreement, remember—it has to be brief, and to the point.

Questions in Advance

Interview subjects often ask if they can have the questions in advance. Normally, that is considered unethical. The interview— particularly on television—is supposed to be a spontaneous, unrehearsed conversation between you and the reporter.

If you know in advance what the questions are going to be, you can go to the experts and memorize their information, then make it look like it's yours.

It's similar to letting the lawyer for a witness at a trial stand behind the witness and whisper the answer to every question.

Most reporters consider it ethical to give you a broad idea of what the interview will cover, but not specific questions.

Questions in Writing

In some cases, however, you can insist, and win. This sometimes happens with highly-placed officials, celebrities, or people facing major charges. Look, they say, I'll answer your questions, but only if you submit them to me in writing. Take it or leave it. Play it my way, or not at all.

In that situation, the media will often play by your rules, but tell their readers, viewers or listeners the terms of the interview so they will not be misled. (See prepared statements in **SKILLS/ Interviews-Print**)

Political Activity

Most journalists consider any kind of political activity unethical. That includes contributions of work or money; bumper stickers on their cars; signs in their yards, attending a political meeting where they are not working as a reporter or editor. Some will even register as "Independent" to avoid any suggestion of bias toward a political party. The extremists do not register at all and do not vote.

Volunteer Work

Purists in the media also refuse to do work for a charitable organization or serve on any board—private or public. Every journalist draws a different line. It is common in many communities for newspaper editors and broadcast executives with news responsibility to work in the United Way fund-raising campaign. Reporters in those newsrooms often chafe when their bosses accept those positions. Hard-liners suspect the people who run United Way chose the boss because they believe they can get better news coverage that way. They probably can.

Sigma Delta Chi's Code

Sigma Delta Chi—the national society of professional journalists—has the most widely recognized code of ethics across the country. It is only a model—a broad guideline. Nothing in it binds reporters. There is no legal or professional commitment for them to live up to it. Many news organizations have much more stringent and specific guidelines for their employees. But this will give you an idea of some broad, general areas that most people in the news media would agree on.

Here's the full text of the Sigma Delta Chi Code of Ethics, adopted at the group's 1973 national convention. The last section—Mutual Trust—was added in 1987.

Serve the Truth

The Society of Professional Journalists, Sigma Delta Chi, believes the duty of journalists is to serve the truth.

We believe the agencies of mass communication are carriers of public discussion and information, acting on their Constitutional mandate and freedom to learn and report the facts.

We believe in public enlightenment as the forerunner of justice, and in our Constitutional role to seek the truth as part of the public's right to know the truth.

Objectivity and Fairness

We believe those responsibilities carry obligations that require journalists to perform with intelligence, objectivity, accuracy, and fairness.

To these ends, we declare acceptance of the standards of practice here set forth:

RESPONSIBILITY: The public's right to know of events of public importance and interest is the overriding mission of the mass media. The purpose of distributing news and enlightened opinion is to serve the general welfare. Journalists who use their professional status as representatives of the public for selfish or other unworthy motives violate a high trust.

Press Freedom

FREEDOM OF THE PRESS: Freedom of the press is to be guarded as an inalienable right of people in a free society. It carries with it the freedom and the responsibility to discuss, question, and challenge actions and utterances of our government and of our public and private institutions. Journalists uphold the right to speak unpopular opinions and the privilege to agree with the majority.

ETHICS: Journalists must be free of obligation to any interest other than the public's right to know the truth.

Gifts, Special Privileges

1. Gifts, favors, free travel, special treatment or privileges can compromise the integrity of journalists and their employers. Nothing of value should be accepted.

2. Secondary employment, political involvement, holding public office, and service in community organizations should be avoided if it compromises the integrity of journalists and their employers. Journalists and their employers should conduct their personal lives in a manner which protects them from conflict of interest, real or apparent. Their responsibilities to the public are paramount. That is the nature of their profession.

3. So-called news communications from private sources should

*not be published or broadcast without substantiation of their claims
to news value.*

*4. Journalists will seek news that serves the public interest,
despite the obstacles. They will make constant efforts to assure that
the public's business is conducted in public and that public records
are open to public inspection.*

Confidential Sources

*5. Journalists acknowledge the newsman's ethic of protecting
confidential sources of information.*

*ACCURACY AND OBJECTIVITY: Good faith with the public
is the foundation of all worthy journalism.*

1. Truth is our ultimate goal.

*2. Objectivity in reporting the news is another goal, which
serves as the mark of an experienced professional. It is a standard of
performance toward which we strive. We honor those who achieve it.*

3. There is no excuse for inaccuracies or lack of thoroughness.

Headline Accuracy

*4. Newspaper headlines should be fully warranted by the con-
tents of the articles they accompany. Photographs and telecasts
should give an accurate picture of an event and not highlight a
minor incident out of context.*

*5. Sound practice makes clear distinction between news reports
and expressions of opinion. News reports should be free of opinion
or bias and represent all sides of an issue.*

*6. Partisanship in editorial comment which knowingly departs
from the truth violates the spirit of American journalism.*

*7. Journalists recognize their responsibility for offering informed
analysis, comment, and editorial opinion on public events and issues. They accept the obligation to present such material by individuals whose competence, experience, and judgment qualify them
for it.*

Labeling Opinion

*8. Special articles or presentations devoted to advocacy or the
writer's own conclusions and interpretations should be labeled as
such.*

FAIR PLAY: *Journalists at all times will show respect for the dignity, privacy, rights, and well-being of people encountered in the course of gathering and presenting the news.*

1. The news media should not communicate unofficial charges affecting reputation or moral character without giving the accused a chance to reply.

Personal Privacy Rights

2. The news media must guard against invading a person's right to privacy.

3. The media should not pander to morbid curiosity about details of vice and crime.

4. It is the duty of news media to make prompt and complete correction of their errors.

5. Journalists should be accountable to the public for their reports and the public should be encouraged to voice its grievances against the media. Open dialogue with our readers, viewers, and listeners should be fostered.

MUTUAL TRUST: *Adherence to this Code of Ethics is intended to preserve the bond of mutual trust and respect between American journalists and the American people. This Society shall thereby work actively in programs of education and other means to encourage individual journalists to understand their responsibility to adhere to these tenets. The Society shall also encourage journalistic publications and broadcasters to recognize their responsibility to frame codes of ethics in concert with their employees to serve as guidelines for journalists in these organizations, so that mutual trust and respect between journalists and their audience will be preserved and strengthened.*

STRATEGY

FIGHTING BACK

I'm Just Not Gonna Take It Any More

When a news story is inaccurate, libelous, unfair, slanted, absurd, or just plain, outrageously incompetent, what can you do about it? In the old days, you challenged the editor or reporter to a duel. Or thrashed him (female editors were extremely rare back then) with your cane. Those techniques have gone out of style, unless you want to be the lead story in tomorrow's newspaper and perhaps make the wire services and network news. Great idea, if that's the kind of coverage you're looking for.

Most people react angrily, in ways that often create more bad stories, and worse public images for themselves. It may make you feel better—just as it would to punch the reporter—but in the end, you'll lose the fight.

Here are some of the most common reactions.

Throw Them Out

Vow never to talk to a reporter—any reporter—again. Hire a bouncer. Issue orders to your staff that any reporter or photographer who sets foot on the premises is to be violently ejected.

This will endear you to all newspaper editors and broadcast news directors. On slow news days, it means they can count on you to liven their news. "Hey, Gorilla," they'll yell across the newsroom, "Go over to Neanderthal's place and try to get in. Keep the camera rolling. We need something to fill the second block."

Great stuff. Will probably earn you a special award at the next Emmy or Pulitzer ceremony. Most Valuable Resource to Increase Ratings and Readership. Marvelous for your public image.

Shut Them Out

Punish the offending station, network, magazine or newspaper by shutting them out. Feed lots of stories to their competition. Hold news conferences and invite everyone else, but conveniently forget to include the offenders.

This is the most common reaction in government agencies—particularly police departments—when they're unhappy with a story.

It rarely works.

Public Records Are Public

Most of the records reporters need for daily coverage of a public agency are—by law—public. If you shut them out, they'll go to court, and win easily. The entire process will get lots of coverage.

The news of your fight with the reporter will prompt disgruntled people within your office to make anonymous calls, leaking new dirt and ammunition to the reporter.

You'll wind up with a big LOSER tag around your neck. It'll look like you're trying to hide something. The story of your shutting them out will be a better story than those you're feeding the competition.

Look at the Compelling C's in **STRATEGY/Selling Your Story**. One of the most powerful elements is CONFLICT. Another NO-WIN RESPONSE.

Stop the Advertising

Cancel your advertising at the offending station or publication. Call your friends who advertise there and urge them to pull their commercials or ads.

In a small town this may have some effect. Otherwise, you're a real candidate for Kamikaze School. Your business needs to advertise a lot worse than the news outlet needs your money. Most TV newscasts sell every available second of commercial time. Other companies are probably lined up, waiting to buy the time you're giving up. Unless you're a major department store or supermarket chain, your advertising dollar is so insignificant, it won't matter.

You Give Them New Vigor

At a station or newspaper with ethical management, the advertising staff is completely divorced from the news operation. To prove that advertisers have no voice in news judgment, the news department may come after you with even more vigor than before.

If it's a station with low ratings, or a declining newspaper, dropping your ads may hurt them a little. But losing the advertising exposure may hurt you more. And it'll hurt a lot more, months from now, when you come back with your hat in your hand, asking if you can place some new advertising with them.

Not a great solution. But in narrow circumstances, better than the first two.

Complaining is Important

It is absolutely vital that you complain when you feel strongly that a newspaper, magazine, TV or radio outlet has published or broadcast an incompetent, unfair, or dishonest story.

You may not want a retraction or correction. That can make matters worse, as I'll explain in a moment. But if you don't complain, the error will be repeated in every future story. Once it is printed three times, the error becomes fact. Almost impossible to correct.

The complaint should not be made in anger. Wait until you've cooled off to decide how you'll complain.

The first time an editor or news director receives a complaint about a reporter's story, you may not get any discernible reaction. But if yours is the second or third complaint about the same reporter or photographer, the editor or news director will begin to wonder whether there is a problem on the staff who could get the newspaper or the station into much more serious trouble.

Truth, the Perfect Defense

Remember that in a libel suit, truth is the perfect defense for a journalist. Editors these days are very concerned about libel suits. More are being filed, and the media often lose. Jurors who feel the media abuse their power have a way to even the score.

We're not talking about small amounts here. Libel and privacy suits usually ask damages in tens of millions of dollars. So a reporter who can't write truthfully. For whatever reason. It can be incompetence. It may be the inability to leave personal prejudices out of the copy. The reporter's supervisors are vitally concerned. (See **INSIDE THE MEDIA/Libel**)

In the same way, privacy suits are often lost because of the way the reporter or photographer acted at the scene of the story. Editors and news directors need to know if they have a staffer who likes to bully people. Who is willing to break the norms of human behavior—perhaps break the law—if that's what it takes to get the story. (See **STRATEGY/Ethics** and **INSIDE THE MEDIA/Privacy.**

Those editors and news directors have no way to know about inaccuracy, incompetence, or improper behavior if you don't tell them.

How to Complain

Let's go through some of the ways in which you can complain with maximum results.

Suppose the story is inaccurate. Name misspelled, titles wrong, errors in numbers that are not really damaging to you or your organization. A letter is probably the best way to complain. I'd suggest writing the reporter, with a copy to the immediate boss. It should read something like this:

"Dear Reporter:

"The story you wrote in yesterday's newspaper/newscast carried several inaccuracies. I thought you should know, so future stories will not repeat those inaccuracies.

"In the first paragraph, you called my organization the Amalgamated Association of Aardvarks. The proper name is The National Association of Aardvark Advocates.

"In the second paragraph, you said we spent $3 million lobbying the state legislature last year. The correct figure was $300,000."

Correction? Be Careful

You may ask for a correction or retraction in print or on the air. But remember that reporters and editors have big egos. To admit they made a mistake is painful. To distract from the mistake, in the same story that corrects the error, they may unload some new information that is even more damaging to you or your group.

If you have any idea of filing a suit because the story damaged you in some way, consult an attorney before you complain. In some states, the form and timing of the complaint can have a major effect on your rights in that future suit. (See **INSIDE THE MEDIA/Libel** and **Privacy** sections)

If an inaccurate or unfair story has caused real problems for you or your organization, a face-to-face meeting may be the best way to make your case. Here again, I'd suggest that you call the reporter and/or the editor to set up the meeting.

You need to be prepared for that meeting. You will need documentation to show how the story distorted the truth, or how outrageously the staffer acted.

You Need to See the Boss

It is critical that you reach the right person with your complaint. The organizational structure at most radio and television stations goes something like this:

The station's **general manager** hires and fires the **news director**, who is responsible for everything in the news department. The news director may have an assistant.

The **assignment editor** decides how the station's news staff will be used every day. How their time will be invested. Who will cover what. The assignment editor is expected to know what's happening in your area, and cover it, if it's important. At most stations, the assignment editor is not responsible for the quality or accuracy of the stories, and will not have much input into how those stories will appear in the newscast.

Each newscast has a **producer**, who's roughly the equivalent of a page editor at a newspaper. The producer decides which stories go into the newscast—how long they'll be, in which order, and in what form.

At larger stations, there will be an **executive producer**, whose duties may include review of scripts for accuracy and fairness. The executive producer is often a sort of assistant news director, with a variety of responsibilities.

Power to Hire & Fire

The news director does all the hiring and firing within the news department. Reporters and photographers work under the direction of producers and the assignment editor, but their competence and any disciplinary action will eventually be decided by the news director.

Most station managers will meet with or talk to their news directors several times a day. Newscasts are the major local image-producer for a television station. Remember, if the station is a network affiliate, the station has no control or responsibility for the network programming it broadcasts.

News directors and station managers are human, too. Their natural reaction will be to defend their employees, and their stories.

Make Your Own Tape

Documenting a broadcast error can be difficult. In the past, the FCC required broadcasters to keep a copy of their scripts or a tape of their broadcasts. Not any more. They are not required to provide you with a copy of what they said.

If you have any advance warning that a story may be slanted or antagonistic, you should at least make an audio recording of the broadcast. A videotape recording of a television story is much better, because part of the inaccuracy or slant may be created visually.

The audio or video tape will be the only way you can prove you were misquoted, or how the story was inaccurate.

The Newspaper Hierarchy

At newspapers, the top editor in charge of everything to do with news is the **managing editor** or **executive editor**, who may or may not have jurisdiction over the editorial page. Many newspapers have an autonomous **editorial page editor**.

The person with overall supervision is the **general manager** or **publisher**. But in most cases, the general manager or publisher is more concerned with the paper's mechanical and financial operations. They leave journalism to the top editor.

At most newspapers there will be a **city editor** or **metro editor** who supervises all stories in the local area. A **state editor** will be in charge of stories and reporters outside the local area but inside the state. There may be a **national editor**, a **political editor**, an **investigative projects editor**. (See **STRATEGY/Selling Your Story**)

Complaining, Step by Step

These are the steps to take if you have a complaint about a story:

Step 1

Call the reporter. Discuss the story. Find out who the immediate supervisor is, or the editor who supervised the story you're unhappy with. If it's a simple complaint to correct numbers or names for future stories, tell the reporter you'll send a letter confirming the call, as I suggested earlier. If you're unhappy with the reporter's response, take the next step.

Step 2

Write the reporter's editor or news director a detailed letter describing your complaint with the story or a staff member's behavior. Quote from the offensive story and write, in detail, your version of what happened; or how the story is inaccurate or unfair.

Repeat. *Don't file your complaint in anger.* Suppose you've headed a study commission that produced a final report. The story about your study is grossly inaccurate. If you're writing a newspaper editor, you may want to include a copy of the study, a copy of the story, and something like, "Dear Editor: I thought you would want to know that a story you printed Monday was very inaccurate. If you'll compare the enclosed study with what your reporter wrote about it, I think you'll come to the same conclusion."

If you are badly misquoted, your letter to the news director should say something like, "Dear News Director: I thought you would want to know that I was quoted entirely out of context in the story you broadcast Monday night. The way in which my interview was edited created a false and very damaging impression. I recorded the entire interview with your reporter, and I'm enclosing a transcript. I think you'll come to the same conclusion. If you'd like to hear the tape, or have a copy of it, I'd be glad to furnish one. And I'd be happy to discuss it with you."

If you're still unhappy with the results, go to Step 3.

Step 3 for Radio & TV

Write the station manager the same kind of detailed letter, but this time make it clear that you're angry. Send a copy to the president of the corporation that owns the station. You can usually get the names and addresses by calling the secretary of the station manager.

If not, go to the station and ask to see the PUBLIC FILE. This is a file required by the FCC which will include fairly complete details of station ownership and corporate officers; and what the station committed to do when it applied for its license with the FCC. If your complaint involves fairness or deception, or something that might lead to a lawsuit, send a copy of this letter to the corporate vice-president for legal affairs.

Step 3 for Newspapers

Write the managing editor or executive editor the same kind of detailed letter, but this time make it clear you're angry. Send a copy to the president of the corporation which owns the newspaper. Ownership will usually be included somewhere in the masthead on the editorial page.

If not, call the general manager's secretary and ask for the name and address of the corporate president.

Step 4

Now it's time to write the president of the corporation, if you're still unhappy.

Local radio and TV stations are usually much more responsive to complaints than newspapers. They're always concerned about their public image. Anything that turns off viewers lowers ratings. What they charge for advertising time is directly related to how many people watch.

Many station managers require their telephone switchboard operators to keep a daily log of calls—both complaints and praise. It gives them a daily survey of audience reaction to their programming.

How To Speak TV, Print & Radio

Until the mid-1980s, the FCC required stations to compile voluminous "ascertainment interviews." These were personal interviews with people from all segments of the community, asking them to list and rate the community's major problems and issues. At license renewal time, the station was supposed to show how its programming had served the community's needs, as outlined in those interviews.

But as part of the gradual deregulation of broadcasting in the 1980s, ascertainment interviews were discontinued. But veterans in the business still reflexively respond when you complain that the station is violating its public trust and responsibility.

If you're contemplating a lawsuit against the station, you should consider having your lawyer look at each of your letters before you send them. The attorney might want to send along a cover letter.

Tell the Competition

Competing local media may be interested in reporting the competition's goof or breach of journalistic ethics.

Regional magazines often cover local media better than newspapers or broadcasters.

This idea of the media tattling on each other is fairly new. In some cities, they still refuse to report each other's indiscretions. After all, the next embarrassing story could be about me, if this thing gets out of hand. But that's changing.

If your complaint involves a broadcaster, write a letter to the editor of the local newspaper. If the newspaper has a television critic, there might be a story there. Newspaper Sunday supplements and regional magazines are often interested in semi-investigative stories that expose shoddy television reporting or policy.

Media Critics

A few television stations have media critics who are always looking for material. They'd love to hear from you if there's a story of sloppy, inaccurate reporting or slanted, unfair treatment. In some cities, public television stations have regular reviews of local reporting.

In 1983, *TV Guide* wrote a scorching story about a CBS documentary that had suggested General William Westmoreland conspired to hide or distort reports on enemy strength and casualties in Vietnam. Hodding Carter, former press secretary for the State Department, also did an investigative special for Public Broadcasting on the same CBS documentary.

Westmoreland vs. CBS

Eventually, Westmoreland sued CBS for libel. It was one of the most costly suits in the history of American journalism. It never reached the jury. After weeks of testimony and high-intensity media coverage, Westmoreland dropped the suit, claiming a moral victory.

In reality, both Westmoreland and CBS suffered heavy casualties as a result of what both sides uncovered in the litigation.

ABC was a pioneer with periodic programs that examine some of its own news coverage. After Geraldo Rivera did a piece for "20/20" claiming aluminum wiring was a serious fire hazard in thousands of American homes, a spokesman for the industry had a chance to sit across from Rivera in the studio and debate the accuracy of that story, with Ted Koppel as referee.

Koppel On the Road

The format was so successful, Koppel took the concept on tour. Called "Viewpoint," or "Town Meeting," the shows are produced periodically in different cities. They have a large studio audience, which can air complaints about media coverage, both local and national. Reporters, editors and producers—as well as the people involved in their coverage—are available to answer questions from the audience and debate the fairness, accuracy, and quality of the stories.

Too Much Sleaze

After Rivera left ABC, he syndicated a talk show called "Geraldo," which quickly settled on a format that invited outrageous guests. The subject matter was usually some form of kinky sex, human degradation, violence—sometimes all the above. For a while, the show did very well. But by early 1990, so many people had complained about the show's subject matter, local stations were threatening to drop it. Rivera quickly hired a public relations agent to help solve the problem, and said he would tone down future content.

Complaining works. In broadcasting particularly, it threatens profits. Executives sit up and listen.

Complaining to a Network

Effectively complaining about a network news story is much more difficult than complaining locally. The networks have regional bureaus across the country. Correspondents work out of those bureaus. They spend about four days a week on the road. If you're interviewed by a network correspondent or producer, chances are you'll never see either of them again. Their immediate supervisor will be a bureau chief hundreds of miles away. The people with the real power are in New York.

Know the Producer

If you're interviewed by the network, find out which bureau is originating the story and the name of the field producer. A network crew will usually include the correspondent, field producer, photographer and sound technician. The correspondent is the one you'll see and hear when the story is broadcast. The producer does most of the work. The producer scouts the story, sets up interviews, gathers documents, manages travel arrangements, figures a way to hustle the videotape to New York by plane or satellite, and may even write the script the correspondent reads.

Work Your Way Up

If you try to call a network bureau to complain to the correspondent or producer, they probably won't be there. They're running to catch a plane halfway around the world. So start working your way up the hierarchy.

1. Phone the bureau chief. Give your assessment of the story and its failings. During the conversation, ask who the bureau chief's immediate supervisor is. Each network is organized differently.

2. Write the superior. At each stage, send a copy of your letter to the next one up the ladder.

3. Write the head of network news. The title of the news division boss varies from time to time. It may be president of XYZ News, which is a division of the XYZ Network. Or the network may have several vice-presidents—one of them in charge of news. Remember to be detailed and specific with your complaint. And if you're still not happy with the response:

4. Write the president of the network. If there's any thought of a lawsuit, send a copy to the vice-president for legal affairs. You can get the names and addresses of network executives by calling ABC, CBS or NBC in New York. CNN is headquartered in Atlanta.

Complaining to the FCC

The FCC processes complaints on virtually every kind of problem in broadcast news—from allegations of unfair or distorted coverage to gripes about the quality of the picture or sound. Most of the people who write get back a form letter asking for more detailed information. Here—more so than with a complaint to a station or network—great detail is extremely important if you expect to have any impact. The local station or network knows exactly which story you're talking about, and precisely what they said. The FCC has no way of knowing.

You Must Give Details

So you have to give them the station or network that broadcast the story, the date, which newscast, the correspondent or anchorperson who read it, quotes from the story (a transcript of exactly what was said will impress them) and why the story is inaccurate, unfair or deceptive.

Send your complaint to:

Federal Communications Commission
Mass Media Bureau
1919 M Street NW
Washington, D.C. 20554

The revocation of a broadcast license is extremely rare. Virtually every revocation in the history of the FCC was based on some kind of deception. But the loss of its license is so threatening, a station always sits up and takes notice if the FCC begins an inquiry.

Nixon-Agnew vs. Media

In the entire history of the United States, government has never used its power to intimidate and harass the news media as energetically as it did during the Nixon Administration. Until he was charged with a federal crime and forced to resign, Nixon's vice-president, Spiro Agnew, was the administration's hatchet man for the press. It was Charles Colson's job at the White House to watch all three network newscasts each evening. If he saw something about the administration he didn't like, he called the network in New York and demanded to talk to the anchorperson immediately, while the newscast was in progress. Occasionally, he succeeded, during a commercial break. It was an effective way to badger the network.

National News Council

Agnew kept suggesting that the news media had become too powerful. That some agency ought to be created to control them. How that could be done without repealing the First Amendment was never explained.

In that atmosphere, the National News Council was born, as a privately financed group to investigate complaints about the news media. For some, it was an idea whose time had come. Others hoped a private review of complaints would slow the campaign to create some kind of governmental control for the press.

Only Power To Embarrass

The council had no power, except the power to embarrass news organizations that were dishonest, inaccurate or unfair. The Council got half its financing from foundations; the rest from individuals and corporate contributors.

Few People Saw the Slap

The council's major drawback was the limited circulation of its findings. They were published in the *Columbia Journalism Review*. A slap from the council was embarrassing within the profession, but few non-professionals ever heard about it. The wire services carried short stories when the council criticized a newspaper, radio or TV station. Many newspapers, including *The New York Times*, wouldn't carry the stories. They opposed, on principle, the idea of the National News Council.

And so, in 1984, the News Council quietly died. But a lot of people keep proposing that the idea be revived.

Columbia Journalism Review

The *Columbia Journalism Review*, founded in 1961, is generally considered the conscience of American journalism. In the first edition, it stated its purpose:

"To assess the performance of journalism in all its forms, to call attention to its shortcomings and strengths, and to help define—or redefine—standards of honest, responsible service . . . to help stimulate continuing improvement in the profession and to speak out for what is right, fair, and decent."

Darts and Laurels

The *Review* is published bi-monthly by the Graduate School of Journalism at Columbia University. In each issue, there is a section called "Darts and Laurels," in which the staff praises or roasts networks, local stations, and the print media, giving details on stories that deserve a dart or a laurel. The editors are always interested in a major story, or a pattern of performance and policy that violates journalistic ethics. If it's serious enough, they'll assign a reporter to investigate and publish a full story in the magazine.

CJR's circulation—about 31,000—makes it the most widely read magazine in this field. Most of its readers are journalists, journalism professors, and public relations people.

If you think the editors would be interested in your complaint, write:

The Columbia Journalism Review
700 Journalism Building
Columbia University
New York, NY 10027

Sigma Delta Chi and Quill

Sigma Delta Chi—also known as The Society for Professional Journalists—has created the most widely-recognized code of ethics for journalists. You'll find the complete text of that code in **STRATEGY/Ethics.** Most major cities have a local Sigma Delta Chi chapter. In most chapters, newspaper people will be much more active than broadcasters. Call the city desk at the local newspaper to find the name of the Sigma Delta Chi president in your city. Call. Talk about your complaint. The initiative and strength of the organization varies a lot from city to city. A strong chapter, incensed over a story that was inaccurate, unfair or unethical, might pass a resolution condemning the offender.

Quill is Sigma Delta Chi's national magazine. *Quill* also publishes articles that criticize journalistic performance, but its circulation and influence are much smaller than the *Columbia Journalism Review.*

You can write the editor at:

The Quill
16 South Jackson St.
Greencastle, IN 46135

American Journalism Review

Founded in 1977 as the *Washington Journalism Review,* the name was changed in early 1993. Its monthly circulation is about 25,000. A 1987 survey by the American Society of Newspaper Editors ranked it the best magazine in the field. It is slickly produced, with sharp, interesting writing, usually by journalists rather than academics. Its stories have the flavor of "insider" gossip and intrigue during power struggles at places like *The New York Times, The Atlanta Journal-Constitution,* and *The Washington Post. AJR* was privately owned until May, 1987, when it was given to the University of Maryland's Journalism School. The journalism school has been able to maintain the commercial look and appeal the original publisher gave it.

You can write *AJR's* editor at:

American Journalism Review
4716 Pontiac St., Suite 310
College Park, MD 20740-2493

Local Journalism Reviews

Some cities have local journalism reviews, often written and distributed free among local journalists. In some cases, they are almost underground publications, where local reporters write anonymously about scandals inside their station or publication. Again, ask the newspaper city desk if it is aware of any local journalism review and how to get in touch with its editor.

Schools of Communications

A school of journalism or communications in your area probably has personal contact with some of the people in local news. The editor or news director may be a graduate.

While a journalism school usually has no formal way to investigate or criticize poor journalistic performance, the dean might be able to quietly shake his finger and influence the station or newspaper the next time a similar situation occurs.

Special Interest Groups

There are a number of national organizations designed to fight for specific causes—particularly television's coverage of those causes. Some lobby for what they believe would be better television. Things like less violence, better children's programming, less sexuality, more programs of one kind or another. Some of these organizations have money and staff to help you carry a complaint to court, to Congress or the FCC. Most of them, however, will be interested in your complaint only if it fits their narrow area of interest.

Accuracy in Media

The most vigorous of the special interest media watchdogs is Accuracy In Media, a conservative non-profit group formed in 1969 to combat what it feels is a liberal slant in American journalism. A.I.M publishes *The A.I.M. Report* twice a month, detailing media coverage it labels inaccurate or unfair. It also administers a Media Victims' Fund, which helps pay the cost of selected lawsuits and FCC complaints against the media.

The group produces a radio report called "Media Monitor," carried by about 90 stations. About 100 newspapers carry a column A.I.M. provides. It buys advertising in *CJR* and *AJR* to castigate the media. A.I.M. also owns a token amount of stock in some major media corporations. An A.I.M. staffer has become a fixture at annual stockholders' meetings, to complain about alleged unfair or inaccurate reporting.

A.I.M.'s Vietnam Rebuttal

After the Public Broadcasting System showed a 13-part series on the Vietnam War, A.I.M. produced two television documentaries to rebut the PBS view of the war. PBS ran one of the A.I.M. documentaries. The other was broadcast by independent stations.

You can send your complaint about media coverage to:

Accuracy in Media
1275 K Street, N.W.
Suite 1150
Washington, DC 20005

F.A.I.R.—a Different View

A liberal perspective on media criticism is available at Fairness and Accuracy in Reporting. With foundation money, F.A.I.R. calls itself a research and information center. Its primary contention is that large corporate ownership of multiple media outlets is not good. That this kind of ownership inhibits media competition, investigative reporting and the broadest possible coverage of major issues in the society.

F.A.I.R. was created in 1986. In mid-1987, it began a monthly newsletter, *EXTRA!* which it offers free to journalists. In late 1992, it began a syndicated radio show called "CounterSpin." F.A.I.R. is concerned about those stories that are never broadcast or published because they might be embarrassing or costly to media owners; that the progressive point of view might not be covered as the result of corporate chain ownership. If you think they'd be interested in your complaint, write:

Fairness and Accuracy in Reporting
130 W. 25th Street
New York, NY 10001

STRATEGY

MEDIA POLICY

You Mean I Can't Tell Them to Buzz Off?

I believe most organizations should have a written media policy. The larger the organization, the more detailed the policy should be. Once the policy is written, the boss should personally tell employees why the policy is there. AND WHAT IT REALLY MEANS. If you don't make your intentions very clear, you'll get a lot of different interpretations. Staffers should be given specific scenarios in which reporters might approach the organization, and how they should handle it.

Too Many Thou Shall Nots

Many media policies are just pages of Thou Shall Nots. Don't talk to reporters. Don't talk about company policy. Don't let reporters or photographers enter without an escort. Don't violate client confidentiality. Don't contradict the governor's political stance.

Don't. Don't. Don't.

After reading all those don'ts, most employees decide the safest course of action is to avoid reporters at all costs. If a reporter shows up, cover your face and hide under the desk.

Corporations and government agencies send their top executives to my seminars, to learn how to deal effectively with the media.

The First Contact

A real problem is that reporters' first contact with an organization is often an entry-level employee who knows nothing about media relations. It scares them. So they become very defensive.

The reporter may interpret that employee's response as the official company line. A story that was slightly critical may suddenly head toward a full expose of scandal in the executive suite.

That's why the written policy is so critical. I suggest that written policies stress the positive aspects of media relations first. Then get around to specific things you should not talk about, and how to refer the reporter up the ladder of command.

It the end of this chapter, I've reproduced portions of model policies I've written for clients. They can be easily modified to fit your organization. Every media policy should contain some basic points:

The Basic Points

1. We need to tell the public who we are and what we do.
2. Public knowledge of the organization is vital to our success.
3. Reporters and photographers need to be treated courteously and diplomatically. Their impression of you becomes their impression of the entire organization, and that is reflected in their stories.
4. Discuss with reporters only those facts you personally know about.
5. If you don't have personal knowledge, help the reporter reach someone who does.
6. If you would give a customer or a client public information the reporter is asking for, give it without hesitation to the reporter.
7. Let a designated executive (usually the PIO) know as soon as possible after any contact with the media. We need to be aware of stories that involve us, so we can provide additional information.
8. Refer media questions about policy or complicated technical issues to the PIO or other designated executive.
9. Return all reporters' calls within 15 minutes. If a message is left and the person the reporter called can't be reached, someone else should return the call. "Can I help you?" We do not want to be surprised by tonight's newscast or tomorrow morning's newspaper. A story about this organization should never say we could not be reached for comment.

10. Every story about this organization should include our perspective or point of view. That can't happen if we don't talk to the reporter.

12. Never say, "No comment." It sounds like you're hiding something.

13. Certain kinds of issues should not be discussed with reporters because of (fill in one or more blanks): (a) the law; (b) our ethics or rules of procedure; (c) client confidentiality; (d) business competition; (e) some major harm that might result. Make sure the reporter understands why you cannot answer the question. Refer the reporter to a designated executive.

14. The news media have a legal right to observe, to photograph and to record any event or any person in a public place.

15. Other elements in **STRATEGY/Ten Commandments of Media Relations.**

Only the Boss Talks

Some organizations have a policy that says only the boss can talk to reporters. That means stories will be written without your point of view when the boss can't be reached.

And reporters get the idea you don't trust your staff. They're either too dumb to speak for the company or have been muzzled because there's something to hide.

There may be a need to designate specific spokespeople for special kinds of situations. In a police department, for instance, the lead investigator working a homicide may be the only proper source for the media on that case. That investigator is best qualified to know whether the release of certain information might harm the investigation.

A Disarming Strategy

A fairly open policy will—in the long run—best serve most organizations. The single most disarming factor for a suspicious reporter is a wide-open media policy.

Private corporations and government agencies need to approach media policy with a slightly different tone. Here are portions of a model policy I suggest for my clients in banking. It can be modified easily to fit other kinds of businesses.

MEDIA POLICY FOR BANKERS

To better serve our customers and the community, we need to tell them more about who we are and what we do here at the bank.

That message is often conveyed by the news media. And so the entire staff needs to be more aware of how we can cooperate with the news media, in ways that will best serve both our customers and the community at large.

CONFIDENTIALITY

Never forget that the confidentiality of our customers' financial affairs is a sacred trust. Every employee of the bank can protect that confidentiality, and still be courteous and cooperative with members of the media.

THEY'RE PART OF THE PUBLIC, TOO

Reporters have the right to answers for any questions you would answer for any member of the public.

EXAMPLE: "What is the bank's current interest rate on new car loans?" We'd answer that question for anybody who asked. Usually, it would be a potential customer who's shopping for a car. So we'd be unusually helpful. You should give reporters that same kind of information and help.

BE SURE OF YOUR FACTS

You should be sure that your answers to reporters' questions are accurate and current. If you don't know the answer, make a special effort to find the person in the bank who CAN get the information for the reporter.

REPORTERS HAVE DEADLINES

Remember, reporters are working against a deadline. They usually need their questions answered quickly. A prompt, courteous reply is good public relations for the bank. It's good business.

BANKING NEWS IS IMPORTANT

The public today is more involved in finance than ever before. Reporting on banking and business is at an all-time high. This is a complicated subject, and good reporters often need explanations and data we can provide. In doing so, we perform a major public service.

When a reporter asks about a generic financial or banking concept, you should—within reason—use your knowledge and the bank's resources to help that reporter.

EXAMPLE: "What is the relationship between banks and the Federal Reserve?" Or, "How does the Federal Deposit Insurance Corporation work? What must a bank do to qualify as a member? What does it cost the bank?"

The answers to these questions are available elsewhere. They're not specifically tied to our bank. But by helping the reporter, we build a relationship with that reporter that's important to us. That reporter will come back to us in the future, both as a reporter and as a customer.

NOTIFY OUR SPECIALIST

As a matter of policy, after you've given this kind of generic information to a reporter, please notify the bank's media specialist. That officer has been assigned the responsibility of working with the news media.

We'd like to keep track of how reporters use the information we give them. Perhaps we'll call later with follow-up suggestions after the story is printed or broadcast. If the reporter's inquiry would call for extensive use of bank employee time or resources, you should also clear that with the bank's media specialist, before you commit to do the research.

MATTERS OF BANK POLICY

If the reporter's question involves a policy of the bank, or a specific incident or personnel decision, the reporter should be courteously referred to the bank's media specialist.

These questions are sometimes sensitive, in terms of our competitive position with other banks. How much information we provide the public is often a policy decision that can only be made at the administrative level of the bank.

EXAMPLE: "We have a tip that you plan to open a new branch and appoint Bob Banker as president of that branch. Can you confirm that?" Or, "To compete with other financial institutions, some banks are offering innovative automatic bill-paying services to checking account customers. Is your bank considering such a service?"

We might be, but we might not want to advertise it just yet. So the bank's media specialist will confer with the top officers of the bank before deciding how the reporter's question should be answered.

Remember, on some questions you can give away the answer just in the way you say you can't answer. So refer the reporter to the media specialist without giving any indication of what the answer is.

NEVER LIE OR TRY TO DECEIVE

It's much better to say, "I'm sorry, I can't answer that question right now," than to give a deceptive answer. Explain why you can't answer. Avoid saying "No comment."

Reporters respect honesty more than any other character trait. So do our customers. In fact, honesty is our stock-in-trade. We must NEVER give even the appearance of being evasive or deceptive. If you give that impression to a reporter, it will probably be passed on to the reporter's readers, viewers or listeners.

OUR BANK IS PEOPLE

Our bank is not a building or a corporation. It is the people who work here. We are constantly judged by the public's perception of the people who represent the bank. When a customer or a reporter finds an employee helpful and friendly, then our bank builds its reputation as a helpful, friendly place.

When an employee is grumpy and uncooperative, then that customer or reporter gets the idea that everybody in the bank is that way.

WHAT IS NEWS?

News is the unusual. It can be good or bad news.

News is information people need in their daily lives.

It can be information that makes their lives more enjoyable and profitable.

It can be information that warns them to take special precautions. Bad news always seems to leak out. Gossips thrive on stories of human frailty or failure. And once they spread their gossip, the media have a responsibility to publish or broadcast it, if they decide it will serve the public interest.

But news is also simple, human stories that remind us of life's joys and special times. Stories that renew our hope in humanity.

"Good news" often goes unreported. Not because the media aren't interested. Because they never hear about it. Gossips don't spread those kinds of stories.

One of your responsibilities here is to make sure our media specialist hears about human interest stories. The media specialist will know who to call in the local media to see if they're interested. But the call will never be made unless you bring the story to the specialist's attention.

EXAMPLE: After a customer had a heart attack in the bank lobby, a group of tellers decided to take CPR classes on their own time. The next time that happens, they'll be better prepared to help until the paramedics arrive.

EXAMPLE: An elderly customer cashed a check and left $100 in cash on the ledge at the teller's window. The next customer in line—a high school student—found the money and told the teller. When the customer who'd misplaced the money returned in panic an hour later, she and her cash were reunited. Without it, she wouldn't have been able to pay her rent.

EXAMPLE: A group of students who couldn't find summer jobs wanted to start a service to "house-sit" the homes of people on vacation. But they had no money to advertise. The bank's loan department decided they were a good risk, and loaned them the money to get started. They've paid off their loan and built a very successful business.

NEWS PEGS

The news media are constantly looking for local stories that tie to a national story. They call these stories "news pegs." They're local stories pegged to a larger, national or international story.

There are many national financial stories that could generate local news pegs. Here again, the local media may not know of the local news peg unless we tell them.

Keep that in mind when you know that we're somehow involved in some banking activity that could be pegged to a national or international incident. Tell the bank's media specialist so the story can be passed along.

CAMERAS IN THE BANK

Reporters and photographers have the same right to enter public areas of the bank as any other citizen.

They do not have the right—in this privately-owned, public place—to interfere with banking business or our customers' expectation of privacy.

When a news photographer enters the bank and begins taking pictures, the media specialist or a bank officer should be notified immediately. The officer should approach the photographer courteously and ask what the pictures are for.

Remember, rudeness—on camera—always gives a bad impression of the bank. If the reporter or photographer is rude, we won't see that in the news. But if YOU are, we'll probably see just HOW rude on tonight's news. And tomorrow's news. And in every future story about this bank.

As a matter of policy, we'll be glad to help the news media photograph banking operations. We'd like to know in advance just what they want and need, so we can arrange the photography with the least interference to our customers, our security, and our normal business.

If the photographer is belligerent and uncooperative, politely ask him to leave. In this kind of conflict with the media, make sure you're not the one who behaves badly.

A Policy for Human Services

The following is a model policy I suggest to human service agencies. By law in most states, these agencies cannot discuss anything about a client. The law and their professional ethic make it extremely difficult to defend the agency when it is attacked unjustly, by people using false allegations. This policy can be easily modified to fit most government agencies.

A SUGGESTED MEDIA POLICY FOR HUMAN SERVICE AGENCIES

This department exists to serve the public.

The people in this community are vitally concerned with human services. How we meet the needs of those who cannot provide for themselves determines, to a large extent, the character of our community—its priorities and standards—its conscience and human dignity.

The people of this community provide the financial support and encouragement that make effective human services possible. They have the right to know, through the news media, how we carry out our duties and responsibilities.

We have nothing to hide. We will not have the support that we deserve as dedicated public servants unless the community is fully aware of the problems we face, and how we deal with them from day to day.

THE NEWS MEDIA CAN HELP

The news media can often help us do our job. Many of our clients and potential clients cannot be reached in any other way. They will not know of our services if they do not hear about them through the media. News stories can rally the community to provide special needs in times of crisis. The news media are often invaluable in helping locate elderly clients who wander away from home; in identifying abandoned babies, and other similar cases.

HELP THE NEWS MEDIA

It is the policy of this department to make information available to the news media as quickly and completely as possible, except in those instances where the release of that information might violate the client's right to confidentiality or interfere with the fair administration of justice. When we cannot release information for legal or ethical reasons, those reasons should be carefully explained to the reporter. In some cases, it might be helpful to give the reporter copies of the law and the regulations governing what we can and cannot discuss publicly.

RETURNING REPORTERS' CALLS

Every reporter's phone call should be returned in less than 15 minutes. If you cannot be reached, make sure your staff returns the call, and refers the reporter to someone who can answer the reporter's questions. We do not want it to be said that we "could not be reached for comment." We do not want to be surprised by tomorrow's headline or tonight's newscast. Stories about us should always include our response or point of view.

CLIENT CONFIDENTIALITY

We have a legal and ethical responsibility to protect the confidentiality of our clients. In some cases, the legal process removes that cloak of confidentiality. If it has not been removed, we can still talk to the media about the way we help clients without naming a specific client. We can explain to reporters, just as we would to anyone who asked, the rules and regulations concerning our services; the way those rules are put into effect; the numbers and amounts of money involved that are a part of the public record, or will eventually become part of the public record.

EVERY STAFFER MAY SPEAK

Every staff member is free to speak to the media about departmental matters so long as the basic policy set forth here is not violated. The employee at the site of our services is often the best witness and can give the most accurate account of what happened.

PUBLIC INFORMATION OFFICE

It is the role of the Public Information Office (PIO) to serve as a coordinator and guide to the media within the department. Reporter's inquiries should be referred to PIO unless they can quickly be handled by the staffer who is contacted. Often, the reporter simply needs a number or an explanation of how a program works. You may be better qualified to give that explanation than PIO. But it is a good idea to call PIO to let PIO know about the reporter's inquiry. There may be other activity on the same subject within the department that you are unaware of. If PIO is fully informed, they may be able to give more assistance to the reporter and improve our rapport with the media.

HAVE PERSONAL KNOWLEDGE

You should speak to the media only about those matters of which you have personal knowledge. This restriction is intended to prevent the relaying of inaccurate information to the news media.

HUMAN INTEREST STORIES

The news media are always looking for strong human interest stories. We often complain that the media cover us when we have problems and ignore us when we do things right. This is a chance for us to tell the public about our successes. It is the responsibility of PIO to suggest these stories to reporters and editors. But PIO cannot know about them unless you alert PIO.

Remember, some of these stories will involve substantial lead time for the media to cover them effectively. Let PIO know as soon as possible about clients or staffers who are involved in human interest situations that offer news story possibilities. Because it is the job of PIO to work closely with the media, they can often arrange ways to cover those stories that do not invade clients' confidentiality.

LEGAL RIGHTS OF PRIVACY

The news media have a legal right to observe, to photograph and to record any event or any person in a public place. On private property, the owner of the property has the final word on who shall be allowed inside the premises. A court order which gives our staff the right of entry does not automatically give that same right to members of the news media. So long as the media are physically on public property—or on private property with the consent of the owner—they have the right to observe, photograph and record events that may be occurring on private property.

ON-SCENE COORDINATION

Many of the conflicts between human services staff and the media occur at the scenes of great human emotion and suffering. Under these difficult and often confusing circumstances, many members of the media will arrive about the same time we do. The ranking staff member on the scene should be responsible for coordinating release of information to the news media until a public information officer arrives.

WHO SHOULD DISCUSS POLICY

Staff members should make every effort to be courteous and diplomatic in dealing with the news media. In matters of policy, the reporter should be referred to a staff member responsible for setting or carrying out that policy.

SHOULD NOT BE RELEASED:

Staff members shall not release for publication, or in a manner which is likely to result in publication, information in the following categories:
    1. The identity of a client, or confirmation that a person is a client, without the written consent of that client.

2. The names and addresses of victims of sex offenses.
3. The names and addresses of juvenile offenders.
4. Until next-of-kin have been notified, the names and addresses of deceased persons. The names shall be released after a reasonable time if notification of next-of-kin cannot be accomplished. Reporters may be given the names of deceased persons so long as they pledge that they will not publish or broadcast them until next-of-kin have been notified, or until the department approves release of the names. This will usually be done as a convenience to the media when notification of next-of-kin is expected before the reporter's deadline.
5. Information which may jeopardize an investigation.
6. Any opinion as to guilt or innocence of a client, or the merits or evidence in a case where a client's identity has become public through an arrest or other action outside this department.
7. The performance of any medical examinations or tests; their results, or the refusal of a client to submit to a medical examination or test.
8. The home address or telephone number of staff members, without the express consent of that staffer. The purpose of this provision is to strengthen the off-duty privacy and safety of the staffer and his/her family, not to make the staffer inaccessible to the media. Media requests for information that may be known only by an off-duty staffer can often be relayed to the staffer by PIO or the staffer's superior without giving reporters a home phone number.

(Insert other localized items)

RECORDS THAT ARE PUBLIC

State and local ordinances provide that the following records shall be open to the public:
(Insert local application)

NON-PUBLIC RECORDS

State and local ordinances and departmental policy provide that the following records shall not be open to the public:
(Insert local application)

Beyond these explicit guidelines, members of this department are encouraged to be open and cooperative with the news media. Although the department has a public information office, its existence does not imply that staff members should refer all inquiries to that office.

Every member of the department is expected to know the contents of this policy, and to abide by it. The director is willing to trust your judgment about what to say to the news media, and how to say it.

Every member of this department is a public information officer.

STRATEGY

PIOS

What Do Public Information Officers Do?

Most companies and government agencies of any size now have at least one public information officer (PIO). When they get that assignment, many PIOs have no training or experience with the media. They don't have the foggiest notion of what they're supposed to do. Or how to do it.

You write press releases, and answer reporter's questions.

Yeah. But there's a lot more to it. The learning process can be very painful for the PIO, the boss, and the organization.

Choosing is Difficult

If you're the boss, choosing a PIO is one of the most difficult decisions you'll have to make.

Should it be a veteran employee who knows the company, but doesn't know much about the media?

Should it be a media person who can be persuaded to leave the news business and represent you? Should it be a man or a woman? Should the job be full-time or part-time?

The PIO's basic ability and personality are much more important than any of those criteria.

Good PIOs Are . . .

- **Good PIOs are bright.** They learn quickly.
- **Good PIOs have great people skills.** They know how to negotiate and mediate.
- **Good PIOs have character.** They project sincerity and credibility. Reporters, photographers and people within their own organization trust them.

How To Speak TV, Print & Radio

The most common misuse of PIOs occurs when the boss creates the position and announces the PIO will now be the spokesperson for the company or agency.

No matter what happens, only the boss or the PIO can speak to the news media. The PIO becomes a buffer. A barrier between the organization, the boss, and the media.

Relays Are Too Slow

In this scenario, the PIO becomes an information relay. It takes a lot of time to gather the answers to a reporter's questions and then get the answer back to the reporter, who by then has thought of several other questions.

You miss the deadline, and your point of view is not in the story.

Every time information passes from one hand to another, it becomes more stale and less personal. The chance for error multiplies.

How Did It Feel?

Most important—the PIO wasn't there when it happened. Can't answer the media's most pressing question. How did it feel? (See **SKILLS/Interviews**)

A police officer is shot in the chest at close range. His only injury is a bad bruise. His bullet-proof vest worked. Reporters want to talk to the officer, not the PIO. They want pictures of the bruise.

How did it feel to be shot and live to tell about it? What went through your mind? How much pain is there when a slug slams into a bulletproof vest? Do you wear the vest all the time? Will you wear it all the time in the future?

Only the officer can answer those questions.

The PIO's function *should be* to arrange the interview, not speak for the officer.

Tour Guides for the Media

PIOs should be tour guides for the media. They are walking encyclopedias. They know the organization as well as the boss—perhaps better. They can quickly lead reporters and photographers to the right place, the right people, the right information.

Good PIOs are credible. They never lie to reporters. If they know the answer, but can't tell the reporter, they say so. One deception, and the trust can never be restored. Reporters have very long memories. They have ways to get even.

Good PIOs are also respected and trusted by their colleagues within the company or agency. They can be trusted not to leak. Unless the organization wants something leaked. Which leads to the chain of command. Who should the PIO answer to?

The Chain of Command

In the best operations, the PIO or public relations director is directly under the chief executive officer. The PIO has constant access to the decision-makers and is included on all major discussions and decisions.

If the PIO is not included, information can be released to the media that's not true. The PIO *thought* it was true. When reporters learn the truth, the PIO becomes—in their minds—either a liar or a front who doesn't even know what's happening in the organization.

Public vs. Private

The PIO for a government agency and a private company should have different perspectives. Similar, but different.

In the private sector, part of the job involves putting the company's best foot forward. It is part public information, part selling the company.

Too many public information officers in government fail to understand the perils if they adopt those same objectives. They think it is their job to make the boss, or the agency, look good. In doing that, they may stall, or try to block a reporter. They may fail to disclose something.

Deception Whets Appetites

Nothing gives reporters more incentive than the belief that you're hiding something. It whets their appetites. There's got to be gold somewhere under that mountain of misinformation, they think. They dig harder. (See **STRATEGY/Ten Commandments of Media Relations**)

The news media seem far less critical of deceptive games when private industry plays them than when the players are government officials or employees.

Who Are You?

The simplest definition of good media relations is:

Effectively telling the public WHO YOU ARE and WHAT YOU DO.

If your organization has good people who do a good job and turn out a good product or service, that's the message you need to convey.

In a society drowning in information, PIOs have to become more and more creative in finding ways to get the public's attention, so they can deliver the basic message. (See **STRATEGY/ Selling Your Story**)

News Conference Role

At news conferences, the PIO's role is to:
* Alert the media.
* Choose the best place and time.
* Act as stage manager, to make sure the physical layout will accommodate both the spokespeople and the news media.
* Provide handouts before the news conference begins.
* Explain any special ground rules for the conference.
* Introduce the people who will take reporters' questions.
* Close the conference when a pre-set time limit is reached, or when questions taper off.
* Help set up individual interviews if reporters ask for them after the conference.

(See **SKILLS/News Conferences**)

PIOs Are Always On Call

PIOs should generally be on call 24 hours a day. News does not operate on a schedule. It happens when it happens, and your organization needs to have its perspective in every story that mentions it.

In some types of operations—fire and emergency services, hospitals, utility companies—you may need assistant PIOs on call at night or on weekends. Otherwise, the PIO will never be able to sleep.

Spend Time With Media

PIOs need to spend time with the reporters and editors who will be covering their organization. The PIO for a large bank should have lunch regularly with the business editor of the dominant newspaper in the area. The PIO for a hospital should do the same with medical reporters.

PIOs should ask to spend a day or half-day occasionally watching news people do their job. Ride with a TV camera crew, then watch them edit the story. Try your hand at writing an accurate newspaper headline in 75 characters or less.

It gives you a much better understanding of the problems media people have getting their stories in the paper or on the air. Accurately and on time.

Enlarge Your List

Watching over their shoulders not only educates you. It sends a strong message that you're interested in what media people do. That you want to do a better job, helping them.

In that visit, you'll enlarge your list of media contacts. Next time you call, trying to sell a story, they're much more likely to listen.

The single most important strategy in dealing with the media is to convince them you're willing and anxious to help them get a better story. That's why my Number One Commandment is: Be Open and Cooperative. (See **STRATEGY/Ten Commandments**)

Becoming a Resource

One of your goals as a PIO should be to have your name, office number and home number in the phone index of every reporter and editor in your community—and perhaps at the networks and major newspapers like *The New York Times* and *The Wall Street Journal*.

Reporters need resource people. Major national associations realize that, and run advertisements in magazines that cater to the media. "If you have questions about the oil industry, we have people with answers," the typical ad says.

How To Speak TV, Print & Radio

Every time you're quoted, with your company affiliation, it's free advertising. It creates prestige and name recognition for the organization. It won't hurt your career, either.

Knowing all that, the full-time, part-time question really depends on how many media contacts the PIO can expect to handle. You may want to begin with a part-time assignment, keep track of how the PIO spends time, and then decide whether it should be expanded to full-time.

(See **STRATEGY/Media Policy**)

STRATEGY

SELLING YOUR STORY

Wow! Have I Got A Story For You!

Many people try to sell a story to the news media, fail repeatedly, and can't understand why. They don't realize that their approach turns off editors. They don't know what news is. Or how to sell it. News is the unusual.

Mayor Sober Today

If the headline says, "Mayor Sober Today," we assume he is drunk most of the time. What would your reaction be if tonight's newscast told you:

- No children were murdered today.
- There were no major airline crashes today.
- No bridges collapsed.
- No banks failed today.

News Is What's Different

News is something different.

It is news when a Vietnam veteran threatens to leap from the roof of a downtown building. It is not news that thousands of other veterans went about their daily lives, never thinking of suicide.

We assume that everything is OK. News is the exception. Something that is not OK. When the media report a government official has been arrested for bribery, we assume thousands of others were honest.

Information You Need

News can also be more than just the unusual. It can be information people need. Information that will in some way affect their lives. In a democratic society, we need to know that the school board is contemplating a tax increase so we can support, or try to stop it. We need to know that a certain brand of sardines is contaminated so we can throw them away and not get seriously ill.

To sell a story, you must know your media market, and the specific needs and tastes of each outlet.

Many of the stories that are staples for newspapers are not visually interesting for television, and have no appeal whatever for radio. Videotape of the school board's hearing on property taxes is not nearly as exciting as a warehouse fire. Because the number of people watching is so critical to television profits, the decision is easy. Air the fire. Dump the school board hearing. They didn't decide anything, anyway.

The Compelling C's

There are seven broad categories for news stories—I call them the Seven Compelling C's:

Catastrophe
Crisis
Conflict
Change
Crime
Corruption
Color (We used to call it human interest.)

If you, your department or your company are going to be in the news, the story will usually have an angle that fits at least one of these categories. And it must be unusual.

A caller says, "I don't want to give you my name, but you should look into what's happening at the Zebra Club. The treasurer embezzled $200,000 and ran off with the president's wife. The children's hospital we support is about to close its doors. They're running out of money because of the theft. There's a big internal fight now, on whether to prosecute the treasurer, or hush it up. Oh, by the way, the treasurer is a minister."

Now, That's News

Now, that's news. Crime, corruption, crisis, conflict, color.
Back to the school board budget hearing.
LIGHTS. CAMERA. ACTION.
School board member: "Looks to me like the school superintendent has sold out **(corruption?)** to the realtors who are fighting this tax increase **(conflict)**. If this tax is not approved, we may have to shut down some of our schools **(crisis)**."

Veteran politicians understand the technique and use it all the time to get news coverage. The people they attack understand the game. They get on their soap box and fight back, and their point of view gets time on the air, space in the paper. Nothing personal. A lot like attorneys who seem to have a grudge match going in court, but play golf together every Sunday.

Manufactured Conflict

The 1988 Democratic convention was a great example of manufactured conflict to hold the media's interest. Gov. Michael Dukakis had the nomination locked up long before the convention. We knew the outcome. The primaries had dissolved any chance for suspense. Sort of like reading a murder mystery, when the author tells you in the preface who did it. Why bother?

So the balloon of a possible dogfight between Dukakis and Jesse Jackson was inflated and released. Jackson had been out of sight. Was he pouting, itching for revenge? Did he plan to torpedo Dukakis? Would it get messy and destroy the harmony the Democrats had worked so hard to promote?

The media hit the bait and ran with it. Many reporters at the convention knew they were being used. But there was nothing else to write about. Everything was cut and dried.

Networks decided to cut back on their convention coverage in 1988, covered less in 1992, and will probably reduce their coverage even more at future conventions. Conflict is news, and that takes place in the primaries.

Wake Up the Stockholders

Want extensive coverage of your next stockholders' meeting? Leak to the news media that a small group of stockholders are planning an insurrection, and will ask for the resignation of the chairman of the board.

If your association's conferences are rarely covered by the media, here's how to change that:

Anti-Yawn Conferences

If you're a medical group, invite a speaker who will attack ambulance-chasing lawyers as the cause of the malpractice insurance crisis.

If you're a bar association, invite a chief executive from a major insurance company who will say outrageous premium increases for auto liability coverage are the result of doctors who milk every dime they can from accident victims.

Or bring opposing points of view to the speaker's platform for a hair-pulling, eye-gouging debate.

The Q&A session after the debate will lead to great quotes and pictures. CONFLICT is the key ingredient that makes most novels and movies work. It is also a certain element in selling your story to the news media.

It Is a Game

It is a game, very much like professional sports. To communicate effectively, you need to learn the game. It must be played very skillfully. If reporters suspect they are being manipulated with a phony issue, the technique can backfire.

One reason professional sports are so popular is that they incorporate most of these basic elements. **Conflict** is central—one team using all its resources to beat the other. There is a new **crisis** every week—what happens if they lose? **Catastrophe** when the star quarterback is injured. **Changes** in team standings or win-lose odds on an hourly basis. And **color** everywhere. Rugged, macho players. Sexy cheerleaders. Big money. Crowds, music, applause. The glory of it all.

In news, the game is life and death, success and failure, power vs. the underdog.

Effect of Community Size

"My civic club elected officers last night, and I knew you'd want to do a story," the caller tells the city editor. In large communities, there are hundreds—perhaps thousands—of civic club elections each year. Not news.

In a small, rural community, with two or three civic clubs, the election of a new Rotary president may grab the front page. News often depends on where it happens.

Timing is Everything

Timing can be everything, when it comes to news coverage. On a slow news day, they still have to fill the print pages and the newscast minutes. If there is still empty space on the page as the deadline approaches, a feature story on the people who make up the Water Buffalo Lodge executive committee gets more and more attractive to the editor.

The day the space shuttle explodes, a five-alarm fire may get two paragraphs.

Newspaper editors need a lot of copy to fill the big Sunday edition. Saturday can be a good day to break a story. Because government and business are away for the weekend, broadcasters have difficulty finding stories for their weekend newscasts. The same is true for Monday morning's paper. It may be easier to place a story then.

The downside is that both newspapers and broadcast stations work weekends with a skeleton staff. One solution: release the story on Friday, with an embargo. The media agree to hold it until Sunday.

Some newspapers traditionally have a large "news hole" on Wednesday or Thursday, because that's the day the grocery stores place their display ads.

Know the Editor

If you expect to sell stories to your local news media, you need to know local editors. (See **STRATEGY/Ten Commandments—#3**) When you call to offer a story, they'll know you. They'll know you have developed a sense of news value. They'll listen a little more closely.

On many story tips, you should notify the editor in advance, in writing. (See **SKILLS/News Releases**)

Then you should follow up the news release with a phone call the day before the story breaks, or early that morning. Try to time your call at the editor's least busy time of day.

How To Speak TV, Print & Radio

For the assignment editor at a radio or TV station, that slack time is mid-to-late-afternoon, the day before the story. The call should sound something like this:

Making Your Story Pitch

"Ed? This is Tom Tipster. I sent you a news release earlier this week about the demonstration we're planning in front of City Hall tomorrow. We expect to have about 500 people there, willing to go to jail, if necessary. I'll be there about 9 a.m. with a handout for your reporter. Just wanted to see if you need any other information."

Be careful not to push too hard. A good story doesn't really need to be sold. Selling too hard makes the editor suspicious that there may not be a real story there. There may be an element that's not obvious. What makes it so unusual?

Timing for City Editors

You'd make a similar call to the editor of an afternoon newspaper about 1 or 2 p.m. the day before the story will break. By that time, the last deadline has passed. Time to work on tomorrow's early morning assignments.

For a morning newspaper, the call should be between noon and about 2:30 p.m. the day before, or in the early evening. In the middle of the day, the city editor has issued today's assignments, and won't be involved yet in afternoon staff meetings that decide which stories will be in tomorrow morning's paper. The call may also lead to a story tomorrow morning telling readers what's going to happen tomorrow.

In the evening, you may tip the night city editor, who leaves lots of notes for the early morning staff.

Radio assignment editors need to know the day before, and may need calls through the day as the story breaks.

Remember—television needs much more advance notice, because they have to collect videotape to cover everything the reporter will say.

Look for News Pegs

You need to contact the media while the issue is hot. If a national story develops on any subject, local editors and news directors look for a local angle. They call it a local "news peg." If you're the first to call with a suggestion, you'll usually be the person they interview and include in their story.

When the Russian nuclear power plant began leaking radiation, almost every local media outlet did a local story "pegged" to the disaster. Could something like that happen here? Does this community have an evacuation plan? How similar is the local nuclear plant to the Russian design? If there was a meltdown, which way would the prevailing wind spread the radiation?

The Easiest Sell

A news peg is the easiest story you'll ever sell to an editor. The national or international story has already established the story's priority. Editors and news directors put the localizing of stories very high on their agenda. But you have to hurry if you or your organization are to be in today's news peg. Your competition may beat you in tipping the local media.

If you work in a hospital or medical research facility, there will be many national health stories you can "peg" to. Call the editor and say, "I saw that story this morning about fingernail transplants. Did you know we've been doing that here for three years, and pioneered the technique?"

If you're a bank executive, there are almost daily financial stories for which you can suggest news pegs to tell your bank's story. "I saw the story on 'The Today Show' about the rising cost of home mortgages. Did you know our interest rates haven't changed in two years? And that we're considerably below other banks in the state?"

Lobbying Your Issue

When legislation is pending, or the courts hand down a decision affecting your special interest, you need to let people know how that law or decision will affect them. Media coverage at the local level has a powerful grass roots effect. In Washington and the state capitol, the officials who will decide the issue are much more influenced by local media stories their constituents read than by coverage in the national media. But local editors may not be aware there IS a local peg unless you call them.

This is one of the most effective ways to campaign for an issue. For most people, a hometown person is more believable, more compelling than a national or state figure. The local person points out specific ways the proposal affects local people.

You'll Become a Regular

Once you develop a reputation as someone who understands difficult issues—who can decipher them, so ordinary people understand them—you'll discover reporters come back to you for future stories. You become an expert they can rely on. If you're skillful, you make their story better. You make them look good.

And the payoff for you (in addition to effectively arguing your point of view) is a subtle form of public relations for your group. It won't hurt your role as community leader, either. Or your standing with your supervisors.

Here's the hierarchy at the local news media, so you'll know who to contact when you have a story to sell:

Managing Editor

At most newspapers, the top editor overseeing daily news stories is the MANAGING EDITOR or EXECUTIVE EDITOR. This editor is the final word on almost everything that happens in the newsroom; supervises all other news editors; and may even have authority over the editorial page editor. At many newspapers, the news and editorial pages are kept separate. This kind of organizational chart is designed to make editorial writers more independent. It is a reminder that editorial writers express their opinions, and news reporters should not.

Publisher & Manager

The managing editor answers to the PUBLISHER. At large newspapers, the publisher has almost nothing to do with daily news coverage. The publisher's function is to represent the owners and give overall supervision to keep the newspaper both financially and editorially healthy. Some publishers write a weekly column. The publisher is often the newspaper's representative in community affairs and civic clubs. At small newspapers, the publisher may also be the GENERAL MANAGER who oversees circulation, advertising, and the mechanical portion of the paper.

General managers traditionally have no voice whatever in news content. This avoids the suggestion that advertisers can influence news coverage.

City News Editors

Local news is supervised by a CITY EDITOR or METRO EDITOR. The city editor is responsible for the local staff, and coverage within the immediate city and nearby suburbs. Many morning papers also have a NIGHT CITY EDITOR, to supervise the local staff from the time the city editor goes home in the evening until the last deadline, sometime after midnight.

State News Editor

State news (news within the state, but outside the local community) is the responsibility of the STATE EDITOR, who may also double as POLITICAL EDITOR, since the reporters at the state capitol bureau are within the state editor's geographic area.

Business News Editor

There's probably a BUSINESS EDITOR at your local newspaper who handles most financial stories. Business news coverage has increased dramatically in the last decade. The stock market, interest rates, banking policy, inflation and unemployment statistics have all become much more newsworthy to average readers. Many newspapers have a special business section, published on the same day every week. That section has a voracious appetite for detailed stories on local firms and the people in them. A great opportunity to sell a story about your company.

Editorial Page Editor

Editorials, syndicated columns, letters to the editor, and other material printed on the page opposite the editorial page (they call it the op-ed page) are under the control of the EDITOR or EDITORIAL PAGE EDITOR. The editor and editorial writers make up the EDITORIAL BOARD. At some newspapers, a representative from the newsroom also sits on the editorial board.

Editorial Board

It is the custom in many communities for political candidates, government officials, and leaders of major causes to visit with the editorial board. It is like an audience with the President or the Pope, in which you respectfully appear, hoping for their blessing. You make the board aware of your cause or point of view and subject yourself to cross examination. The goal is to garner editorial support or endorsement for yourself or your issue. Each editorial writer is usually assigned specific areas of expertise.

Feature Editor

The FEATURE EDITOR supervises long-term reporting projects that are normally not produced on deadline. Stories like profiles of people in the news; an extensive look at controversial issues; magazine-length pieces where writing style is encouraged and enhanced. With the advent of gender equality, the old Women's Section has been abandoned. The section is now given a variety of names. Style or Lifestyle are popular. Many of the stories that would have once been in the Women's Section are now in this section. The favorite topics are personality profiles, psychology, marriage and family issues, health and diet, moral conflicts like abortion and capital punishment. The feature editor may be called editor of this section, whatever its name.

Investigations Editor

Some newspapers with long traditions of investigative reporting have an INVESTIGATIONS EDITOR who supervises a team of specialists. At most papers, investigative projects will be supervised by the editor who would normally supervise other stories in the same area. The overseer of political corruption investigations will be the political editor. Investigations of local government will be monitored by the metro editor, etc.

News Directors

At radio and television stations, the person in charge of all news operations is the NEWS DIRECTOR. The news director is in charge of all hiring and firing—roughly the equivalent of the managing editor or executive editor at a newspaper. The news director answers to the GENERAL MANAGER, who reports to the station owner.

Assignment Editors

The ASSIGNMENT EDITOR is the person who decides how reporters and photographers will be dispatched to cover stories. If you'd like to have broadcast coverage of something you're involved in, you need to let the assignment editor know about it.

Assignment editors are the most harried people in television news. The typical assignment editor sits in the center of the newsroom, totally immersed in noise and confusion. On the desk, a bank of telephones are constantly ringing. With one ear, the assignment editor must monitor several squawking police and fire department radio scanners.

Noise and Confusion

On top of that, a dozen camera crews out in their cars need directions to addresses they can't find. They are reporting by radio every few minutes to say their camera or tape recorder has broken down; they arrived 30 seconds too late to catch the bridge collapse; the convention they're supposed to cover doesn't begin until next week, that the massive protest against police brutality is actually a little old man who hand-delivered a letter to the mayor's secretary.

Assignment editors also eavesdrop on the two-way radio conversations of the competition.

No Respect

If the assignment editor happens to get a crew to the right place at the right time, and they come away with a great visual story, the reporter and photographer usually get the credit. If the assignment editor misses a story, the news director has a nasty habit of screaming, banging on the desk and shouting obscenities. Good assignment editors are born. Those that aren't, but try to remake themselves into assignment editors, often have nervous breakdowns.

Show & Story Producers

The PRODUCER of the newscast decides the length of stories, their format, and their placement in the newscast—the equivalent of a page or section editor at a newspaper. The stories gathered at the direction of the assignment editor are turned over to the show producer. Network television crews have a FIELD PRODUCER who travels with the correspondent and photographer and manages most of the details.

The field producer may also videotape an interview, but is rarely seen or heard on the air. Local stations will occasionally assign a field producer to a crew for a major series or documentary. Since there are several newscasts each day, the producers of each show may be supervised at larger stations by an EXECUTIVE PRODUCER.

Public Affairs Director

The PUBLIC AFFAIRS DIRECTOR was created back when the FCC required licensed radio and television stations to dedicate a certain amount of air time to public affairs. The standard format for public affairs programming was a weekly talk show. (See **SKILLS/Talk Shows**) With the deregulation of broadcasting, many stations are phasing out their public affairs departments. The talk show may be produced now by the news department.

Editorials & Commentary

Broadcast editorials and commentary are written, produced and performed by the station's EDITORIAL WRITER or COMMENTATOR. They are usually supervised by the station's general manager or public affairs director. At some stations, the editorials are delivered on the air by the general manager. Under the old FCC Fairness Doctrine, stations were required to give opposing points of view a chance to air their position. Although the doctrine is in limbo as this book goes to press, most stations still abide by it, and that gives you another opportunity to sell your story.

The FCC's rules on Personal Attack and Political Editorials are still in effect, and you may demand response time on the air under certain conditions. (See **INSIDE THE MEDIA/Fairness and Equal Time**)

When you have a story to sell, you should try to place it so it will reach the widest possible audience. Consider all the possibilities. There are many you may not have thought of. Here's a checklist:

Radio Story Opportunities

News.
Talk shows.
Special reports & documentaries.
Editorials and editorial replies.
Commentary and commentary replies.

Television Opportunities

Daily newscasts.
Special issue coverage.
Live interviews inserted in newscasts.
Talk shows.
Series and documentaries.
Editorials and editorial replies.
Commentary and commentary replies.

Newspaper Opportunities

Local news.
State news.
Special sections. Sunday newspapers often devote entire sections to longer, more thoughtful pieces that explore pending legislation, controversial issues, or follow-ups to major stories.
Editorials and editorial replies.
Letters to the editor.
Columnists and columnist replies.
Special columns written by outsiders.

Local Magazines

Don't forget the local and state-oriented magazines that are always looking for fresh ideas involving local people and issues. Many local chambers of commerce now publish magazines that concentrate on business, finance, and community development.

Association Newsletters

Virtually every association publishes some kind of newsletter. You may not realize how many associations there are in America. Professional associations. Business associations. Associations to promote the use of dairy products or nuclear energy. Associations for virtually every major issue. Most states have several hundred associations. Nationwide, there are tens of thousands. They're always looking for stories to fill those newsletters. To find the association that might be interested in your story, there's a two-volume *Encyclopedia of Associations* at most public libraries. The American Society of Association Executives is headquartered in Washington, D. C. The state association of association executives will usually be located in your state capital, and most of them publish an annual directory. Obtain a copy so you'll have a specific name and address to call when you have a story idea that would appeal to their members.

Don't Tell Me—Show Me

In TV newsrooms all over the world, there is a sign: Don't Tell Me—Show Me.

It is a reminder to reporters and photographers that the television story *must* be visual. We are no longer satisfied to read or hear about someone trying to shoot the President. We expect to see the assassin, and hear the shots, in living color and natural sound.

Sports coverage, again, illustrates state-of-the-art storytelling with pictures. Half a dozen live cameras shooting from every conceivable angle. At least one camera always at the point of impact, much closer than if we had 50-yard-line seats. It can replay the fumble or the winning pass again and again, in slow motion, so we can study and savor it.

Think Pictures That Sell

Your success in selling a story idea to a radio or television assignment editor will often hinge on your suggestions for sound and pictures. In many cases, you can supply the sound and pictures. Broadcasters are so understaffed, they'll grab them and use them, exactly as you supply them. (See applications of this idea in **SKILLS/News Conferences, News Releases, Talk Shows**)

Unfortunately, much of government and business is dull, by comparison with other, more visual stories. How do you show a smooth-running water department? How do you photograph a record stock dividend? So much of government that has been traditionally covered by newspapers is almost entirely ignored by television.

Even Watergate—the biggest story of the 1970s—was poorly covered by television. There was little that television could show until the impeachment hearings began. Most of the Watergate story had to be *told*.

Photo Opportunities

Public relations agencies and government public information officers have created a new event—the "photo opportunity." This is an event generated specifically for news media pictures. It is neither spontaneous nor unrehearsed. In many respects, it is phony. Everybody knows it's phony. But the appetite and demand for pictures is so great, the media play along. Your success in selling a story may depend on your ingenuity in creating a photo opportunity.

Television and radio miss many stories simply because they don't know about them in time to get a camera or microphone there. A newspaper will usually have about five local reporters for each reporter at a TV station.

Newspapers assign reporters to beats, and those reporters spend their entire day at city hall or the courthouse or the police station. They're expected to know, and report, everything that happens there.

Television and radio depend on newspapers, and on listeners and viewers who call to tip them to stories.

Don't Cry Wolf

Public relations firms have a bad habit of trying to sell stories that really aren't newsworthy. Once an editor gets burned by sending a crew to a story that flops, you'll have a hard time when you call with the next story idea.

Broadcast news and small newspapers are terribly understaffed. Their reporters and photographers spend the entire day rushing from one story to another. Give the editor accurate times so the staff won't waste valuable minutes waiting for people to show up or the event to begin.

Who Gets it First?

If the story is not an event that needs to be photographed, you sometimes have to decide whether to give it first to newspapers or TV, or to both at the same time. It's very rare to choose radio as the medium that will get it first on an exclusive basis, largely because coverage will be brief. It will not reach nearly as many people.

There is intense dislike among newspaper people for television news, which can affect how your story will be covered. In many cities, newspapers try to ignore television. If television beats them to a story, they won't touch it. It is an ego thing. Newspaper people look down their noses at both the TV medium and the people who work in it.

The Newspaper-TV Feud

Television, in their minds, is fleeting, shallow, delivered by people who are hired for their looks, not their ability or intelligence. It is showbiz, not journalism.

If television got it first, it's hard for newspaper editors and reporters to admit they were beaten by the medium they spend so much time criticizing. So they decide it's not much of a story. Several weeks later, they may revive the story with a new twist, trying to make it look like they found the story and broke it first.

It's Not Old For TV

Television is not so concerned about competing with newspapers. News directors will kill to beat a competing TV station to a story, but they assume most viewers don't read newspapers. Just because it's in the newspaper this morning doesn't make it old news for the TV audience.

The rivalry between TV and newspapers over being first with a story varies from place to place. You have to test it in your market area.

Some PIOs and public relations agencies almost always give stories to the newspaper first. The newspaper coverage makes TV more interested in a story that may be visually dull.

Post-Times Certification

The same phenomenon takes place with national stories. TV network bureaus send story proposals to New York. New York says it's not interested, and the story idea is trashed. Two months later, the story appears in *The New York Times* or *Washington Post*. The network news desk in New York jerks the bureau chief in Los Angeles out of bed at 5 a.m. Rent a jet. We want this story for tonight's newscast.

"Hey, I told you about that story two months ago, and you didn't want it," the grumpy bureau chief complains.

"It wasn't news then," New York says. "It's in *The New York Times* this morning."

Public Affairs Programs

Most local stations produce other types of news-related programs that are the responsibility of the public affairs director. Interview shows on weekends; early morning shows that feature invited guests; audience call-in shows, and late-night shows that may have a studio audience are often produced locally.

Some of them have regular guests, like the county agent in farm areas, who gets ten minutes every day at 5:30 a.m. The county agent's time slot was apparently chosen because they thought the farm audience had to be up that early to milk the cows.

Public affairs directors are hungry for ideas and guests, particularly if they can be tied in some way to a current news story.

If you're looking for ways to get your message or your people on television, watch for an opportunity in public affairs programming, where you can be an expert on some item in the news. If you turn out to be a good interview subject, the news director and assignment editor will remember, and come to you for comment when they need expert analysis for future news coverage.

Talk shows have an enormous appetite for people and subject matter. The producer is always looking for ideas. (See **SKILLS/ Talk Shows**)

STRATEGY

TEN COMMANDMENTS

Basic Techniques for Better Media Relations

Unless you've been caught in the cross fire of a pitched media battle, you will have a hard time understanding what it is like. It may be the most difficult experience of your life. Remember the scene in "Apocalypse Now" when the helicopters are staging an early morning attack on the Vietnamese village? The air is thick with choppers. They swarm like dragonflies. Napalm is exploding. There is gunfire from all directions.

Everything moves so swiftly it is hard to keep your sense of balance and direction. It is confusing. You feel naked, out in the open, not knowing when the incoming fire will suddenly target you. It is frightening. You feel death and disfigurement whistling by, very close. People around you, people you know well, are dropping.

An All-Out Media Attack

That's what it feels like when you become the center of a national or international story. Reporters and photographers arrive by the thousands, from all over the world, in helicopters and Learjets, armed with tons of exotic, space-age equipment. They surround your office, your home, your church. They camp there, round-the-clock, crushing the tulips. Throwing their Big Mac wrappers and coffee cups on the lawn.

You and your family cannot move without running the gauntlet of microphones and cameras. You may be followed everywhere you go for weeks at a time. You will feel invaded. Under siege. A captive. Your life, your career, the stability of your home and family will seem suddenly at great risk.

Fight or Flee Syndrome

That's the worst-case scenario. But the Fight or Flee Syndrome will also seize you when a reporter shows up, unannounced, and begins to ask questions. If it is a television crew, stage fright will be added to the stress.

To help you cope, I developed the Ten Commandments of Media Relations. Some of them are just basic common sense. But your fear of the media often leads you to do strange things. The commandments should also help you develop some regular routines and policy for coping with reporters, editors and photographers on an everyday basis.

The Ten Commandments

I	Be Open and Cooperative. Never lie.
II	Personalize the Organization.
III	Develop Media Contacts.
IV	Take Good Stories to Them.
V	Respond Quickly.
VI	Never Say, "No Comment."
VII	It's OK to Say, "I Don't Know."
	(But I'll Find Out)
VIII	If You Screw Up, Confess and Repent.
IX	Use the Big Dump.
X	Prepare for a Media Disaster.

1—Be Open and Cooperative

Let's go over them, one at a time. I'll explain what I mean.

When you close the door in the face of a reporter, or refuse to provide a document, you do not realize the visceral reaction you trigger. Particularly if the reporter has a legal right to enter that door, or see that document.

As a young reporter, I quickly realized I was too sensitive covering stories that involved death and human tragedy. The emotions got in the way of my objectivity. They prevented my seeing and hearing everything.

So I set out to desensitize myself. I attended executions. As a college student, I covered a shooting one afternoon. The deputy asked me if I'd like to attend the autopsy that night. I ate a big dinner and then watched the coroner open the skull and chest cavity of the shooting victim. I knew my exercises were succeeding as I watched, fascinated, with no sense of nausea.

Those exercises were extremely valuable to me later in my reporting career. I was caught in the middle of several riots. I was a block away when two major industrial accidents occurred, each killing half a dozen people and injuring many others. I was able to walk through the carnage, taking notes, shooting pictures, cool and deliberate. Surgically recording what was happening so I could give my readers or viewers an objective, clear picture of what really happened.

You Challenge the Reporter

And yet, after 30 years of conditioning to be unemotional on a story, I often felt an adrenaline rush that made my pulse jump and the hair stand up on the back of my neck. It happened whenever someone told me I could not enter. Or I couldn't look at a public record. They challenged my skill as a reporter. They sharpened every combative instinct I possessed. They were hiding something. It was my job to find what they were hiding and tell the entire world.

I was no longer Clark Kent. I stepped into the phone booth and came out—SUPERMAN! Fighting for truth, justice, and the American Way. I usually found what they were hiding and told my readers about it on the front page. I was able to obtain a copy of the document they hid, and put it, full-screen, on the next newscast.

Nixon's Private Meeting

Richard Nixon thought I bugged him during the 1968 Republican Convention. I didn't. But he pulled the trigger that challenged my reporting skill when he announced he would hold a private meeting with all the Southern delegates to discuss his position on school busing. School busing to end racial segregation was a big issue that year. The night before the private meeting, my managing editor called me over to his desk. "Jones," he said, "You're a good reporter. I'd like to know what Nixon says tomorrow morning about school busing."

My first attempt to crash the meeting didn't work. The guards on the door were too good. So I stood out of earshot, looking for delegates I knew. I was carrying a large audio tape

How To Speak TV, Print & Radio

recorder. Two delegates refused to help me. The third grinned and said, "Sure." He slung the tape recorder over his shoulder, in plain sight, flashed his credentials at the guards, and waltzed in. He sat under a loudspeaker. When Nixon began speaking, my secret agent turned on the recorder. He brought me back a studio-quality tape. The next morning, across the front page of the *Miami Herald,* we ran the complete transcript. Nixon had violated the First Commandment.

 # 1A—Never Lie

There is a sub-commandment here. Never lie. The lie, in the Media Morality scale, is often worse than the sin you lie about. As an investigative reporter in television, I did whatever I could to get you to talk to me on camera. If you were the villain I thought you were, you would lie. And I could use the lie to destroy you.

In the past, people who lied to reporters could later claim they were misquoted. No longer. With audio and videotape, you do not lie once. You lie at 6 o'clock; at 11 o'clock; on the morning show; again at noon. We may hear the lie played over and over as long as you live. Even after you die. Break some of the other commandments, but don't lie.

 # 2—Personalize

Help me with an experiment. I want you to record the first thing that comes to your mind when you read the next paragraph.

Ready?

Chrysler.

If you're like most Americans, an image of Lee Iacocca popped into your head.

That's because Chrysler's media mavens wrote the book on personalizing the organization. Let's go back to Chrysler's problems in the 1970s. They'd been making mediocre cars. Overpriced cars. Cars that couldn't compete with the flood of imports. People stopped buying their cars. Their profits evaporated. Their stock hit the skids.

They were on the verge of bankruptcy. Nobody would lend them any money. The economists said at least 300,000 people would be out of work in one fell swoop if Chrysler went down the tubes. And that would probably trigger another Great Depression. One last-ditch proposal was made—ask Congress to guarantee the loans it would take to reform the company and make it profitable again.

Big, We Don't Like

One small problem—why should the American taxpayer bail out Chrysler? Why should the good faith and credit of ordinary Americans be put at risk for a company that had made stupid decisions in the marketplace? Americans do not love big corporations. In fact, they have a negative mindset for almost anything that smacks of bigness and bureaucracy. They carp about the phone company, the military, the legal profession, doctors, public schools—you name it.

But their attitude about any large organization changes when they get to know personally someone in that organization. The medical profession is just a big collection of quacks, my next-door neighbor says. You go in for an operation and they cut off the wrong leg. You have dandruff and the prescription to stop the flakes gives you cancer. Except for my cardiologist. A saint. The reason I'm alive today.

My Kinda Guy

So the publicists at Chrysler set out to give Iacocca massive media exposure. Their goal? Make Iacocca equal Chrysler. They were amazingly successful. He was on every magazine cover, talk show, front page. Of course, they had good material to work with. Bright, tough, colorful. The emigrant kid with smarts and sass who made not one, but two fortunes. Risk-taker. Creator of the Mustang. Hated Henry Ford. My kinda guy. Yeah, I'll gamble on Iacocca. Go ahead, Congress, guarantee the loans.

I Am the NRA

Other organizations quickly copied the idea. The National Rifle Association for years has been running the same basic ad in national magazines. A full page, color picture of a gray-haired lady in tennis shoes, her long-barrel .357 magnum at the ready. A famous baseball player with his Winchester pump in a duck blind. A school teacher or electrician at the target range. Under every ad, one simple phrase: "I Am the NRA." See? Not a crazy with Uzis in each fist, a bullet belt over each shoulder. Just ordinary people. People like you, personalizing the organization.

What Do You Do?

To be successful with the media, you have to become very creative at showing us real people in your organization. All public relations boils down to one simple concept—**Who are you? What do you do?**

I asked a group of agents representing every FBI office in the country that question. In an earlier age, J. Edgar Hoover was a master at media relations. We saw G-men under massive headlines when they captured bank robbers or rescued kidnapped kids. The Ten Most Wanted List was a clever media device to promote the FBI. Yet today's FBI hasn't caught up with the times. If we asked Joe Sixpack today what FBI agents do, he might say they're the guys in coats and ties who walk handcuffed people in and out of the federal building. That's all we see them do.

3—Develop Contacts

Let's be frank. You develop personal relationships with reporters and editors so you can use them to get better coverage. As you cultivate the contact, you know that. They know that. But you never say that. It is a strange game in which you collect poker chips which you will someday cash in. But it is done without a word.

As a young newspaper reporter, I covered federal court arraignments every morning. I would write small stories about the procession of car thieves, pimps, moonshiners and occasional bank robbers who appeared to plead and have their bonds set.

My Doctor, the Defendant

I walk into court one morning, glance over at the group of defendants, and my jaw drops. In the group is a prominent local surgeon whom I know very well. He had corrected my hernia a few months earlier. Before I can check the docket to see what he was arrested for, his attorney scurries over to me. I know the attorney, too. He is a state senator I have covered on a daily basis during legislative sessions at the state capitol. "I'm here representing your doctor," the senator says earnestly. "Please, please don't write a story. It will destroy him."

My curiosity is really aroused. What did they get him for?

"Please, Clarence, no story."

Why is he here, senator?

"The game warden caught him. He shot too many ducks."

A Strange Ethic

Normally, I would not have written a game warden arrest story. But that day, I was compelled to. Why? To prove my relationship with the defendant and his attorney could not influence my unbiased, objective coverage. In retrospect, it is a strange ethic.

How do you develop contacts? Invite them to lunch. They'll probably insist on paying their own check. (See **STRATEGY/ Ethics**) At lunch, make it clear that you are available when they need a resource. Emphasize Commandment # 1. Just want you to know that we have an open door to reporters and photographers at our place. Call. We'll do our best to help you.

Good Reporters Need You

Good reporters have many contacts. They depend on them. Contacts call with story tips. Contacts volunteer inside information they know will help on today's major story. And when it's time for a story about your profession or organization, the contact will be quoted. It enhances the positive image of your group, and it won't hurt your career.

Remember, all stories are not black and white. Reporters have tremendous power in deciding which stories will be written— which will be thrown away. Stories take a slant or tone by the choice of a word or a phrase. The reporter who knows you personally—respects your competence and integrity—will write a very different story when you're having problems than the reporter who is a stranger.

After you develop contacts, they call you when they get tips suggesting something's wrong at your place. Rumors—and the stories they generate—die when you assure your reporter contact the rumors are false. When the rumors are true, you must NEVER, NEVER suggest that the reporter owes you a break. If you do that, the game is over. You lose all your chips, and a good media contact. Go directly to the front page. Do not pass go.

 # 4—Take Good Stories

The side dish with most American dinners now is a generous helping of blood and guts. Night after night, we watch bodies dragged across the screen. If not a double murder, then a plane crash. If not a terrorist bombing, then a tenement house fire, with mothers dropping their babies to the pavement. From every corner of the world, we see tears, pain and human suffering.

National Public Radio wakes us each morning with news of the latest terrorist bombing in the Middle East.

Why Always Bad News?

Why do they always bring bad news?
Because people want to hear and see it.
Because they *need* to know.

It is not just morbid curiosity. It is part of our instinct for self-preservation. We *need* to know there is a killer stalking children so we can protect our children. We *want* to know there is a serious design defect in a new airplane so we can take a different flight. We have always pictured ourselves as caring people who value human life. But because most of us never venture into the ghetto, we do not think about inadequate or unenforced building codes until we see children die there.

We have become so isolated from each other, so insulated from our own neighborhoods, we do not notice problems unless there is a disaster to grab our attention. In a nation so overloaded with crises, we seem now to tend only those that have most recently shocked and sickened us.

The Media Set the Agenda

Once the news media bring those issues to our attention, we put them on our agenda. The reform of drunk driving laws in the United States swept across the nation in the 1980s as local and national media focused on the terrible toll of death and permanent disability caused by drunk drivers.

The same thing happened with child abuse and the destruction of the environment.

In modern-day America, we do not believe a problem exists unless we *see* that problem spotlighted in the news media.

And if you are a problem-solver, we will not believe you are doing anything until we see you working to solve that problem.

We Are Insulated from Life

There is another theory, too, about the crowds that gather to stare at people dead, or dying, in the street. In this sterile, high-tech society, most of us never see or experience life's most basic components. Most of us have never seen the struggle and wonder of birth, the anguish of a nervous breakdown, the courage of self-sacrifice, the loneliness of old age. Most of us have never seen someone die.

We hide life's basics in hospitals and nursing homes, or in a code of behavior that says we must never, never let anyone know what we are feeling, or who we really are.

We are terribly alone, and often bored, in our plastic packages. We need to touch reality. And so we are drawn to—fascinated by—death and violence, human triumph and tragedy. That is one reason cops, reporters, doctors and criminal lawyers are the central figures in so much of contemporary television drama. Their jobs put them in touch with humanity. We want to look over their shoulders. We envy their opportunity to experience life with the wraps off.

How Much Gore?

In newsrooms everywhere, there is constant debate over just how much to show. How much blood should they let seep into your living room? How close shall the camera zoom on the face of the dead child?

There are excesses, and after a long string of bodies every night, editors and news directors write memos ordering less blood and gore. The media are always trying to sense just the right balance. Enough to satisfy the viewers' cravings—not so much to disgust them and make them stop watching, listening, or reading. Enough to inform and motivate without turning them off. (See **INSIDE THE MEDIA/Privacy**)

We Forget Good News

There is another phenomenon here. We remember the BAD NEWS stories and forget the rest. In every newscast, newspaper or magazine, there are lots of GOOD NEWS stories. Many local stations now have their equivalent of "Charles Kuralt On The Road." Newspapers were doing it long before Kuralt. Folksy visits with little old ladies who still chop wood for their kitchen stoves. Trained pigs that bring in the newspaper. Kids who have defeated birth defects through sheer courage and determination.

For some reason or another, we forget the story about the cop who saved a life, and remember the story about the one who sold his badge to the dope peddler.

Looking For a "Kicker"

In more than a thousand TV newsrooms across America, they are searching right now for tonight's "kicker." By decree in the television news industry, every newscast must have a kicker.

The kicker is the last story in the newscast. It is a warm, fuzzy, feel-good, overcome handicaps, success story. It is a story that picks us up and makes us feel that people are basically good, despite what we've been told in the previous 28 minutes.

The kicker decree was ordered years ago by TV news consultants who interviewed focus groups on their reaction to TV news. They kept picking up the same kind of response—

"You know, we watch the news every night while we eat dinner. And after all that blood and pain and tears, we get indigestion. We've talked about watching 'Gilligan's Island' re-runs instead of news."

Every Newscast Has One

The consultants came up with an easy cure—run a kicker as the last story, and the audience will forget the blood and pain and tears. They'll feel good, and come back tomorrow night. And so virtually every newscast in America—local or network—ends with a kicker.

The bad news almost always leaks out. You assume that good news leaks, too. It doesn't. Gossips inside your organization take bad news to the media. It is a natural phenomenon. There is no natural counterpart for good stories leaking.

You must create a system where everyone in the organization is sensitive to good stories. There must be a way for those ideas to reach the person who is responsible for public relations. It's that person's job to try to sell the good story. Thousands of good stories die every day simply because the media never hear about them.

5—Respond Quickly

If you are under attack, YOU MUST RESPOND BY 3 P.M. TODAY.

Your lawyer can be a real problem here. Lawyers often give good legal advice, with horrible media results.

When someone planted cyanide in Tylenol capsules, the attorneys at Johnson and Johnson counselled CEO James Burke to say absolutely nothing. The giant corporation would surely be sued for billions of dollars. Whatever was said could come back to haunt them in court. Tylenol was responsible for a third of the corporation's revenue.

The Tylenol PR Victory

Burke thanked his lawyers for their opinion, and then did exactly the opposite. The doors of the corporation were flung open to any reporter who called. Burke went on the "Phil Donahue Show" and took questions from the audience and anonymous callers. Mike Wallace and a "60 Minutes" camera crew were allowed to cover a top-level executive meeting at the height of the crisis, with no holds barred.

Most people in the public relations business consider Burke's gutsy decision the most successful PR coup of the century. If Burke had followed the legal advice, the company might have gone belly-up.

Legal Training

Lawyers give that advice because of their training and experience. Never ask a question until you know the answer. Never discuss a case until you have all the pieces of the puzzle together. Something said before you have the entire picture can be damning once you know what really happened. Wait until all the facts are in.

Lawyers have also designed a system where there are no absolute deadlines. Trials are set months in advance. The trial day comes, and one side or the other asks for a continuance. A key witness is ill. A piece of evidence needs further testing in the lab. New evidence has just been discovered and both sides need to examine it. In the interest of truth, justice and fairness, the judge grants a continuance. That is as it should be. But the media do not grant continuances. Once the allegation surfaces, the trial will be scheduled for tonight's newscast. The longer version will be in tomorrow morning's newspaper.

The Media Trial

Let's look at what happens when you stonewall. The nightly newscast opens with the anchor saying, "Well, there's more trouble at Widgetworks tonight. Frank Ferrett, our investigative reporter, has been following that story and tonight he has the latest. Frank—"

It is 20 seconds after six o'clock. Ferrett now assumes the role of prosecutor, or plaintiff's attorney. His opening statement to the jury lays out the charges and allegations. He calls several witnesses to the stand. In those interviews, they are not cross-examined. Ferrett puts several documents into evidence. We see them on the screen, with key portions circled or enlarged for emphasis. They are not challenged or questioned.

The Prosecution Rests

Then Ferrett rests.

If you have attended courtroom trials, you know that the prosecutor presents his case to the jury first. Then the defense is presented. In this media courtroom, the defense decides to make no argument, present no witnesses, introduce no evidence. The decision is announced: "Officials at Widgetworks refused to talk to us." Perhaps we see them going into their offices, covering their faces. Or their attorney says curtly, "We will have no statement at this time."

Ferrett now makes his closing argument. He sums up all the evidence, which has not been challenged. The case goes to the jury. This is a speedy trial process. It is now one minute and 40 seconds after six. At 6:01:45, the jury returns with a verdict.

Guilty On All Counts

I know, before the clerk reads it, what the verdict is. GUILTY ON ALL COUNTS.

Several days or weeks later, the attorneys go to the CEO. Let's ask for a rehearing in the media. A new trial. We can show we are absolutely innocent.

The media court has different rules of procedure. New trials are extremely rare. Rehearings, if they take place at all, are often two paragraphs back by the hemorrhoid ads.

Once you are cast as the villain in a story, it is extremely difficult—often impossible—to change that image, no matter what you do.

The media policies I write for clients have rules that require staff to return all reporters' phone calls within 15 minutes. If the person the reporter is trying to reach is out of touch, someone else should return the call. "We can't reach the boss. Can I help you?"

This will prevent you from being surprised on tomorrow's front page. You need to know what the reporter is working on. Every story about you should include your viewpoint.

Sometimes, the reporter simply needs information. You become a resource. Your image is enhanced. You're an expert. (See **STRATEGY/Media Policy**)

 # 6—Never Say No Comment

Never say, "No Comment."

Why?

It violates Commandment Number One.

We hear something else. We assume you are hiding something. Evading. If you haven't done anything wrong, why not talk to us?

In reality, however, there are times when you simply can't tell everything to the media. If the detectives tell us too much about the kidnapping, the child may die.

If the CEO discusses the proposed merger, the negotiations may fall apart.

The grand jury witness who tells reporters what happened in the jury room will be held in contempt and jailed.

If the human services caseworker discloses anything about a client, the law calls for prosecution and dismissal. The worker can be sued for invasion of privacy. The lawyer, banker, accountant or physician who tells reporters about conversations with a patient or client violates a sacred trust.

So what do you say when reporters ask questions you truly can't answer?

The Oliver North Posture

During his first appearance before the Iran-Contra Congressional committee, Marine Col. Oliver North told the committee almost nothing. But he never said, "No comment."

His handlers knew he would look bad. No Comment is very much like the Fifth Amendment. The Fifth Amendment is a perfectly valid Constitutional right guaranteed every person in this country. But because so many shady characters have used it in appearances before Congressional committees, it has fallen on hard times. Like "No Comment," we hear something else.

I Wish I Could Help You

North took a different posture. When he did not—or could not—answer a question, his response was, "Senator, I wish I could tell you what really happened. . . . People in America would feel safer tonight if I could disclose the truth and put those rumors to rest."

It was a way to stonewall without appearing to stonewall. His stance appeared to be trustworthy, helpful, friendly, courteous, kind, cooperative, humble.

If you can take that posture and be truthful about it, you avoid the negative message that "No Comment" sends. But you must follow it with a complete explanation of why you can't answer the question. "Because my lawyer won't let me," is not good enough.

Explain Why You Can't

North frequently based his failure to respond to the question on national security.

Sometimes you will not be able to answer because the law forbids it. Explain the law. Perhaps give the reporter a copy of the law.

Media Morality values accuracy and fairness. Explain that because so little is known at this time, you don't want to be inaccurate or unfair. Explain in great detail how you plan to investigate and find the truth.

As Soon As I Can, I Will

Close the conversation with a promise that you will get back to the reporter with a full answer just as soon as you can—as soon as the investigation is completed; the negotiations finished; the arrest made; the trial over; the contract signed; the deal sealed.

BE SURE YOU KEEP THAT PROMISE.

In real life, if you are successful at the media game, you will also learn how to talk to reporters in confidence. (See **SKILLS/Off-the-Record**)

 # 7—It's OK to Say I Don't Know

If you don't know the answer to a reporter's question, don't try to fake it. Don't assume your employees did what they were trained to do. Don't use statistics unless you're absolutely sure of the numbers.

Reporters don't expect you to have the Library of Congress in your head. But they do expect you to know where the information is, and to be able to retrieve it quickly.

I recommend that you include a staff member in any complicated interview or news conference. (See **SKILLS/Interviews** and **News Conferences**) The staffer's job is to answer complicated technical questions in their area of expertise. Or to fetch the records you need to answer the reporter's question.

But I'll Find Out

"I can't remember the exact figure," you tell the reporter. "But Bill, if you'll get the 1987 committee report, that'll have it. We can give you those numbers before you leave the building."

In this way, you appear helpful, open, cooperative. I DON'T KNOW. BUT I'LL FIND OUT AND GET WHAT YOU NEED.

8—Confess & Repent

This is another basic in the American character. We respect people who admit they made a mistake. IF THEY DO WHATEVER THEY CAN TO MAKE IT RIGHT.

How different our tribal character would be if George Washington had said to his father, "Cherry tree? What cherry tree?"

In the new Media Morality, the lie, the cover-up, the insensitivity are greater sins than the crime itself.

Nixon's Failure to Confess

Richard Nixon did not lose the presidency because of the Watergate burglary. There was never any evidence that he knew about the burglary in advance, or helped plan it. He was disgraced because of the cover-up, not the crime.

Nixon would have been a very different figure in history if he had gone on television shortly after the Watergate burglars were caught to announce that someone at Republican Headquarters had made a dreadful mistake; that he, as the party nominee, would accept the blame and see that those responsible were brought to justice.

Long after he had resigned in disgrace, Nixon consented to a series of televised interviews with David Frost. The most emotional moment in those hours of conversation came when Frost told Nixon he wished the fallen President could admit that he made a mistake in trying to cover up the break-in. Nixon stonewalled. Frost tried again, almost begging Nixon to confess and ask forgiveness.

The Cardinal Sin

"Mr. President, can't you just say you're sorry?"

The cameras were close, flicking from Frost to Nixon, then Frost, and back again. You could almost hear the former President's heart pounding. It was like that moment in the revival tent when everybody is singing and praying that the town sinner in the back row will walk down the aisle to repent and be saved.

After a pause that seemed forever, Nixon said he had done nothing to be sorry for, and turned away.

We find it very hard to forgive the sinner who will not confess and repent. But if you confess to the media, you must also repent in the same breath. After "How to you feel about . . ." Reporters have a guaranteed follow-up question:

"What are you going to do about it?"

A Time to Repent

One of the favorite hypotheticals in my seminars is one in which the person on camera is playing the role of a construction company owner. The company has a multi-million-dollar contract to build a new civic center downtown. Today is a major event in the construction project. They finished clearing the site this morning. By sunset, the digging for the foundation will be well underway. Within a few days, there will be steel and concrete in the hole. You will be able to see the building taking shape.

There is one small problem, however. One of the houses your workers bulldozed this morning was not on the site. It was just over the line. There was nobody at home to stop them. The widow who lives in the house was at the hospital, visiting her mother, who is dying of cancer.

And now, the widow (who lives on Social Security) is digging through the rubble, looking for the only picture she has of her only son. He was the marine who died in Vietnam and was awarded the Medal of Honor for heroism.

What Do You Do Now?

What do you do now? I ask my audience.

"Take a six-month vacation in Hawaii," one man suggested.

No. Confess.

This drives attorneys crazy. We all carry in our wallets the little card our auto insurance company mailed us. IF YOU HAVE AN ACCIDENT, it says, DO NOT ADMIT FAULT.

Look, I tell the lawyers in the audience. I don't care where you try this case—who the judge is—who the jurors are—who the opposing attorney is—they're going to find out you knocked

down the wrong house. So go ahead and confess, once you're
sure you made a mistake.

Do Your Penance

And in the same breath, do your penance.

What are you going to do about it?

Build her a new house. Does she want it here? In the mountains? By the seashore?

"Just tell me where, and we'll start that new house tomorrow
morning. You'll need a place to stay during construction. I've
arranged for you to be my guest at the Hyatt Regency. Meals
included.

"It looks like we've torn up your furniture and clothes. I've
arranged a credit for you at the Furniture Gallery. When the
house is finished, furnish it any way you'd like. And Saks Fifth
Avenue will provide you a new wardrobe."

She will still sue. But any juror who hears about your confes-
sion and penance will get angry. Not at you.

"That greedy bitch," the juror will say. "And she wants
$20 million? Get out of here."

 # 9—Use the Big Dump

When you have bad news to dump, dump it all at once.

Don't let it dribble out. That will prolong the stories and
multiply the damage.

Once you decide to confess and repent, you may be tempted
to confess only part of your sins. That's human nature. But then
you find follow-up stories repeating the original allegations as
they add tiny bits of new information. With each new story, the
damage increases.

Two months from now, a tiny detail that has not surfaced will
be discovered by an enterprising reporter. LOOK WHAT WE
FOUND the headline screams. EXCLUSIVE INVESTIGATIVE
REPORT. The new finding is so insignificant, it would not have
been considered news if you had dumped it the first day.

No Time or Space

Far better to dump everything you reasonably believe the media might find. There will not be time on the air or space in print

to disclose it all. And then it will be old news. You can move on past the problem.

Dirt that you disclose is always less newsworthy than dirt reporters dig by themselves. So long as the news media believe there is more to be mined, they will continue to dig. That's their job. When they believe the mine is exhausted, they move on to more fertile subjects.

 # 10—Prepare

Most organizations have carefully prepared disaster plans. They conduct fire drills, tornado drills, earthquake drills, hurricane drills. They buy insurance and prepare for the worst.

It is much more likely that you or your organization will experience a media disaster before you have a fire or an earthquake or a tornado. Yet few companies or government agencies have prepared for that more likely hazard.

A first step is a written media policy. (See **STRATEGY/Media Policy**)

Key spokespeople ought to be trained to deal with the media. And they need to practice those skills often. Otherwise they get rusty. They lose their reflexes. (See **STRATEGY/PIOs**)

What Would We Do If?

Hypothetical media incidents should be studied by your command staff. What if we suddenly discovered a major internal theft? How will our police department react if one of our officers makes a major mistake and kills an innocent person? What will the hospital say to the media if a major slipup occurs in the operating room and a famous patient dies? How will the bank explain an employee who helped a drug smuggler launder millions of dollars? What will be the position of the human services agency when it returns a battered child to its parents and the parents kill that child? What will the judge say when he releases a career criminal and that criminal murders a little girl within a week?

All these things happen with some regularity. We are human. We make mistakes. Our systems are imperfect. If we do not prepare for disaster, it can easily destroy us.

Part 3
INSIDE THE MEDIA

Editing

Fairness & Equal Time

Jargon

Libel

Networks

Newscast

Newspapers

Privacy

Ratings

Technology

INSIDE THE MEDIA

EDITING

Did I Really Say That?

Editing is an art form. Your interview can be edited so skillfully, you can't tell what they took out, or stitched together. You can't see the scar where a good plastic surgeon makes the incision. Or—when they've finished editing what you said, you may think the editor used a chain saw. Once you've given an interview, you are at the mercy of the reporter and the editor. A tiny fraction of what you say in the interview will ever be published or broadcast. Maybe none of it. You may wind up on the editing room floor. Simply a notation in the print reporter's shorthand pad.

Broadcast Interviews

The usual hallway interview, on the run, as you go in or out of a meeting, will last about five minutes. A sit-down session for radio or TV may go 10 to 20 minutes. Out of that, a maximum of 20 to 30 seconds will be used—and that much, only if they use several of your sound bites, separated by reporter narration or bites from other interviews. They'll normally use only about 10 seconds of what you said.

Newspaper reporters may spend an hour or two with you for a daily story; a day or two for a lengthy profile. Magazine writers may live with you for a week.

FACE Formula for Print

An interesting phenomenon is taking place. Print reporters are choosing the same kind of formularized quotes for their stories that radio and TV use. They simply use more of them. The

FACE Formula applies for all media. (See **SKILLS/Interviews-Broadcast**) The editing for television is more complicated, because it must deal simultaneously with both words and pictures.

People who work in broadcasting for a while change the way they listen to conversation. At a party, even when they're not working, they find themselves involuntarily scanning what you're saying, marking off usable sound bites. It is like panning for gold. Somewhere in that muddy dialogue, there must be a few bright, memorable nuggets.

TV News Editing

Let's watch the TV editing process.

At a city council meeting, Councilman Luther "Red" Light proposes that the city revoke its current prostitution ordinances. He wants to make prostitution legal in a specially-zoned area near the downtown convention center. A local television crew catches up with him in a hallway after the meeting. He is persuaded to come back to his desk in the council chamber for an on-camera interview. This is a transcript:

1   REPORTER: Councilman, you

2   proposed tonight that the city le-

3   galize prostitution. Why?

4   LIGHT: It seems to me that

5   we've wasted enough time and

6   money and law enforcement re-

7   sources chasing them from one

8   street corner to the next. Have

9   you ever tried to figure what it's

10   costing this town to bring a

11   hooker to court, so she can laugh

12   at the law, pay her $50 fine, and

13   get back on the street in time to

14   catch the lunch-hour customers?

15   It's ridiculous. An absolute waste

16   of time and resources. It's time

17   we had policemen chasing mur-

18   derers and rapists and robbers

19   who terrorize and kill and maim,

20   instead of a few women trying

21   to make a living, supplying a

22   service for which there seems to

23   be a great demand.

24   REPORTER: You say a few

25   women. It's hard for a man to

26   walk from City Hall to the police

27   station without being propo-

28   sitioned. Aren't you just—

29   LIGHT: Exactly. The present

30   law doesn't work. The vice squad

31   made 84 arrests for prostitution

32   last month. You know how many

33   of those arrested spent any time

34   in jail? I'll tell you. None. Not a

35   single one. I've done my home-

36   work on this. The vice squad con-

37   sists of eight detectives, a lieuten-

38   ant and a captain. Ten altogether,

39   who draw total salaries of $23,280

40   per month. Add cars, medical in-

41   surance, other fringe benefits,

42   and the price to the taxpayers is

43   roughly $30,000 per month—

44   $360,000 per year. Now, they ar-

45   rested 84 prostitutes last month—

46   alleged prostitutes. Thirty-two

47   of those arrests were thrown out

48   by the prosecutor's office and

49   never got to court. That leaves

50   52. Twenty-one of those were dis-

51   missed by the judge. That leaves

52   31. Every one of them pleaded

53   guilty and paid a $50 fine. A total

54   of $1,550 for the city coffers.

55   Why, that won't even pay for the

56   gasoline to run the cars for the

57   vice squad, much less their salar-

58   ies, and the salaries of the clerks,

59   the prosecutors, the judges and

60   secretaries and bailiffs. It's not

61   cost-productive. Never has been.

62   And it doesn't stop prostitution

63 The world's oldest profession is

64 here to stay. I say zone it into an

65 area where we can control it.

66 Properly done, it might even draw

67 more people to the city. Might

68 as well make some money from it

69 instead of wasting half a million

70 dollars a year, trying to enforce

71 stupid, hypocritical laws that

72 don't work.

73   REPORTER: You realize the

74 preachers will organize to fight

75 your proposal?

76   LIGHT: Sure, I do. But every

77 single preacher knows, down

78 deep in his heart, I'm right.

79 They've got their job to do, I've

80 got mine. But hellfire, this is the

81 20th century. Sex isn't going to go

82 away. It's time we quit pretend-

83 ing it will. I know the preachers

84 will come after me. But in their

85 hearts, they know I'm right.

86   REPORTER: The opponents of

87 legalized prostitution say it in-

88   creases violent crime.

89   LIGHT: What do you think ten

90   policemen fighting crime, instead

91   of chasing little girls down the

92   sidewalk, would accomplish?

93   That's a lot of crap. Put those ten

94   officers to work catching robbers,

95   rapists, killers and thieves, and

96   you'll see the crime rate in this

97   town go down, not up.

98   REPORTER: Thank you,

99   Councilman.

Let's see, now, what a little judicious editing can do. This is what the finished script looks like:

Legalize Hookers
Lead-in
ANCHOR LIVE   CITY POLICE SHOULD QUIT CHASING
PROSTITUTES AND CONCENTRATE ON
VIOLENT CRIME. THAT'S WHAT CITY
COUNCILMAN "RED" LIGHT PROPOSED
AT TONIGHT'S COUNCIL MEETING.
NEWSWATCH REPORTER SUSAN SCOOP
SAYS THE COUNCILMAN WANTS TO
CREATE A ZONE FOR LEGALIZED
PROSTITUTION NEAR THE DOWNTOWN
CONVENTION CENTER.

Videotape begins
SCOOP V/O   THIS IS GOODTIME STREET, JUST TWO
(Hookers waving   BLOCKS FROM THE POLICE STATION.
at cars)   IT COSTS THE CITY ABOUT $300,000

	A YEAR TO OPERATE THE VICE SQUAD. COUNCILMAN LIGHT SAYS THE EXPENSE IS A WASTE OF TIME AND MONEY.
SOT Light (Line 80)	This is the 20th century. Sex isn't going to go away . . .
(Line 29)	The present law doesn't work . . .
(Line 15)	It's ridiculous. An absolute waste of time and resources. It's time we had policemen chasing murderers and rapists and robbers.
V/O (File tape of vice squad raid)	LIGHT SAYS THE VICE SQUAD MADE 84 ARRESTS LAST MONTH. MOST OF THE CASES WERE DISMISSED BEFORE THEY WENT TO TRIAL. THIRTY-ONE PLEADED GUILTY AND PAID $50 FINES. NOBODY WENT TO JAIL.
SOT Light (Line 55)	That won't even pay for the gasoline to run the cars for the vice squad . . .
(Line 63)	The world's oldest profession is here to stay. I say zone it into an area where we can control it.
SOT STANDUP (Scoop)	LIGHT SAYS THE CITY'S RELIGIOUS LEADERS WILL ATTACK HIM AND HIS PROPOSAL—BUT IN THEIR HEARTS, THEY KNOW HE'S RIGHT. I'M SUSAN SCOOP, ON THE NIGHT BEAT FOR NEWSWATCH ELEVEN.

Building the Tape

Phrases can be shuffled and spliced together, and your ear can't hear the edit. But editing the video requires some finesse. Here's how they do it:

The reporter first reviews the interview tape and decides which sound bites she'll use. The story will be built around the interview. She may have recorded the interview separately on a small audio recorder. She can listen to it in the car, on the way back to the television station, and save valuable time if she's close to deadline.

When the script is written and approved, the reporter and editor work together in the editing booth. At most stations, the photographer who shoots the tape also edits it. Networks and stations in large cities are more specialized. Photographers shoot, and editors edit.

The Editing Console

The editing console is two large videocassette recorders (VCRs), each with its own TV monitor. There is a microphone and a sound mixer in the booth. The videocassette recorders are wired together so that what is played on the LEFT VCR can be copied by the RIGHT VCR.

The editor puts a blank videocassette in the RIGHT VCR. The story in its final, broadcast form will be assembled on this cassette.

Reporter's Voice, No Video

The script begins with reporter voice-over. Susan reads the first section of script into the microphone. Her voice is recorded on the blank cassette in the RIGHT VCR. There is no picture to go with the voice. That comes later. The RIGHT VCR can record sound, or picture, or both at the same time.

Sound Bite Voice & Video

The first sound bite from Councilman Light comes next. The editor puts the interview tape, recorded at City Hall, into the LEFT VCR. He rolls to the section Susan has selected. Susan gives him the "in-cue"—the words at the beginning of the sound bite—and the "out-cue."

In-and Out-Cues

In-cue: This is the . . ."
Out-cue: " . . . going to go away."
Leaving a half-second pause after the reporter's voice, the editor copies from LEFT VCR to RIGHT VCR Councilman Light

saying, "This is the 20th century. Sex isn't going to go away." Both audio and video are copied at the same time. Then they search for the next phrase in the script and edit it to the first one—"The present law doesn't work." And then a third one— "It's ridiculous. An absolute waste of resources."

Susan records more voice-over onto the tape in the RIGHT VCR, then another section of edited interview, and finally, Susan's videotaped standup in the council chamber closes the story.

Standups

When we see a reporter talking on camera, it is called a standup. Whether she's sitting, walking, riding or standing, it's still a standup.

If we looked at the tape in the RIGHT VCR now, we would see blank screen while reporter Scoop talks; Councilman Light talking; blank screen while Scoop talks; Councilman Light talking; Scoop talking.

Covering Video Holes

They will go back now, to "cover" the video holes in the story. As the crew left the council meeting, they took time to shoot some streetwalkers waving at cars near City Hall. They now edit this video under Scoop's voice, mixing in some of the natural sound from the street. The same process puts file tape video of a police raid to cover the second section of reporter voice-over.

Now for the sleight-of-hand that will hide the way they edited what Councilman Light said.

Jump Cuts

The edits are clearly visible. Dramatically visible. You can't miss them. They're called jump cuts. At the beginning of the interview, Light was leaning forward, elbows on his desk. Then he lit a cigar. At one point, he shifted back in his swivel chair and put his hands behind his head.

In the first phrase they edited, Light is puffing on his cigar. The next phrase, butted against it, shows his hands, but no cigar. On arm is on the desk. In the third sound bite, he is leaning back with his hands behind his head. As you watch the edited tape, it looks like the councilman suffers from a strange nerve disorder that makes him suddenly jerk from elbows-on-table to hands-behind-head. He also seems to do magic tricks that make cigars disappear.

Cosmetic Cutaways

At the place where the film or tape is edited, the speaker will suddenly jump to another position. This happens at every edit point. In the early days of television news, they decided jump cuts were too distracting. They developed the "cutaway" technique to hide them.

After they finished the interview at City Hall, Scoop and her photographer took several minutes to shoot cutaways. The two most often used cutaways are:

Two-Shots

A wide-angle "two-shot" that shows both the reporter and the subject of the interview. The interviewee is talking, but the camera is too far away for us to tell whether the movement of his lips matches the words we are hearing.

Listeners

A "listener." The reporter listening, or the reporter making notes. It is sometimes shot from behind, and over the shoulder, of the person being interviewed. Reporters have a bad habit of nodding during cutaways, like those little toy dogs that sit in the rear windows of automobiles.

How Quickly We Forget

The cutaway shot is edited onto the story cassette for only a second or two. It replaces the picture of the councilman, so that your eyes cut away to something else. The sound is not changed. As soon as the jump cut passes, you see Councilman Light again.

In that brief cutaway second or two, you forget that he was smoking a cigar before you looked away. Your mind assumes that in that cutaway moment, he put out his cigar, or leaned back in his chair. If you diagram the finished videocassette as it will play on the air, it will look like the next page.

EDITED
VIDEOTAPE

AUDIO TRACK		VIDEO TRACK
Reporter voice/over mixed with natural sound		Streetwalkers
Councilman Light's voice	---(EDIT)--- ---(EDIT)---	Councilman
		Reporter listening
		Councilman
Reporter voice/over mixed with natural sound		File tape of police raid
Councilman Light's voice	---(EDIT)---	Councilman
		"Two-shot" cutaway
		Councilman
Reporter sound-on-tape shot at City Hall		Reporter standing in council chamber

Print Also Edits

Print journalism interviews are heavily edited, too. Unless the full transcript is printed, a newspaper story takes a phrase here, a phrase there, often out of sequence. But if the words are direct quotes, the ethics of print require three dots (. . .) to tell readers where the edit points are. That's the difference. People who work in television understand that a cutaway means an edit point, but most viewers don't know that. Many complaints about television news accuracy and distortion are based on the cutaway editing technique.

Did He Really Say That?

"The Selling of the Pentagon," a CBS documentary, caused a major furor—eventually a congressional investigation—in the early 1970s. The criticism was based largely on editing of the interviews. "I said those words, but not in that order," the military spokesman argued. "When you string the phrases together in a different order, it changes the meaning of what I said."

Broadcasting Needs a Signal

If broadcasting would create some signal to tell viewers where an interview is edited, much of that kind of criticism could be avoided. During the cutaway, for instance, an audio beep could be inserted to tell the audience an edit took place. If the beep were standardized, it could become broadcasting's equivalent of the three-dot ellipsis.

In both broadcasting and print, an ethical reporter is very careful to make sure the edited version of an interview does not change the meaning or intent of what was said in the original version.

Jump-Cut Commercials

In the 1960s, the hidden camera was a favorite technique for television commercials. A housewife, supposedly unaware of the camera, was asked to compare her laundry before and after it was washed in Brand X. An old man described his headache in great detail and then told about his miraculous relief after taking two of the new pain killers.

Those interviews were heavily edited. Somewhere along the line, somebody said they were misleading if the edit points were hidden with cutaways. So commercials began letting the jump cuts show. As a result, we have become much more accustomed to jump-cuts. Some news organizations, concerned that they will be accused of distortion, now let jump cuts show in a sensitive interview.

Reverse Questions

Another editing device for broadcasting uses the "reverse question" between answers. When the interview is finished, everyone is told to stay in position. The photographer shoots cutaways. The reporter is shot asking the same questions asked during the interview. The camera is reversed, shooting in the opposite direction, over the shoulder of the interview subject. The reverse-shot question can then be used as a bridge to get from one answer to another.

Instead of a cutaway at the edit point, we see the reporter asking a question. Then we jump to an answer that may be five minutes away from the last answer. The effect is a continuously flowing conversation. While the question is being asked, the viewer forgets about the cigar or how the person answering the questions was sitting when we last saw him.

Radio Does It, Too

Radio can do the same thing. In the audiotaped interview, the reporter has his original questions, and doesn't have to worry about video jump-cuts. But sometimes the mike was pointed at the interview subject while the reporter was speaking, and the quality of the reporter's voice is poor. Or the reporter asked the question in a clumsy, stumbling way. To cover the stumble, the reporter records the question again—this time more clearly or eloquently than in the original interview.

The danger in this technique is that the question may not be phrased exactly as it was when you answered it the first time. The new question, spliced to the old answer, may be misleading.

Listen Carefully

When a broadcast reporter completes your interview, listen carefully as reverse questions are taped. If they're not restated exactly as they were when you were answering the question, politely point that out to the reporter. If you have some reason to suspect the reporter's integrity, have a staff member make a shorthand transcript of the reporter's questions during the interview. The staffer can then compare the shorthand notes with the reverse questions as they're taped.

Make Your Own Tape

It's also a good idea—if you have any reason to doubt the reporter's competence or integrity—to make an audio tape of the entire interview. Make sure the reporter knows you're recording the interview, to avoid legal problems. The audio tape is the only proof you have if you complain that the editing was unfair or out of context. (See **SKILLS/Interviews-General** and **Defending Yourself**)

Double-Shooting

On a major TV network documentary—particularly a sensitive, controversial subject—interviews will be "double-shot." The entire interview is recorded by two cameras—one on the interview subject, the other on the reporter. In that way, reporter questions and reactions are recorded exactly the way the interview subject saw and heard them. There can be no reverse question distortion. But few local stations or network field crews are given the resources to double-shoot interviews.

Sloppy Shorthand for Print

The big problem for print interviews is reporters whose shorthand is sloppy. They scribble furiously, and you think they're capturing your every word. Actually, they're only getting key phrases. So when it's time to write their story, they reconstruct the quote as best they remember it.

Sometimes the quote is distorted. Sometimes it's improved. Or it can be changed in such a way that it has no resemblance to what you really said.

Print Uses Tape, Too

Many print reporters now use audio recorders. The spread of the technique was prompted partly by readers' ability to compare quotes in newspapers with the same quotes on radio or TV. A news conference, for example, where a number of reporters are using the same quotes. Newspaper reporters discovered their shorthand wasn't always accurate. So they started using recorders.

The problem is that going back to review audio tape is a slow, tedious process. Even though there is a tape, the print reporter will usually make extensive notes. It's a lot easier to use the notes and ignore the tape. The tape becomes a backup for the notes.

One of your goals should be learning how to craft a quote so the reporter—whether print or broadcast—will use it exactly as you spoke it, without editing or taking it out of context. (See **SKILLS**/**Accuracy** & **Interviews** Sections)

Editing by Headline

A perennial complaint about newspapers is the inaccuracy of headlines. That, too, is a form of editing. When the headline distorts the story, you should complain. (See **SKILLS**/**Accuracy** and **STRATEGY**/**Fighting Back**)

Headline writers are true specialists. They must condense the thrust of the story into five or six words. And the words must fit the column, very much like a crossword puzzle. On deadline, the headline writers sometimes write the headline after reading only three or four paragraphs of the story. If they had read a little further, they would have a very different perspective, and a more accurate headline.

Editing by Committee

Newspaper and magazine stories go through the hands of a series of editors. At each stage, the story may be changed to suit the whim of the latest editor. That process can gradually distort the story and make it inaccurate or misleading.

The traditional newspaper story formula was designed to make shortening stories easy. It is called the pyramid formula. The main point of the story up top. You put the who, what, where, when, why and how in the first paragraph or two, then added details below the lead paragraphs.

Chopping from the Bottom

Ideally, the reporter put those details in diminishing order. The farther down in the story, the less important. In that way, when the page editor placed the story into empty space on the page, it could be cut from the bottom to make it fit and not damage the story.

But today's newspaper stories often use "soft" leads. The first paragraph describes David Dentz getting out of bed, stretching, yawning, brushing his teeth. He wondered why he hadn't heard his son, who usually got up before his parents.

Dentz checked his son's room. He wasn't there. The TV was dark. Then Dentz looked out the patio door and stark terror gripped him. There, on the patio, was a huge Bengal tiger, licking his chops.

The tiger had devoured David Jr.

Soft Leads

Sports writers, competing against live coverage of the ball game, go all-out to give us a feature slant on yesterday's game. So much so, they sometimes forget to tell us the final score.

Stories with soft leads are much harder to edit. They take time and skill. Chopping a story from the bottom to make it fit can be done by someone who's illiterate. In the time crunch just before deadline, the editing can badly distort a story.

When it does, you need to complain. (See **STRATEGY/ Fighting Back**)

INSIDE THE MEDIA

FAIRNESS & EQUAL TIME

Only Politicians Get Equal Time

"Congress shall make no law respecting an establishment of religion, or prohibiting the free exercise thereof; or abridging the freedom of speech or of the press; or the right of the people peaceably to assemble, and to petition the government for a redress of grievances."

The First Amendment to the U. S. Constitution is a simple, straightforward statement. *Congress shall make no law* abridging freedom of speech or press.

The press shall be free, the Constitution says. Nowhere does it say the news media in America shall be fair.

Early History

The early journalists in this country were revolutionary philosophers—zealots who used their printing presses to spread politics and religion. The American Revolution was conceived and sustained by writers, not soldiers. Men like Thomas Jefferson and Tom Paine. They believed with religious intensity that ideas—and the freedom to express those ideas—were sacred. So they protected that belief in the Constitution. It was a novel idea. A noble experiment. And it became part of the psyche, the historical heritage of the early newspaper editors.

Dan Rather: Wimp

Newspaper stories were grossly distorted to make the editor's friends appear saintly, his enemies grotesque. During the Nixon presidency, many people thought Dan Rather—CBS White

House correspondent at the time—did not show the proper respect at presidential news conferences. Journalists of the 19th Century would have considered Rather and Sam Donaldson wimps. Editorial cartoonists who disagreed with Abraham Lincoln drew the President as a caricature—a gorilla. Until early in this century, most newspapers announced their political bias on their front pages or mastheads. You didn't need to look at their declaration of political point of view. You knew, from reading their stories, they were Whigs or Tories, Republicans or Populists.

Preaching to the Choir

Economic pressure forced newspapers to be more fair. The early crusading newspaper editors had been much more interested in their causes than in their credit ratings. Their papers were sometimes distributed free, to a small group of readers who usually agreed with the editor's point of view. The more outrageous the editor's attack on his enemies, the better his readers like it.

Occasionally, the early papers entertained. But primarily, they printed ideas and information, often without hoping to make a profit. It was a labor of love and ego, conscience and politics.

Advertising's Influence

As advertising became an accepted part of daily and weekly newspapers, the stories were toned down. It was important not to alienate large sections of advertisers, or the readers advertisers paid to reach. The mass circulation dailies in the early 1900s were not exactly fair. Sensational stories that became the battleground for the circulation wars mangled both truth and the small group of people they wrote about—people unfortunate enough to be caught in the crossfire.

The news media in America are probably more fair today than at any time in our history. The problem is that fairness—like beauty—is in the eye of the beholder.

The Sense of Fairness

Public censure has become a more realistic threat to keep both print and broadcast news honest and fair. The audience has developed its own sense of how the game is played, and what is expected in terms of fairness. The media are more willing to report on each other—to embarrass their competition when they go outside the bounds of good taste or accepted standards. The media's own publications attack stories that are unfair. Magazines like *The Columbia Journalism Review, Washington Journalism Review, Nieman Reports* and *Quill* can be devastating to a newspaper, television or radio station that goes outside the recognized boundaries of fairness. (See **STRATEGY/Fighting Back**)

Sigma Delta Chi's Code

Sigma Delta Chi, the national society of professional journalists, has a model Code of Ethics that says this about fairness:

We believe in public enlightenment as the forerunner of justice, and in our Constitutional role to seek the truth as part of the public's right to know the truth.

We believe those responsibilities carry obligations that require journalists to perform with intelligence, objectivity, accuracy, and fairness.

. . . News reports should be free of opinion or bias and represent all sides of an issue.

(For complete text, see **STRATEGY/Ethics**)

While the Sigma Delta Chi Code of Ethics suggests, but doesn't spell it out clearly—**the accepted standard of fairness now requires a reporter to contact you if a story is critical of you,** to get your response. The contact should be made BEFORE the story is published or broadcast so your point of view will be included to balance the story.

Skirting the Ethic

Reporters sometimes squeeze around that ethic when they call you a few minutes or hours before the story breaks. You're not in, so they leave a message. You don't return the call until after their deadline. So the story says you "could not be reached for comment." They skirt the ethic, claiming they tried to reach you. We are not told how hard they tried.

That kind of fudging with fairness may sometimes be justified if the story breaks just before a deadline. But the next edition or news broadcast should have your reply.

How To Speak TV, Print & Radio

Return Calls Quickly

That's why I suggest in the model press policies I write that you have a rule of thumb in your organization—**No reporter's call should ever go unanswered for more than 15 minutes.** If you're not in, someone else should return the call. If that staffer learns the reporter is working on a story that will be critical of you or your organization, someone should act as spokesperson and defend you in the first version of the story. Even if the story is not critical, if it involves you or your organization, fairness requires your input and perspective. (See **STRATEGY/Media Policy**)

Government Control

There are no laws requiring newspapers or magazines to be fair. U. S. Supreme Court decisions have made it very clear that government cannot interfere in any way with the content of the printed press. Civil suits can be filed against newspapers and magazines if they damage you or invade your privacy (See **INSIDE THE MEDIA/Libel** and **Privacy**), but government cannot censor or control what they write.

There are some laws making it a crime to publish national defense secrets. The courts have said government can punish the publisher, but cannot prevent the publishing. To do so is called prior restraint. That is unconstitutional, the U. S. Supreme Court decided.

Broadcasting is Different

As this book goes to press, the question of how far government should go in controlling radio and TV programming may become a major issue once more. The concept is called the Fairness Doctrine.

The Fairness Doctrine

Most people in America now get their news from radio and television. The government's regulation of broadcasting seems a strange contradiction in a nation that preaches press freedom as a basic requirement for democracy.

How did we get here?

Early Radio

As AM radio spread across the world in the 1920s, the broadcast band became crowded. Radio signals began to override each other, much like the spread of CB radio in the 1970s. An investor in a radio station in 1925 quickly discovered nobody could hear what he was broadcasting. If another station within a hundred miles was using the same frequency, everything was garbled. At that time, you were completely free to broadcast on any frequency, at any power level you chose. As the number of stations grew, finding a clear channel became more and more difficult. Even if you found one, there was no guarantee it would stay clear very long.

Broadcasters went to Washington to solve the problem. Their lawyers came up with a theory that would get around the First Amendment and allow Congress to regulate the industry.

It goes something like this: Radio waves cross state lines. Therefore, broadcasting is interstate commerce. The Constitution gives Congress the right to regulate interstate commerce.

The Public Sky Theory

Of course, newspapers cross state lines, too. So a second argument was devised. Broadcasters do not own the medium that carries their signal—the sky. Radio waves must go through the sky. The sky belongs to the public. Therefore, the public has a right to regulate how its sky is used.

Federal Radio Commission

In 1927, Congress created the Federal Radio Commission to regulate all broadcasting in America. The commission was to give order and decency to the airwaves. Anybody using the public sky had to get a license. The commission decided who was fit to hold a license.

1934—the FCC

In 1934, Congress rewrote the Radio Act and created today's Federal Communications Commission. There was no question that Congress, through the FCC, restricted freedom of both speech and the press. Most people accepted it as a practical, though unconstitutional solution to a technical problem. Either you regulate broadcasting, or nobody will be able to broadcast. Simple as that.

Shortly after it was created, the old Radio Commission began to regulate not only the signals and equipment broadcasters used, but what they said over the air, and how they allocated their time.

Equal Time

Licensing radio stations created an immediate political problem. In many towns, there was only one station. In a political campaign, the owner could use his station to help one side and hurt—or ignore—the other. Equal Time and the Fairness Doctrine were born.

For Politicians Only

Many people confuse fairness and Equal Time. If a radio or television story criticizes them or their business, they demand equal time to reply. Only politicians get equal time. Congress, in its wisdom, made it that way.

If a station gives air time to a politician during a campaign, federal law says it must give equal time to the opponents. If the station runs an editorial endorsing a candidate or a campaign issue, it must give equal time to the other side—or sides.

To carry out the pretense of press freedom, the Equal Time Law has a clause exempting news coverage. The same kind of convoluted reasoning that enabled Congress to waltz around the First Amendment can also take Equal Time for a spin.

Presidential Debates

In 1960, after Richard Nixon and John F. Kennedy agreed to a series of nationally televised debates, Congress passed a special suspension of Equal Time requirements for that year's presidential campaign so every candidate wouldn't have to be included.

The question came up again in 1976, when the networks planned a series of debates between challenger Jimmy Carter and incumbent Gerald Ford. Both agreed to participate. Everything was all set.

Carter vs. Ford vs. Chisolm

Then Cong. Shirley Chisolm, also a candidate for President, demanded that she be included. The law seemed to be on her side. Without another congressional suspension, if you give Carter and Ford air time to debate, you have to put Chisolm on the platform and on the networks. There were other, more obscure candidates out there, too, who would all get equal time. Candidates for the Socialist Party, the Prohibition Party, the Vegetarian Party—you name it, there's a candidate out there for it somewhere, and they all get equal network time.

The networks called their lawyers. What do we do now? A debate between a dozen candidates will be a zoo. Nobody will watch. It will run all night.

Bending the Law

Some legal contortionist came forward with the solution.

The networks decided to cancel the debate. Forget the whole thing.

Then the League of Women Voters announced it would sponsor a debate between Jimmy Carter and Gerald Ford. The League made it clear that Chisolm and all those other tag-along candidates would not be included. The Equal Time Law doesn't apply to the League of Women Voters.

Aha! the networks said. If you sponsor a debate between the two major candidates, it will be a news event, and we'll cover it.

FCC: Debates are News

Chisolm and the National Organization for Women ran to the FCC. The FCC announced it had been misinterpreting Congress' intent all those years in requiring equal time for all candidates if debates were broadcast. If the League of Women Voters wanted to invite two candidates to debate, and the networks covered it as a bona fide news event, then Equal Time did not apply, the FCC decided.

Chisolm v. FCC

538 F.2d 349 [D.C. Circ.] (1976)

Chisolm and NOW took the FCC decision to court. They lost. A panel of U. S. Circuit judges agreed with the FCC's new policy. Government can't make news judgments for broadcasters, the court decided. The U. S. Supreme Court refused to hear an appeal. The debate was televised, just as originally planned, with only Carter and Ford on the platform.

Compare television's equal time requirement with an almost exact parallel in the print media.

Equal Newspaper Space

In 1913, the Florida Legislature passed a law protecting the election process from unfair newspaper influence. It was introduced by a lawmaker who was a newspaperman and signed by a governor who was a newspaper publisher. It said that candidates had the right to reply to newspaper attacks during a political campaign. Before the election, the newspaper had to give equal space to the other side, and print it in the same general section of the newspaper.

Tornillo vs. Miami Herald

It is the fall of 1972, and the Florida Equal Space Law has never been seriously challenged. Pat Tornillo, leader of the teachers' union in Miami, is running for the Florida Legislature.

Tornillo and the editor of the *Miami Herald* are old enemies. The *Herald* is a dominant newspaper that, even today, does not have a single union anywhere in its operation. Its editorial page will almost always side with management and against unions. The animosity between the *Herald* editor and Tornillo had be-

come much more personal and intense in 1968, when Tornillo led
a teachers' strike the *Herald* felt was illegal.

Hydrofoils and Hoopla

Tornillo is a flamboyant, clever strategist with an eye for the
grand gesture. During that 1968 strike, he had rented a stadium
on Biscayne Bay for teacher rallies. Tornillo would roar up to the
floating platform in a rented hydrofoil to the applause of his followers.

So it is 1972, four years later, and Tornillo has his eye on the
state capitol. The Herald opposes him with two scathing editorials:

> *"The screeds say the strike is not an issue. We say maybe it*
> *wouldn't be were it not a part of a continuation of disregard of any*
> *and all laws the Classroom Teachers' Association might find aggra-*
> *vating. . . . What's good for CTA is good for CTA and that is natu-*
> *ral law. Tornillo's law, maybe. For years now he has been kicking*
> *the public shin to call attention to his shakedown statesmanship. He*
> *and whichever acerbic prexy is in alleged office have always felt their*
> *private ventures so chock-full of public weal that we should leap at*
> *the chance to nab the tab, be it half the Glorious Leader's salary or*
> *the dues checkoff or anything else except perhaps mileage on the*
> *staff hydrofoil. Give him public office, says Pat, and he will no*
> *doubt live by the Golden Rule. Our translation reads that as more*
> *gold and more rule."*

So Pat Tornillo and his lawyer go to the *Herald* to demand
equal space to reply. The *Herald* tells him to jump in the bay.

Tornillo Wins at First

Tornillo goes to court to force the *Herald* to comply with the
1913 law. Meanwhile, Tornillo loses his campaign for the legislature. The Florida Supreme Court sides with Tornillo. The justices
there decide that equal space is not a violation of the First
Amendment. After all, they note, federal law gives candidates
equal time to reply on the airwaves. The Florida decision quotes
heavily from the U. S. Supreme Court opinion that had upheld
the FCC's Fairness Doctrine and government's right to regulate
what broadcasters put on the air.

Miami Herald Publishing Co. v. Tornillo
418 U.S. 241, 94 S.Ct. 2831, 41 L.Ed.2d. 730 (1974)

This time, Tornillo and Florida's Equal Space Law lose. Writing the opinion for a unanimous court in June, 1974, Chief Justice Warren Burger says:

> *"The issue in this case is whether a state statute granting a political candidate a right to equal space to reply to criticisms and attacks on his record by a newspaper violates the guarantee of a free press. . . . The choice of material to go into a newspaper . . . whether fair or unfair . . . constitutes exercise of editorial control and judgment. It has yet to be demonstrated how governmental regulation of this crucial process can be exercised consistent with First Amendment guarantees of a free press."*

TV is Not The Press

In his opinion striking down all equal space laws, the Chief Justice does not mention the court's very different attitude about equal time and the regulation of broadcast journalism. To justify that regulation, the court had decided years earlier that electronic media are not "The Press" the framers of the Constitution had in mind when they wrote the First Amendment.

Justice Byron White, writing a concurring opinion in the Tornillo case, reflects that difference of attitude when he says:

> *"The First Amendment erects a virtually insurmountable barrier between government and the print media."*

Equal time, as you've seen, is a very narrow concept, applied only to political issues and candidates.

The Fairness Doctrine

The Fairness Doctrine was a much broader concept which evolved over a period of years as the FCC heard complaints about broadcasters being unfair, abusing their license to use the public airwaves. The Fairness Doctrine said broadcasters must be fair in covering "controversial issues of public importance."

The FCC said television stations have an *obligation* to carry all points of view on those issues.

The theory said the broadcast license was created to serve the public. That the public needed to hear every conceivable point of view from broadcasters on those issues of public importance. And since the number of stations was limited, without this requirement, the public's need to know could be seriously shortchanged.

Supreme Court

The Fairness Doctrine was not tested at the U. S. Supreme Court until 1969, when the court ruled in *Red Lion Broadcasting Co. v. FCC* that the scarcity of broadcast channels required a different kind of Constitutional interpretation for broadcasters. Broadcasters, because of their special license and the privilege to use the public sky, had to be fair, the court said.

The Fairness Doctrine concept was a radical departure from the way the printed press has operated in this country. There was never any legal obligation for newspapers to be fair. Justice White, in that same concurring Tornillo opinion, said:

> *"Of course, the press is not always accurate, or even responsible, and may not present full and fair debate on important public issues. But the balance struck by the First Amendment with respect to the press is that society must take the risk that occasionally debate on vital matters will not be comprehensive and that all viewpoints may not be expressed. The press would be unlicensed because, in Jefferson's words, 'where the press is free, and every man able to read, all is safe.' Any other accommodation—any other system that would supplant private control of the press with the heavy hand of government intrusion would make the government the censor of what the people may read and know."*

TV—A Different Heritage

The heritage for broadcasting is very different. From the beginning, television was conceived as an entertainment medium. For most decisions, the highest priority was profit. Television also depended on a large audience. Fear of offending that audience, and the chilling effect of government looking over their shoulders, made many television outlets shy away from anything even slightly controversial.

Conflict in the streets made good film, but few stations took the risk of saying anything editorially about that conflict. Edward R. Murrow became a legend because he was willing to tackle subjects like Sen. Joseph McCarthy's witch hunt for communists, and the abuse of migrant farm labor.

Until 1963, 15 Minutes

News was—and still is—a small fraction of television's programming day. Until September, 1963, network news totalled 15 minutes per day—including commercials. The entire news staff at many local stations was one man who served as reporter, photographer and anchorman.

The public's thirst for news is an acquired taste. In the early 1970s, staff at CBS's "60 Minutes" constantly kept feelers out for other jobs. Whether the program could survive with such low ratings was questionable. Ten years later, it became the most-watched show in the country.

"60 Minutes"

The Watergate scandal may have been the story that whetted the public appetite for public punishment of rascals on the tube. In the basic format for a "60 Minutes" story, complex issues are boiled down to a simple morality play.

Good Guy vs. Bad Guy. It has the same appeal as the classic western movie. Show us the bad guy. Make us dislike him. Tease us toward that inevitable, face-to-face confrontation with the marshal where the fastest draw, the steadiest hand, the coolest courage will decide the winner.

High Noon in Prime Time

And if the marshal is not as skilled—if he is outgunned and outnumbered, as in "High Noon"—the tension builds. We root for the underdog, pin our hopes, our faith, on Good conquering Evil. The more powerful the target of investigative reporting, the harder the fall. We sit, nervously munching our popcorn, waiting for the "60 Minutes" marshal to fire the fatal question. We feel good when the bad guy bites the dust.

Few things in our lives are so organized, so manageable, so easy to understand. We sometimes lose faith that the bad guys who acquire power and position, wealth and control over our lives, will be punished for their sins. Investigative reporting—where we watch the shootout up close—helps assure us of that basic morality we were taught as children.

Courts interpreting what the Fairness Doctrine meant decided fairness did not require equal time.

Measuring Fairness

One clear court interpretation of fairness is a U. S. Circuit Court opinion written in the District of Columbia. The case involved an NBC documentary narrated by Edwin Newman, "Pensions: the Broken Promise."

Accuracy in Media—a group concerned with the growing power of the press—filed a formal complaint with the FCC, saying, "The NBC report gave the viewers a grotesquely distorted picture of the private pension system of the United States."

The FCC ruled NBC had not lived up to its fairness obligation and ordered more air time for opposing views. NBC challenged the FCC ruling in court.

The Pensions Documentary

The documentary shows a series of old people, who had worked for a company most of their lives, looking forward to retirement and their pensions. In each of the personal stories, the pension was never paid. Some companies went bankrupt, and there was no money for pensions. Some workers moved from one union to another, not realizing they lost benefits when they transferred. In some cases, the companies simply fired workers shortly before they were eligible to draw their pensions.

NBC, Inc. v. FCC

516 F.2d 1101 [D.C. Circ.] (1974)

The appellate court ruled that Newman and NBC had met the Fairness Doctrine requirements. A broadcast report, the court said, does not have to give equal time and attention to every part of its subject. It must focus on the unusual—the newsworthy—the court said, quoting from a memo that had been filed in the case by the American Society of Newspapers:

> *"Newspapers investigate and expose policemen who are on the 'take' in the dope rackets. If equivalent time must be given to policemen who are not on the 'take' the whole campaign becomes so unwieldy and pointless as to be useless."*

The judges who ruled in favor of NBC were impressed with the two-minute monologue that closed the documentary. In it, the court said, Newman met the fairness standard. The decision quotes it in full:

> NEWMAN: *"This has been a depressing program to work on, but we don't want to give the impression that there are no good private pension plans. There are many good ones, and there are many people for whom the promise has become reality. That should be said."*

Newman summed up all the problems the program had explored, and then concluded:

> *"These are matters for Congress to consider and, indeed, the Senate Labor Committee is considering them now. They are also matters for those who are in pension plans. If you're in one, you might find it useful to take a close look at it. Our own conclusion about all of this is that it is almost inconceivable that this enormous thing has been allowed to grow up with so little understanding of it and with so little protection and such uneven results for those involved. The situation, as we've seen it, is deplorable. Edwin Newman, NBC News."*

In the early 1980s, government began deregulating private industry. The telephone company, airlines, and broadcasting were three major areas. Many of the old arguments for regulating broadcasting are no longer valid. Technology has opened up a huge variety of broadcast, cable and satellite channels.

The FCC's Fairness Report

As part of its philosophical belief in deregulation, the FCC conducted a series of hearings on the Fairness Doctrine and issued the 1985 Fairness Report. It concluded that the explosion of new technology has made the old argument about scarcity of channels obsolete. The Commission found:

> *"The public has access to a multitude of viewpoints without the need or danger of regulatory intervention. . . . In stark contravention of its purpose, [the doctrine] operates as a pervasive and significant impediment to the broadcasting of controversial issues of public importance."*

In that 1985 report, the FCC said the Fairness Doctrine had actually "chilled" free speech, rather than enhancing it. That it had inhibited expressions of unpopular opinion; had placed the government in the intrusive role of scrutinizing program content; had created the opportunity for abuse for partisan political purposes; and had imposed unnecessary costs on both broadcasters and the FCC.

While the 1985 report said the FCC felt the Fairness Doctrine was unconstitutional, the Commission refused to repeal it, saying it would leave that decision up to Congress or the courts.

Fairness Doctrine Repealed

Concerned that the FCC might change its mind, Congress in early 1987 wrote the Fairness Doctrine into law. In June, 1987, President Reagan vetoed it. Congress could not muster enough votes to override the veto. And in August, 1987, the FCC repealed the doctrine. Some of the reasoning from its order:

> *"The fairness doctrine provides broadcasters with a powerful incentive not to air controversial issue programming. . . . Each time a broadcaster presents what may be construed as a controversial issue of public importance, it runs the risk of a complaint being filed, resulting in litigation and penalties, including loss of license. This risk still exists even if a broadcaster has met its obligations by airing contrasting viewpoints, because the process necessarily involves a vague standard. . . .*
>
> *"In the 1985 Fairness Report, the Commission gave specific examples of instances in which broadcasters declined to air programming on such important controversial issues such as the nuclear arms race, religious cults, municipal salaries, and other significant matters of public concern. In each instance, the broadcaster identified the fairness doctrine as the cause for its decision. . . . Some stations refuse to present editorials; other stations will not accept*

political advertisements; still others decline to air public issue (or editorial) advertising; and others have policies to decline acceptance of nationally produced programming that discusses controversial subjects or to have their news staffs avoid controversial issues as a matter of routine. . . . In sum, the fairness doctrine in operation disserves both the public's right to diverse sources of information and the broadcaster's interest in free expression. Its chilling effect thwarts its intended purpose, and it results in excessive and unnecessary government intervention into the editorial processes of broadcast journalists. We hold, therefore, that under the constitutional standard established by Red Lion and its progeny, the fairness doctrine contravenes the First Amendment and its enforcement is no longer in the public interest."

But the FCC made it clear, as it abolished the Fairness Doctrine, that two other, related rules, were still in effect:

The Personal Attack Rule

The FCC requires that any person whose character is attacked during a public affairs broadcast (as distinguished from news) must be given a "reasonable offer" to respond on the air. Public affairs programming at most stations is limited to talk shows, where guests discuss with a host some current issue. The Personal Attack Rule tends to keep those discussions bland. Because the FCC has relaxed many of its other rules requiring news and public affairs programming, talk shows are dwindling.

The Political Editorial Rule

Another FCC rule says political candidates must be given a "reasonable opportunity" to respond on the air if a radio or TV editorial opposes them or endorses their opponents. This is similar to the Equal Time Law.

George Bush made it clear that because of his Republican philosophy against government regulation, he would veto any attempt by Congress to revive the Fairness Doctrine. As this book goes to press, Democrat Bill Clinton is the new President. Some members of Congress want to resurrect the Fairness Doctrine. If they are successful, the U. S. Supreme Court may have to review once more whether it violates the First Amendment.

Stay tuned.

INSIDE THE MEDIA

JARGON

Strange Things
Media People Say

A-B Roll
An old term from the days of film in television news, where the director in the control room could switch video from the "A" roll of film to the "B" roll while audio continued on the "A" roll. See Cutaway for one of the most common uses of A-B roll technique.

ABC
The Audit Bureau of Circulations, which audits and certifies the circulation of print media to make sure advertisers reach the audience they pay for.

Actuality
Radio term for recorded sound from the scene of the story, in contrast to sound originating in the studio. Can be natural sound captured during an event, or a taped interview.

Ambush Interview
A sudden confrontation with a TV news crew, in which the interview subject is physically ambushed, caught by surprise, and frequently appears guilty or furtive.

Anchor
The person who introduces news stories, usually in the radio or TV studio, during a newscast. The anchor will also read stories alone where a reporter is not seen or heard. The job gets its name from a ship anchor, which is supposed to hold the ship firm, no matter which way the wind blows. In TV news, most formats revolve

around the anchor or anchor team, as the focal point giving the newscast its style and direction, moving it from one story to another.

Arbitron

One of the two major national rating services which measure audiences for TV and radio.

Ascertainment Interviews

Before deregulation, the FCC required broadcast stations to interview people from all segments of the community, asking them what they thought the community's major problems were and how to solve them. The station as part of its license renewal process was required to show how its programming had met those community needs and problems. No longer required, but some stations continue similar programs as a public relations technique.

Assignment Editor

The person in a radio or TV newsroom who decides each day how the station's reporters and photographers will be used. Expected to know what is happening, and dispatch the station's resources to best cover them. One of the most hectic jobs in television news. The person to notify when you think you have a story for broadcast media.

Audio

The sound you hear during a TV newscast, as distinguished from video—what you see. During the editing process, audio and video are sometimes inserted separately into the videocassette that will eventually be broadcast as a reporter's story.

Below the Fold

Anything in the lower half of the front page of a newspaper section. Used to denote placement of a story. More important stories are usually above the fold.

Bird

TV slang for a satellite in space. As in, "I'll send it to you by the bird this afternoon. We've got time (reserved) on the bird between 2 and 2:30."

Bite

Short for sound bite. A small portion of an audio or videotaped interview which is edited into the reporter's story. Usually less than 15 seconds. In network news stories, frequently less than 10 seconds. One bite is sometimes edited to another in a way that makes it appear both sentences or phrases were spoken together, in sequence.

Black
A blank television screen. Can occur when a TV station loses its transmitter. The screen goes black. Or a brief moment when a shot is faded, before the next scene or sequence. Called "going to black."

Block
A "block" of broadcast news stories. From the opening of the newscast to the first commercial break is the first "block." The next section of stories—between the first commercial break and the second commercial break—is the second "block."

Break
In TV, the interruption in the newscast for commercials. In newspapers, the place where a story is cut on the first page and continued on an inside page. In print, also called the jump.

Bright
A short, funny news story.

Bug
A very small radio transmitter, used to secretly broadcast conversation to a receiver, usually several blocks away. Illegal under FCC rules and regulations, except for police. A felony under federal law if nobody in that intercepted conversation is aware of the electronic eavesdropping. In some states, illegal under state law even if one party to the conversation is aware.

Bulldog Edition
The first edition of a newspaper. The edition with the earliest deadline.

Bullets
The dark circles used to highlight major points in a print story.

Call Letters
A broadcast station's unique identifying letters. Some early stations had only three letters. A system developed later to give all stations

four letters. Most of those east of the Mississippi begin with W. Most of those west of the Mississippi begin with K.

Canned Story.

A story that is finished and ready for publication or broadcast. The story is "in the can." Sometimes used to distinguish a wire or network story that is transmitted to the newspaper or broadcast station—a "canned" story rather than one produced by the local staff.

Chroma-Key

An electronic device used by a TV station to insert graphics or video in the broadcast picture. Often used to insert a generic graphic over the shoulder of the anchor.

City Room

Old newspaper term for the newsroom.

Color Bars

The row of rainbow-colored bars transmitted when TV stations are off the air. These can be used to check and adjust the signal being transmitted or received. Also used internally to check the accuracy of the color being transmitted.

Control Room

The nerve center of the television station, where a director, sitting at a huge board of lights, switches and TV monitors, controls what goes out over the air. The buttons and switches in the control room start and stop machines in other parts of the station—cameras, microphones, videotape players, film projectors, etc.

Copy Boy

Old newspaper term for boys who carried reporters' copy to the editor's desk, tore wire service stories off the teletype machines and delivered them to the proper editors. No longer applicable in newsrooms that are computerized.

Copy Desk

Before computers, the desk where editors and headline writers reviewed copy before it was sent to the composing room to be set in type.

Copy Story
A news story read by the anchor in which there is no reporter and no videotape. Sometimes called a "reader."

Correspondent
The proper title for network reporters, probably because they are always on the road. They were given this title in the early days of radio and TV news, in the same way that newspapers have traditionally called their out-of-town reporters correspondents.

Countdown
A countdown similar to those marking the moment of ignition and liftoff during a rocket launch. Used to help editors find the exact spot where a quote on audio or videotape begins. A correspondent calls his station or network to dictate a story. Once he is told the recorder is rolling at the other end, he says, "Three—Two—One—This is Dave Doomsday reporting from Armageddon. The world ended today at exactly 2:17 p.m."

Crawl
Information, usually words and numbers, that "crawl" across the bottom of a TV screen while the regular programming continues. Often used to give weather bulletins or election results without interrupting the regular program.

Cross-Cutting
See intercut.

Cutaway
An editing shot, used to cover a TV edit point, or "jump cut." The most frequently used cutaways show the reporter listening or taking notes; the crowd during a meeting or a speech; or a "two-shot," in which we see both the reporter and the interview subject from a great distance—far enough away that we cannot tell whether the movement of the interview subject's lips matches the words we're hearing.

Dateline
In newspapers and magazines, the first words used to indicate the story was not produced locally. Frequently at the beginning of wire service copy, as in NEW YORK (AP)—. Before stories could be transmitted to newspapers the same day, the dateline included the date

the story was written. Most newspapers have now dropped the date, but the city where the story originated is still called the dateline.

Dish
A parabolic antenna to receive satellite signals.

Display Advertising
Large blocks of advertising in newspapers, to distinguish them from classified ads with small print and no drawings or pictures.

Dissolve
The fading out of one picture while another fades in. Frequently used to make the transition from one place to another less jarring.

Double-Truck
Two facing pages of newspaper advertising or copy.

Dub
A copy of an audio or videotape. The sound and picture are dubbed from one cassette onto another.

Dummy
A schematic drawing of a newspaper or magazine page, showing where the ads, headlines and news stories will be placed.

Ear
The small box in the upper corner of a newspaper front page on either side of the newspaper's name. Often carries weather information, the newspaper's slogan, etc.

ENG
Shorthand for electronic news gathering—the revolution in technology which took place in the 1970s, when most TV networks and local stations switched from film to videotape.

Equal Time
A requirement by the FCC and federal law that any broadcast licensee who gives time to a political candidate during the election process must give equal time to his opponent. Only politicians during political campaigns get equal time.

Exclusive
Used correctly if no other news outlet has the story. Sometimes used fudgingly if the newspaper, magazine or broadcast outlet has a portion of the story that nobody else has.

Fairness Doctrine
An old FCC requirement that broadcast licensees must present all sides of controversial issues of public importance. Not to be confused with Equal Time. Congress tried to make it law, but President Reagan vetoed the bill. Repealed by the FCC in 1987. At press time, some in Congress are trying to resurrect it.

FCC
The Federal Communications Commission, appointed by the President and confirmed by the Senate, to regulate broadcasting in the United States.

Feed
To transmit audio or video via radio or wires. Each afternoon, network TV crews use satellites to feed their stories to New York. You can call a radio station and feed the station sound bites from your recorder if you have the proper connecting wires to attach your recorder to a telephone or telephone jack.

Field Interview
An interview videotaped in the field—away from a radio or television studio.

Field Producer
A radio or TV producer assigned to work with a reporter or camera crew in the field, as distinguished from a producer who acts as editor and production manager for a specific newscast.

Flack
Derogatory term for a public relations person. Can also be a verb, as in "He's flacking for the mayor."

FOI
Freedom of Information Act. A federal law which makes certain records public. To gain access to many of them, however, reporters must file an FOI request.

Freeze Frame
A single frame of video, taken from a moving videotaped picture. Sometimes used when the picture is so fleeting most viewers will not get a chance to see what the camera recorded. In effect, a still picture taken from movie film or videotape.

Graphic
A picture, drawn by an artist, or a graph used to help illustrate a TV story. Graphics are often used when there is no videotape to cover a section of the reporter's script. Sometimes used to distinguish between a still picture or drawing and video that has movement and sound.

Grip
Another name for the camera assistant who works with a TV news photographer. Grips will usually double as sound technicians, monitoring the quality and level of sound picked up by the mike and recorded on videotape. Becoming more rare as size and weight of TV equipment become smaller.

Hot
Broadcast term for sound that is too loud or light that is too bright. Can also refer to an open microphone that can pick up conversation not intended for broadcast. As in, "Be careful, that mike's hot."

HUT
Stands for Households Using Television. The HUT-level is the same as Share in TV ratings lingo. A HUT-level of 30 means 30 per cent of the households watching TV were watching your show.

In-Cue
The first words of a sound bite. Sometimes written into the script to help an editor find the bite the reporter wants edited into the story at that point.

Intercut
An editing technique, where two interviews are cut so the videotape switches back and forth between interviews without interruption by the reporter. Used to heighten conflict between opposing points of view. Also called cross-cutting.

JOA

Stands for Joint Operating Agreement. This is an agreement between two newspapers who use the same printing and circulation facilities to produce two separate newspapers. In many cities, JOAs were created to prevent the death of the afternoon paper. Because this could lead to a monopoly over newspaper publishing in many communities, a JOA in most cases must be approved by the U. S. Justice Department.

Jump

The place at which a front-page story jumps to an inside page. The continuation of the story carries a "jump head," and that part of the story is called the "jump." As in, "I read the beginning of the story, but didn't go to the jump."

Jump Cut

The point at which a TV interview is edited, where a second phrase or sentence is spliced to the first. Gets its name because the interview subject appears to suddenly jump where the videotape was edited. (With videotape, unlike film, cutting and splicing are done electronically. The original version of the interview remains intact. The edited version is a dub on a second cassette.) Jump cuts are usually covered by a cutaway shot for esthetic reasons. TV news has not yet agreed on a system like the print journalist's ellipsis, which would tell viewers an edit was made.

Key

Short for Chroma-Key. The picture inserted, or "keyed" into a small section of the television screen.

Kicker

The last story in the newscast. Almost always a feature or human interest story that is upbeat, to wash away the bad feelings viewers have after watching a long string of stories involving death, destruction and pain.

Lead-In

The introduction to a TV news story read by the anchor. Usually less than 15 seconds. A headline, designed to tell you what the story is about and alert you to pay attention.

Leak

A covert release of information to the news media. Usually done by a confidential source who does not want to be identified. A standard technique, widely used by both government and corporate executives with political, competitive or revenge motives. Also used as a last resort by frustrated whistle-blowers who come to believe they must go to the media because they cannot cannot cure problems within the system.

Listener

Another name for the cutaway shot in television, used for editing purposes, in which we see the reporter listening as the person interviewed speaks.

Live Shot

A reporter standup or interview relayed back to the TV station for immediate, live broadcast during a newscast.

Make-Good

A commercial offered free or at a discounted price to a broadcasting advertiser when a show fails to draw the expected audience. The station or network "makes good" its promise to deliver a certain number of people per dollar spent on advertising in the show.

Makeover

Changing a newspaper page, usually to get late-breaking stories into this edition, or to update stories. Also called a "replate."

Market

The area served by a radio or television station. Usually about 50 to 75 miles in all directions for FM radio and TV, depending on topography that can block the broadcast signal.

Masthead

The box that shows the newspaper name, owner, and editors. Usually on the editorial page.

Meters

An electronic device wired to a TV set to give a constant measure of whether the set is on, and which station it is tuned to. Used extensively to determine TV ratings. Updated in 1987 with People Meters, which also electronically determine who is watching when the set is turned on.

Microwave
The radio frequency used to transmit audio and video back to a television station for re-broadcast. Live shots are microwaved to the station, then converted to the broadcast band for immediate, live transmission.

Mixer
An electronic device which allows an editor to mix two sounds and edit them onto one cassette. The reporter's voice is sometimes mixed with natural sound from the scene that is described, or in television, the video which covers the narration.

Morgue
The library that keeps newspaper clippings and tape of previously broadcast stories. Reporters go to the morgue to get background and history on a story or person they are covering.

Natural Sound
Sometimes called "wild sound." The background noise that is present everywhere except in an acoustically padded booth. Adds realism to audio or videotape. A reporter will sometimes use natural sound, full volume, at the beginning of the story to set the scene. You will hear the noise of a gun battle, the crackle of a fire, the collapse of a building that was recorded on tape. In TV news, natural sound is usually mixed with the reporter's voice when narrating videotape, voice-over.

Network
An organization to broadcast radio and TV programs to member stations. Local stations affiliated with a network agree to broadcast locally the network's programming, but are not owned or controlled by that network. Each major network owns some stations, which are under its control. Originally ABC, CBS and NBC. New networks have been formed in recent years which feed cable systems as well as broadcast stations.

News Director

The person in charge of everything in a local radio or TV station's news department. The person who hires and fires reporters, anchors and photographers.

News Hole

The space in a newspaper for news stories. On days when there is more advertising, the news hole is larger. On slow advertising days, the news hole shrinks.

News Peg

A local story pegged to a national or international story. The local view or angle on that story.

Nielsen

A. C. Nielsen Co., one of the two major national rating services which measure audiences for TV and radio.

O and O

One of the local stations owned and operated by a network.

Op-Ed

The page opposite the editorial page in a newspaper. Often used for columns and letters to the editor.

Out-Cue

The last phrase in a sound bite. Sometimes written into the script, along with the in-cue, to help an editor find the bite the reporter wants edited into the story at that point.

Out-Takes

Film, audio or videotape shot by a news crew which is not broadcast. Often the center of conflict between government and broadcast news operations. Some organizations, as a matter of principle, refuse to give up out-takes, even if they are subpoenaed.

Package

The term used at some stations for a reporter's story, complete within itself, "packaged" on an audio or videocassette. Will usually include one or more interviews. Sometimes called a "wrap" or a "Sony Sandwich."

Peanut
TV term for a small microphone, about the size of a peanut, that clips to your tie or collar.

People Meters
A new kind of electronic measuring device to determine how many people are watching TV at any given time. First used for national network ratings in the fall of 1987. Differs from older, passive meter systems in that family members must "log in" through remote control devices when the set is turned on, or when the channel is changed.

PIO
Short for Public Information Officer. The person designated by governmental agencies or private business to act as spokesman and to help reporters find people and information within the organization.

Plug
Mentioning an item or service that will promote that item or service. In effect, free advertising. Highly unethical for reporters in any medium to accept anything of value for a "plug."

Plumbers
Staffers assigned to find and stop leaks of information to the news media from inside an organization. The term was coined by the Nixon White House staff during the Watergate investigation.

Pool
An agreement by a group of reporters and photographers in which one of them will cover a story and provide information and/or pictures to other members of the pool. The Pentagon created a complicated pool agreement after the Grenada invasion to invite small numbers of media people to accompany the military on combat or secret missions. First used during the U. S. invasion of Panama in 1989.

Pot
Broadcast term for a volume control. Sound is "potted up" or "potted down."

Producer

The person who decides how a radio or TV newscast will be organized; the order of the stories; how long they will be, and how they will be produced. Roughly the equivalent of a page editor or section editor at a newspaper. Also see Field Producer, above.

Promo

Short for promotion. A commercial touting a TV show later tonight is called a "promo."

Public File

A public record required by the FCC to be available at each broadcast licensee's office, giving corporate or ownership information about the station, its application for licensing, and certain publications explaining how the FCC regulates broadcasters.

Pyramid Story Formula

Another name for the who-what-when-where-why formula for newspaper stories. All main facts are at the top of the story. Additional information that is less important follows, so that information at the bottom is small and trivial. With this formula, editors could chop from the bottom to make a story fit a hole in the page and not lose essential information.

Rating

The percentage of households in a market area who own a radio or television set who are listening to or watching a certain program or station at any given time. A rating point is one percent of the entire potential audience listening to or watching a show.

Reader

A story read by an anchor without visuals or reporter involvement. Also called a "copy story."

Release

The written agreement a person signs giving permission for the media to use his or her picture or voice. Not needed for news coverage. But if the person's likeness is used for commercial purposes, they can sue for invasion of privacy if they have not signed a release. Sometimes called a "model release."

Reverses
Videotape of a reporter asking an interview subject a question. Usually shot over the shoulder of the interview subject after the interview is finished, so the question can be edited to an answer already videotaped. Can distort a TV story if the question is not worded and spoken exactly as it was when the answer was given. Another way to avoid a jump cut.

Rim
The outer edge of a horseshoe-shaped desk used in traditional newspaper newsrooms to process copy and write headlines. The copyreaders and headline writers sat around the rim while the editor who approved their work sat in the "slot."

Scoop
An exclusive. A story that nobody else has. Also called a "beat."

Second-Day Story
A followup story.

Second Generation
An audio or videotape copy, made from the original. If that tape is dubbed, the new copy would be "third generation." With each generation, audio and video quality decrease. Digital technology will provide exact copies with no loss of quality, in the same way that computer disk copies are copied.

Share
The percentage of the radio audience or households using television (HUT) who are listening to or watching a specific program at any given time. A share is that station or network's share of those who are listening or watching. A show's rating is the percentage of the potential audience in the entire market area who are listening to or watching your station or network. Unless everybody in the market is listening or watching, your share will always be higher than your rating.

Shield Law
A state law giving reporters the right to shield the identity of confidential sources from governmental inquiries.

Shotgun Mike

An elongated, directional microphone which can be pointed at a person and pick up conversation at a greater distance than the ordinary mike. Often used by broadcast crews where there is a large crowd and they are not able to get close to the person talking.

Sidebar

A secondary story involving some element of a major story. Often played in a newspaper beside the primary coverage. Often a profile of a major character in the main story, or a feature-type treatment of some factor in the primary story.

Sig Out

The close of a broadcast reporter's "package" or "wrap" in which the reporter signs out. "I'm Earl Egotist, Channel 14 Action News."

Slow News Day

A day in which very little of interest is happening. A good day to sell your story to an editor.

Soft Lead

The lead paragraph or paragraphs in a print story that use a feature approach to make the story seem more interesting. Often used by sportswriters because the basics of yesterday's game—the score, most valuable player, etc. are already old news. Writer can be so carried away, he forgets to tell you the main points in the story.

Sony Sandwich

TV term for a reporter "package" or "wrap." At some stations, the Sony Sandwich is used to denote only live shots, in which the reporter speaks, then interviews someone, then closes the story. The interview, or videotape used in the middle of a live shot is the meat in the Sony Sandwich. The reporter's introduction and close are the bread.

SOT

Short for Sound-on-Tape. Used in a script to tell the editor both the audio and video are on the same section of videotape.

Sound Bite

A short portion of an audio or videotaped interview which is edited into the reporter's story. Frequently shortened in broadcast jargon to "bite."

How To Speak TV, Print & Radio

Squeeze Zoom

An electronic device that enables the director to insert a videotape or live picture in a small area of the TV screen, then zoom it out to fill the entire screen, or vice versa.

Staging

Creating an event or encouraging people to do something for television, which viewers believe is spontaneous and unrehearsed. A serious violation of FCC guidelines, and media ethics. There is a current national controversy over dramatizations and re-enactments—whether they are a form of staging.

Standup

A TV reporter's narration where we hear and see the reporter talking. Whether the reporter is standing, sitting, talking, driving or lying down, it's still a standup.

Super

Writing which is superimposed over video during a TV broadcast. The name of the reporter or interview subject is supered when we first see them, to tell us who they are. A super saves time. The person appearing on camera does not have to be introduced.

Sweeps

Four standard rating periods in which TV audiences have been measured, and on which advertising rates are based.

Talent

TV talk for those staffers who are seen on TV. Reporters, anchors, sportscasters and weather forecasters are "talent."

Talking Head

Just what it says. Someone talking on camera with nothing to break the visual monotony.

Tap

Short for wiretap.

TelePrompTer

The device which projects a script onto a pane of glass in front of a studio camera, allowing TV anchors to read it while they appear to be looking directly into the camera lens.

Think Piece

An analysis of a complicated story or event. An essay about an ongoing news story.

-30-

The traditional sign that ends newspaper copy. Used as shorthand to tell the typesetter this is "the end."

Tight Shot

A closeup or telephoto shot, where the scene or person appears to be very close to the camera. A tight shot of a person might fill the TV screen with just the face. A wide shot will show half the room from the same camera position.

Tombstone

Two newspaper headlines of similar size and width side-by-side on the page, so readers might read the first line of the right-hand headline as a continuation of the left-hand headline. To be avoided.

Two-Shot

A picture that includes two people, usually the reporter and the interview subject. Also used when two people are on camera at the same time in a TV studio.

Typo

Short for typographical error.

UHF

Ultra High Frequency TV band. Channels 14 and higher.

VCR

Short for videocassette recorder.

VHF

Very High Frequency TV band. Channels 2 through 13.

Video

The picture you see on TV, as distinguished from audio—what you hear. Video and audio are carried on separate tracks of the videotape. During the editing process, the audio that originally was recorded when the tape was shot can be replaced with other audio, or mixed with it. The most common mixing involves editing a reporter's voice over the natural sounds on the shooting tape, so we can hear, in the background, what was going on when the tape was shot.

Voice-Over
This can be done live, or edited onto videotape. We hear the voice of the reporter or anchor while we see video—usually what the narrator is talking about. On videotape, the reporter's voice is mixed with the original sound on the tape, which we can still hear in the background. In live voice-over, the sound on the tape is turned down. We can hear that sound under the voice of the anchor, who is talking over the sound on the tape.

Voting
The process where viewers in a ratings sample cheat and log a favorite program in their daily diaries, even if they didn't watch it. Viewers in rating samples also are inclined to vote for cultural or educational programs when they were actually watching wrestling or sit-com reruns.

VTR
Short for videotape recording. Is being replaced in the jargon by VCR. Videotape recorders were originally reel-to-reel machines, and the VTR term was created. Most videotape cameras and recorders now use videocassettes.

Wallpapered Story
In television, a story with lots of visuals. The story is wallpapered, beginning to end, with pictures while the reporter's voice narrates. Producers love wallpaper. The pictures can have so much impact, however, the content of what the reporter is saying can be lost on the average viewer.

Wide Shot
A wide-angle camera shot, showing a broad area. A wide shot in an office would show half the room. A tight shot would fill the screen with the face of the person being interviewed.

Wild Sound
See Natural Sound.

Wireless

Short for wireless microphone. This is a small microphone and radio transmitter frequently used to pick up a reporter's voice or natural sound, and transmit it to a receiver, where it is then broadcast or recorded simultaneously with the video. Referees in sporting events wear wireless mikes so the audience can hear their calls. Reporters on the floor of a political convention use wireless mikes. Their picture is sometimes being shot by a camera halfway across the convention hall. The wireless enables them to talk to the camera without running a wire there. A wireless is legal so long as one person in range of the microphone is aware it is transmitting. Under some state laws, all persons whose voices are transmitted over the wireless must be aware for it to be legal. A hidden wireless, secretly transmitting conversation, becomes a "bug."

Wiretap

A physical connection to a wire that secretly intercepts information carried on that wire. Usually a telephone line. Always illegal for private citizens, under both federal and state laws. Law enforcement agencies are allowed to wiretap under court authorization that lets them search for conversation that might be evidence of a crime. Sometimes called a tap. Pickups that use inductance microphones are technically not a wiretap. Inductance pickups are legal in some states, illegal in others, depending on how they are used.

Wrap

TV term for a reporter story that includes a videotaped interview. The interview is wrapped inside a reporter introduction at the beginning of the story, and a reporter conclusion after the interview. In some places, called a "package" or a "Sony Sandwich."

Zoom Lens

A lens with a variable focal length that allows it to zoom from a wide shot to a tight shot, or vice versa. When the camera appears to be moving in close, the photographer is actually "zooming in." The camera remains stationary, as the lens gradually swings from wide-angle to telephoto.

INSIDE THE MEDIA

LIBEL

Can They Do That and Get Away With It?

It depends on who you are, as well as what they show and tell. No matter how powerful the media seem to be, there usually are ways to get even if a story damages you unjustly. Sue. For libel, or invasion of privacy. The jury might make you a millionaire. But before you rush to the courthouse, you should know what you're getting into. Collecting damages can take years. You'll need a very good attorney, because this area of law is complicated. It's still evolving.

A Long, Painful Process

The station, network, newspaper or magazine will have on its side some of the best legal counsel available. If your suit has no merit, the judge might make you pay the attorneys' fees for the other side when the suit is dismissed.

Don't expect a quick settlement. Some major publishing and broadcasting firms have a policy of never settling out of court. Settlements tend to encourage other suits. In the long run, it's cheaper to fight to the bitter end—and lose—than to put up with the hassle of a new lawsuit every week.

Your Life An Open Book

Once you file suit, you open your entire life. If there is anything in your past that could be embarrassing or painful, it will almost surely be found and publicized. One of the best defenses in a civil suit is a good offense.

Your suit will give the defendant subpoena power to get records, and drag in witnesses who must testify under oath. They will explore everything about your finances, your family, your medical history, your professional career, your education and your sex life.

Still want to sue? OK. Let's look at the two areas of law. They're similar in some respects, but also very different.

In matters of governmental regulation (see **INSIDE THE MEDIA/Fairness & Equal Time**) the courts have treated print and broadcasting differently. In libel and privacy, the courts make few distinctions between the media.

Libel and Defamation

You have been defamed if a publication or broadcast damages you. It becomes libel if there is no justification for the defamation. If your friends, your family, the people at work or the club think less of you after they see or hear the story, you have evidence of your damage. The people who see the report don't have to know you for it to damage your reputation.

The story can hurt you financially, by decreasing your future income, or your ability to borrow money. It can damage you emotionally, by causing embarrassment, ridicule and anguish.

News stories defame hundreds of people every day in America, yet few suits are filed. The law provides several defenses for the media, based on freedom of press and speech.

Defense #1: Truth

The law says they can defame you and get away with it if the story is true. Truth is an almost perfect defense in a libel suit.

How do you prove something is true? How many witnesses does it take, what kind of evidence?

There are no rigid rules. **Truth is what a jury will believe.**

A half-dozen burglars and robbers testify they met you at your jewelry store every Sunday morning at 11 o'clock to fence what they'd stolen. Your priest says you never missed 11 o'clock Mass on Sunday morning. The jury will probably believe the priest, even though the witness score is 6–1.

Relaying the Libel

A journalist does not have to initiate the libel. If the media pass on something someone else says about you, the media outlet generally must take responsibility for the truth of that statement.

Suppose you fire one of your employees. The employee then holds a news conference and says you are a drug user who regularly encourages teenage employees to use cocaine, and supplies them with the drug. A reporter covers the news conference and reports what the disgruntled employee says about you.

It's True You're Accused

It is *true* that the accusation was made. But that will not protect the reporter who publishes or broadcasts what the employee says. The damaging information must be true.

If the media act as a relay for the employee's accusations, they must be prepared to prove to a jury that you are indeed, a drug dealer who encourages teenage employees to use cocaine and supplies them with the drug.

If they convince a jury that you do those things, then you cannot win a libel suit, no matter how much damage has been done to you.

Defense #2: Privilege

If the damaging information comes from a part of the governmental process, the news media have limited responsibility for the truth of that information. This is called privilege.

The legal theory says government officials should be able to do their jobs freely, without having to worry about libel suits. A Supreme Court justice once said freedom of speech does not give you the right to yell "Fire!" in a crowded theater when there is no fire.

But a senator can run up and down the aisles of the Senate Chamber yelling "Fire!"—or anything else—without fear of reprisal. And the media can report what the senator says. In a free society, the public needs to know—through the news media—what its public officials are doing and saying.

But It's Not True

Suppose that during a debate in the Senate Chamber, a U. S. Senator announces that you are a war criminal who murdered hundreds of innocent civilians in Viet Nam. The story is widely reported. As a result, you lose your job. An angry crowd sets fire to your house. Your children are beaten on their way to school. What the senator said was absolutely false. But you cannot sue. And you cannot win a libel suit against the media for publishing or broadcasting what the senator said. It is privileged.

Judicial Process Privileged

If you are charged with a crime, anything in the criminal justice system records—part of the governmental process—is privileged. Anything in a court suit—records or testimony—the contents of a governmental audit, what a policeman says during the investigation of a crime—will almost always be privileged.

Notice as we go through this chapter how often I hedge with qualifiers like probably—almost always—generally—usually. The rules are not firm. They can be bent—and often are—by judges and juries who feel they should cure an injustice.

Most judges would probably extend privilege to what is said in political campaigns, or presidential press conferences, even though they technically are not part of the governmental process.

Defense #3: Absence of Malice

It is the early 1960s. Martin Luther King is waging war against racial segregation in Alabama. He moves from city to city, encouraging black followers to break the law. Use segregated rest rooms, he tells them. Sit in segregated sections of the bus. Enter restaurants and hotels that bar blacks.

King knows that if the law is bad, the only way it will be changed will be to get media coverage of public officials enforcing bad law. His movement becomes a major national story. The police who enforce the law become the villains as they use clubs, fire hoses, attack dogs and tear gas to drive back the demonstrators.

King becomes a master at using the media in his campaign. A committee goes to *The New York Times* and pays for a full-page ad attacking the public officials in Montgomery who lead the segregationist forces. *The New York Times* publishes the ad without checking its accuracy. As it turns out, some of the charges are not true.

New York Times Co. v. Sullivan,

376 U.S. 254, 84 S.Ct. 710, 11 L.Ed.2d 686 (1964)

The Alabama officials sue *The New York Times* for libel. In Montgomery, a jury finds the *Times* has, indeed, libeled those local public servants and must be punished by paying them damages.

The New York Times appeals the verdict all the way to the U. S. Supreme Court. In 1964, *New York Times Co. v. Sullivan* makes new libel law for the nation. The press cannot be held responsible for the libel of a public official, the Supreme Court says, unless it publishes the libel with malice in its heart, knowing the information is false.

The media must be found guilty of *reckless disregard for truth* before a public official can collect for libel, the court decides.

If You Can't Take the Heat . . .

In their decision, the justices acknowledge that many public officials will be damaged by untrue, libelous stories as this new ruling is applied. But the democratic process demands full and free debate—continuous open season on public officials—the court rules.

The public must be able to hear every accusation thrown at those in public office, and decide whether they deserve a position of public trust. If you can't take the political heat, stay out of the kitchen, the court warns.

What Is Reckless Disregard?

How far must a reporter go to check out damaging information about a public official to meet the absence of malice test?

That's up to a judge or jury. In *New York Times Co. v. Sullivan,* the Supreme Court felt the *Times* had no obligation to check the accuracy of the paid advertisement.

Suppose the mayor has been waging war against local chemical companies that have polluted the river and some neighborhoods near the chemical plants. The mayor has a reputation as Mr. Environment. His campaign has persuaded many local firms to stop buying from the local polluters. They have switched to suppliers in other nearby cities. An anonymous caller tells a reporter the real motive for the mayor's crusade: Mr. Environment has a hidden interest in a Chicago company that has inherited business as a result of the mayor's crusade. And the company in which the mayor is involved is even worse, in terms of pollution.

Anonymous Tip = Reckless

To be fair, the reporter asks the mayor if the charge is true. The reporter gets an angry denial, and then runs a story that says, "Our sources tell us the real reason for the mayor's crusade. He holds a financial interest in a Chicago chemical company that signed a contract with the city after the mayor's environmental campaign put three local firms out of business. The mayor denies it."

Reckless disregard for truth? Almost certainly. If the only evidence is an anonymous tip, most juries will say the reporter and the newspaper or broadcast station were reckless with the truth. They should be punished by paying damages to the mayor.

But suppose the reporter pursues the tip, drives to Chicago, and finds two employees at the chemical company who say, on tape, that the mayor is in the main office of the plant where they work at least one day every week, and seems to tell the manager what to do. The mayor has also been talking to employees at the plant, asking them for ideas that would make it more profitable. During one of those sessions, the mayor told them he owns a controlling interest in the company.

The outcome of a libel suit may now depend on the skill of the opposing attorneys.

Defense #3A: Public Persons

Back to the 1960s. As integration spreads across the South under court edicts and the muzzles of army rifles, a federal court orders the University of Mississippi to admit its first black student. He is escorted to the campus by a squad of U. S. marshals.

That night, the marshals and a small army of reporters are driven into the university administration building by an angry mob. As the night wears on, the administration building comes under attack. The mob begins to shoot at the marshals and the building.

Small groups charge, carrying Confederate flags, trying to break in. A reporter is killed. The federal government is once again in a shooting war with the rebellious South.

The Truth Battle at Oxford

In the heat of the battle, someone runs into the Associated Press office and says a famous general is leading the charges at the Old Miss administration building—former U. S. Army General Edwin Walker. A bulletin is quickly typed. The story goes over the wire. It is published all over the world the next day.

General Walker had been a career soldier who believed strongly in the communist threat to America. As commander of U. S. forces in Europe, he had recommended that his troops read the John Birch Society's *Blue Book*, which accused former President Dwight D. Eisenhower and other national leaders of being communist dupes.

Walker was relieved of his command. He retired and went on the lecture circuit. The wire services transmitted a picture of the general, flying an American flag upside down as a distress signal that the country was in trouble. He was a big enough celebrity that Lee Harvey Oswald took a shot at him. Oswald missed, then went on to Dallas.

Associated Press v. Walker,
388 U.S. 130, 87 S.Ct. 1975, 18 L.Ed.2d 1094 (1967)

So the AP reports this famous general is leading the charge against the U. S. marshals. Walker sues for libel. The AP cannot trace the source of its information. It cannot even prove that Walker was on the campus that night. Walker wins the libel suit.

The AP appeals, and again the U. S. Supreme Court reverses. In 1967, the court extends the *New York Times v. Sullivan* guidelines to "public persons." Public persons, like public officials, cannot win a libel judgment, the court rules, unless the media show reckless disregard for truth.

In the heat and stress of the battle situation that night on the university campus, the court decides, the AP cannot be penalized for making an honest mistake.

Tabloids & Public People

Now you can understand why the tabloids are devoted to public officials and entertainers. The libel rules are much more lenient for public people. The media don't have to be absolutely sure the story is true, so long as they don't know it's false.

But the present Supreme Court seems more uneasy with that broad libel immunity. Later decisions have muddied the guidelines. Juries, too—as in the Carol Burnett case against the *National Enquirer*—sometimes try to re-draw the line.

Defense #4: Fair Comment

British law developed another area where the press could defame people and get away with it—theater critics. If a critic says an actor's performance is shoddy, and the script miserable, the review does great damage to everyone involved with the play. Not just their reputations—their livelihood. Some critics have the ability to shut down a play within days if they give it a bad review. Their opinions are as devastating as any false statement of fact.

Yet the law recognizes that different people are entitled to express different opinions. If you go on stage to display yourself in public, journalists have the right to throw figurative tomatoes if they don't like what they see. That same kind of license has been extended now to journalists who test cars, rate restaurants, or review other kinds of consumer services and products.

A damaging story can kill a new business. A favorable story, in the right place, can make millions for a new product.

There are *some* restrictions. Most courts would rule that the journalist who decides to judge artistic or engineering merit can be successfully sued for libel if the facts are misstated in the review.

INSIDE THE MEDIA

NETWORKS

An Endangered Species Struggles to Survive

Broadcasting networks are going through a rapid evolutionary process. Nobody is sure what they'll look like ten years from now. Some pessimistic observers say the networks—as we've known them—will be extinct. The massive audiences they once captured are gradually drifting away to other shows on cable, to satellite-delivered programming, to movies rented at the nearby video store.

Network Share Dropping

During the 1978-79 television season, 92 per cent of the people watching television were tuned to stations affiliated with the three major networks. By 1992-93 their share of the national TV audience was only 61 per cent.

The entire financial structure of the networks was created with the assumption of a massive, nationwide audience. There were three—ABC, CBS and NBC—to split that audience.

In the early days of television, few cities had more than three stations. Local stations affiliated with the networks produced two or three newscasts per day, some weekly talk shows, and an occasional special or documentary. Everything else on the tube came from the network.

The network affiliates were generally VHF stations. Channels 2-13. UHF signals in those early days were inferior, both in quality and in reach.

Independent Meant Cheap

Independent stations (no network affiliation) were often UHF stations with small audiences. To be profitable, they had few employees. Some had a short broadcast day. They ran sit-com reruns, very old movies, and no news.

Cable in those days could deliver a high-quality picture for a UHF station, but very few homes had cable. There was no incentive to produce original programming for cable. Too few viewers were connected.

It's a very different story today.

Majority Now Have Cable

By early 1993, 61 per cent of American households were connected to cable TV systems. Cable systems had expanded so that only three per cent of the homes in the nation did not have cable service as an option.

Cable finally conquered its major obstacle in the late 1980s when—for the first time—a majority of American homes were hooked up to a cable system.

Once most homes were subscribers, the rate of growth in the cable industry rapidly accelerated. With a larger audience, cable advertising also grew, raising the money to stimulate more channels and new cable programs.

By the early 1990s, most metropolitan-area cable systems were offering 50 to 100 channels. As the choices increased, the number of viewers watching the original Big Three networks—and network profits—steadily declined.

The National News Monopoly

The networks originally had a monopoly on national and international news. They built their own coaxial cable system connected to their affiliate stations in virtually every American city. It was the only way you could send television signals more than 75 miles.

Satellites changed all that. They may make the network system obsolete.

Originally, the networks were the primary customers for satellite transmissions. Their field crews could send videotape to New York instantly to be edited for tonight's newscast. Or they could cover stories live. The correspondent in the field transmitted to New York via satellite, and the network then fed that picture to its affiliates on the coaxial cable.

But more and more communications satellites were

launched. By the late 1980s, most local television news operations had their own satellite capability.

Local News by Satellite

They could send reporters anywhere in the world and beam stories back instantly. Once they could do that, and give the story a local angle, the network coverage was redundant. Second-rate, compared to the localized version of the story.

If the networks' monopoly on a national audience AND the ability to report live from anywhere in the world no longer exist, how much longer can the networks hold enough audience to remain profitable? What should networks be doing that will be unique and profitable? The people who run the networks are still trying to resolve those questions.

Add to the competition a growing number of "networks" using cable to distribute their product and their advertising. There is ESPN, CNN, FNN, A&E—an almost endless supply of specialized programming that continues to grow as the cable audience increases.

FCC's Network Definition

The FCC definition of a broadcast network is a central source offering at least 15 hours a week of programming. Fox Broadcasting Co., contracting with broadcast stations that were previously independents, met that goal in late 1990, and by early 1993 was providing programming every night.

The relationship between the networks and their local affiliates is confusing. Many people think of their hometown newscast as "ABC's local news," or "CBS in Atlanta."

The tie between a network and its affiliates is much more distant. Networks and local stations have contracts to supply services to each other. But there's usually no ownership interest between the two.

Network O and O's

The exceptions are network-owned-and-operated stations. In the business, they're called "O and O's."

Until 1985, the FCC limited the number of television outlets one company could own to five VHF stations (channels 2 through

13) and two UHF stations (channel 14 and higher). The rule was established to prevent monopolies that could narrow the control of television news.

Each network, for many years, owned and operated five stations.

TV Ownership Expanded

In 1985, the rules were rewritten. One company can now own 12 stations as long as they do not reach more than 25 per cent of the national audience. UHF stations are assessed at half the homes in the market, because their signals don't go as far.

One company can own 14 stations and reach 30 per cent of the national audience if two of those stations are controlled by minorities.

After the rules were rewritten, the networks branched out with new O and O's. In some cities, the station they bought had been affiliated with one of the other networks. Very confusing for the viewers.

Fox also owns and operates stations. The stations owned by the four networks are:

ABC
Chicago—WLS-TV
Durham, NC—WTVD-TV
Fresno, CA—KFSN-TV
Houston—KTRK-TV
Los Angeles—KABC-TV
New York—WABC-TV
Philadelphia—WPVI-TV
San Francisco—KGO-TV

CBS
Chicago—WBBM-TV
Green Bay, WI—WFRV-TV
Los Angeles—KCBS-TV
Miami—WCIX-TV
Minneapolis-St. Paul—WCCO-TV
New York—WCBS-TV
Philadelphia—WCAU-TV

FOX
Chicago—WFLD-TV
Dallas—KDAF-TV

Houston—KRIV-TV
Los Angeles—KTTV-TV
New York—WNYW-TV
Salt Lake City—KSTU-TV
Washington—WTTG-TV

NBC
Chicago—WMAQ-TV
Denver—KCNC-TV
Los Angeles—KNBC-TV
Miami—WTVJ-TV
New York—WNBC-TV
Washington—WRC-TV

No Network Control

At about 1,120 other commercially-operated stations around the country, the networks have no ownership interest, and no control over local programming.

About 650 of those commercial stations are affiliated with one of the three major networks, and the number contracting with each network is fairly even.

The number of stations, and the number of affiliates, varies from year to year. New stations are gradually added. About half the commercial TV stations in the country are VHF and half are UHF.

There are about 360 educational TV channels. Just over a third of them are VHF stations.

The Network Contract

When advertisers buy network time, they want to reach the entire country. So the network has a contract with a local station to broadcast network programming in that area. The local affiliate has some options to pre-empt network programming, but they're severely limited.

The network wants to be sure that its advertising will reach the mass audience it promised when it sold the commercial time.

In return for that service, the network pays the local station a fee. The fee is negotiated with each station, and varies according to market size. It's not a large fee. Not much more than it costs to provide the equipment, engineers and overhead to keep the local station on the air for network shows.

The Local Station's Cut

In effect, the local affiliate gets free network programming to fill most of its broadcast day.

The real money for the affiliate comes from local advertising slots that are built into network programming. Each hour of a network show carries about 10 minutes of commercials. About three minutes of that 10 minutes is set aside for the local affiliate to insert local commercials. The money the affiliate gets for those commercials is pure profit.

Watch a network show. Most of the advertising will be national—cars, detergents, aspirin, beer or office machines. But some of the commercial breaks will advertise Aunt Millie's Delicatessen or a local diaper service.

The cost of producing an hour of entertainment is more than the price of commercial time in most local markets. There just aren't enough people in one city to justify the kind of advertising rates necessary to pay for those shows.

Panic at the Networks

As the network audience slipped away and network profits diminished at the end of the 1980s, a national economic recession hit. Scrambling to cut their losses, network news divisions began massive layoffs. Bureaus were closed in some major cities and foreign countries.

As part of their belt-tightening, networks proposed cutting back on payments to affiliates. Some plans suggested affiliate payments based on local audience ratings for network shows. There were proposals that the affiliates pay the networks for network programming, instead of the other way around.

In 1992, CBS ordered a dramatic cut in payments to affiliates, and the stations rebelled. Eventually, CBS backed down. The networks and their affiliates need each other, but changing technology and declining profits are creating huge conflicts. All that is in transition as this book goes to press.

Local News is Expensive

Many local news operations cost more than the advertising they bring in. A documentary that requires travel halfway around the world and six months' work by a reporter and camera crew will cost more than the local commercial time in that hour can earn.

There is usually a cooperative working relationship between network news organizations and the local stations. Suppose a tornado touches down in your area. There's no network correspondent available to cover the story. The network will call the local affiliate and ask for a copy of its tornado videotape.

Locals on the Network

Sometimes, the network will ask for a complete "package" from a reporter at the local affiliate. When the reporter "sigs out" at the close of the story, you can tell whether he's network or local.

If he's local, he says, "In Topeka, I'm William Windy, for NBC News." If the story is done for the network, the reporter is not part of the network staff.

A network correspondent would close his piece, "In Topeka, I'm William Windy, NBC News."

When a network uses videotape shot by an affiliate, it usually pays the reporter and camera crew a fee. They're moonlighting for the network.

If the network news desk decides to send a crew to a town where it has no bureau, the crew will often use the local affiliate's newsroom, telephones and editing facilities. The same cable and satellite systems that bring network programming to the local affiliate can also be used to transmit stories to New York or Washington for tonight's network newscast.

The Rise of News

Until the middle 1970s, news was rarely a money-maker for local stations or networks. It was considered a prestige item, which built viewer loyalty for entertainment shows.

But something happened—perhaps Watergate—to make Americans more news-hungry. "60 Minutes" became one of the most-watched television shows on the air in the early 1980s, and ranked regularly in the top ten shows throughout the decade.

There are millions of news junkies who will watch three and four hours of news at a sitting, even if many of the stories are repeated, in slightly different form, every 30 minutes. Cable and satellite news services now offer 24-hour, non-stop news.

When Ted Turner started his first Cable News Network in 1980, few people believed the country could absorb that kind of news saturation. Most of the experts thought Turner was on an ego binge that would drive him to bankruptcy. Instead, he opened a second non-stop cable news network in 1982—Headline News—with quicker, shorter stories.

Independent News Networks

The independent news networks have now made local independent stations much more competitive. Stations with no network affiliation have to buy their programming from syndicates and independent producers.

Those independents can now buy slickly produced newscasts that give international and national coverage. The news shows vastly increase the prestige of the independent station.

Earlier Bedtime News

Independent stations also have more flexibility in scheduling their programs. In the South and Northeast, for instance, prime time network programming runs until 11 p.m. Most local affiliates run their late-night newscasts at 11. But a lot of people can't stay up that late, so many independents run their newscasts at 10 p.m. A substantial chunk of the audience will switch from network programming at 10 o'clock so they can catch up with the news before they go to bed.

INSIDE THE MEDIA

NEWSCAST

For the End of the World, Two Minutes

Time dictates almost everything in radio and television news. Broadcast deadlines are absolute. The news begins at exactly six o'clock, or ten, or eleven. The lead story in broadcast news must be ready when the anchor says, "Good evening." Sure, you could place that story later in the newscast. But if the audience is expecting today's big story and it's not ready at the top of the newscast, they'll switch to the competition.

Time restricts broadcast stories in another way. The producer—who assembles the newscast—must build a collection of taped stories and live material that will fit the newscast time slot exactly. A television newscast, in its entirety, will be 30 or 60 minutes long. The time slot is rigid, just as the "news hole" in a newspaper (the space set aside for news stories) can't be stretched.

Radio Even Shorter

A radio newscast producer will have only five or ten minutes. Unless it's National Public Radio. Most radio news stories will be 10 or 15 seconds long. Thirty seconds for radio is a very long story.

The 17-Minute Newscast

Time is absolute, and it is precious. After you subtract commercials, weather, sports, good evening and goodbye, a 30-minute local TV newscast is only about 17 minutes of news. Most stories will run 30 seconds, or less. A few will have the luxury of a full minute. For a major story—90 seconds.

How To Speak TV, Print & Radio

Half-hour network newscasts contain about 22 minutes of news. They don't have weather and sports segments.

Producers have an inside joke they scream when young reporters say they need more time for a story. "What do you think you're covering?" they yell. "This story is worth 90 seconds. For the end of the world, two minutes. But only if it's really good."

TV Altered The Mind

Television has radically altered the way most Americans receive, retain, and react to information. Thirty years ago, first graders had an average attention span of 20 to 30 seconds. Today, that is the limit for most adults. Television's ability to flick from one picture to another—sometimes several times per second—has conditioned us to expect frequent changes of scenery on the tube. When it doesn't happen, our attention begins to drift.

Television stations and networks hire consulting firms to study viewers—to learn what turns them on, and what makes them switch to another channel.

Do Not Exceed 90 Seconds

It was those consulting firms that issued the Ninety-second Commandment. Sure, the commandment is broken. But unless it is exceptionally well done, any story longer than 90 seconds tends to make viewers go to the kitchen, the bathroom, the bedroom, to sleep in their chair—or worse—switch stations.

Those same studies led to another time commandment: Never let anybody talk on camera for more than about 15 seconds. The voice can continue, but you must constantly give viewers new video. If you want to retain or improve your audience ratings, change the picture more often.

Under 10 Seconds

Network news has whittled down considerably that time edict for interviews. When you watch the news tonight, time the interviews. They will probably run less than ten seconds. In radio, many sound bites will be less than five seconds.

How can you possibly say anything about a complicated, controversial subject in ten seconds or less?

It is a skill that can be learned, no more difficult than driving a car or playing bridge.

The fear of doing it wrong, of embarrassment and public ridicule, make talking to television or radio reporters seem so terribly difficult. (See **SKILLS/Interviews-Broadcast** and **Interviews-General**)

Understanding Their Needs

Understanding what reporters need and how they must assemble stories will take away some of the fear. And, like driving a car or playing bridge or public speaking, the more you do it, the easier it becomes.

In **SKILLS/Interviews-Broadcast**, I give you exercises to develop mental agility for simplifying complicated subjects. How to get to the point quickly. If you expect to communicate effectively on radio or television, it is a skill you MUST learn.

Talking to a newspaper reporter, you don't sense the time pressure as much. Compared to broadcasting, newspapers have many more reporters to cover the same ground. Print reporters have the luxury of time to gather volumes of material before they boil it down to fit their assigned length.

If you talk too long to a newspaper reporter, you wander away from the point you want to make. That rambling conversation can easily steer the story elsewhere. The ability to condense your thoughts is an element of control that affects the final version of the story in all news media—TV, radio and print.

If you don't boil it down, the reporter will. You're the expert. Your summary is more likely to be accurate.

Transferring Skills

Once you develop that skill, you'll discover it works in many other places where you need to communicate—to sell ideas. You'll be much more effective if you use some of TV's techniques for your next civic club speech—when you testify at a legislative hearing—or when you're trying to convince your staff or your board of directors.

Those people, too, have been affected by television. You need to be brief. You need to persuade with pictures.

Newspapers are adopting many of television's formulas. The price of newsprint keeps going up. There is less space in most newspapers for news. Stories must be shorter, brighter, better illustrated.

The Sony Sandwich

The most common formula for a TV news story that involves a reporter is the Sony Sandwich. Some stations call it a "wrap" or a "package." Most television reporters' stories will follow this simple formula, or some variation. Radio uses a very similar sandwich form. And now newspapers are adopting it, too. (See **SKILLS/Interviews-Broadcast** and **Interviews-General**)

Walter Cronkite once said television provides a headline service. Newspaper people love that quote. For much of television coverage, Cronkite was right. But there are other times when neither the written nor the spoken word can come close to the awesome impact of the television news camera and microphone.

Television has unified us more than any other force in history. The storytellers in ancient tribes gave people their sense of time and place and identity. But each person crouched around the campfire came away with a very different mental picture of what the chief or medicine man was reciting.

Then books served that purpose for civilization. But still, no matter how well written, every reader had a different mental image.

Identical Memories

We are the first generation to have identical memories of the major events in our lives. Those moments, captured by television, bind us together as a people. More powerful, more intimate, more emotional than books, they are engraved in our collective past. So much so that we sometimes have to think a minute—did I see it on television, or was I really there?

- The Vietnam War.
- Martin Luther King speaking at the Lincoln Memorial.
- The first step onto the lunar surface.
- The explosion of the Challenger spacecraft.
- The shooting of Robert Kennedy, and George Wallace, and Ronald Reagan.

For those stories, television forgot about time. When it does, and when luck and skill put a camera in just the right place, no other medium can even come close.

Newscast Mechanics

As a first step for coping with broadcast news, you need to understand some of the mechanics of producing a newscast. Some of the things they do are very puzzling if you don't know about the gadgets, the formats, and the way they dictate the production of both stories and the newscast itself.

Many of the story forms for television news are dictated by attention-span requirements. That's why the double or triple anchor format was invented. If viewers begin to nod, the new face and voice bring them back to attention. Many local stations believe male-female anchor teams offer maximum appeal and attention-span advantages.

The Anchor Balancing Act

The anchors are usually attractive people, easy to look at and listen to. The shift back and forth between male and female voices offers constant attention fresheners. If they're not listening closely, men in the audience enjoy looking at a beautiful woman. Female viewers like to watch a good-looking anchorman. And the chemistry between a man and a woman on camera makes ad-libs more interesting.

Television stations balance their anchor teams in the same way a political party tries to balance its ticket. A city with a large black population needs black anchors. Stations with significant ethnic communities search for anchors who've lost their accents, but have identifiable ethnic names and look Spanish, or Italian, or Polish.

TV & Radio Monotony

Television and radio amplify monotony. Fifteen seconds of a blank screen, or dead silence on the radio, seems like forever. Listen carefully to good disk jockeys—the way they talk to keep you listening. Broadcasters train themselves to read so their voices go up and down, now slower, then faster without a breath, then a long pause. Paul Harvey—one of radio's most successful commentators—has a style that exaggerates the technique.

In putting together a newscast, the producer tries to pace the show the same way. A long TV story (90 seconds) will be followed by several short ones. The plane crash report may be played just before a break. When they come back from the commercial, there will be a fluffy, breezy story to make you feel better.

Copy Stories

The simplest and briefest television story is called a "copy story" or "reader." The anchor reads the entire story, on camera, with no visual effects. It is usually no longer than 15 or 20 seconds.

TelePrompTers

While we're talking about copy stories, you may wonder how anchors read the news without looking at the script in their hands—and why they bother to have it there.

TelePrompTer devices enable anchors to read stories while looking directly into the camera lens.

The pages are actually on a small conveyor belt, across the studio, out of sight. A tiny, closed-circuit television camera is mounted over the conveyor belt.

On top of—or under—the big studio camera, a black-and-white TV set receives the picture of the pages on the conveyor belt.

The picture is reflected onto a plate of clear glass in front of the studio camera lens. The angle of the glass is fixed so the anchor can see the reflection of the pages, but the camera can't. In fact, the anchor can't really see the lens very well.

You Don't See the Eyes Move

The script is printed in large type and very short lines—usually two or three words to the line—so it can be scanned without noticeable eye movement. An operator at the conveyor belt runs the belt to match the anchor's reading speed.

A carbon of the script pages passing by on the conveyor belt is in the anchor's hands. Each time a page goes by, the anchor

The TelePrompTer operator feeds script sheets to a conveyor belt that passes under a closed-circuit TV camera.

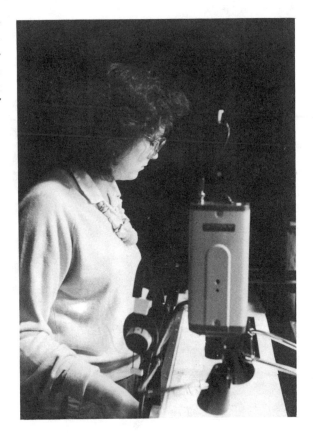

turns a page on the desk, in case something goes wrong with the TelePrompTer.

TelePrompTer Problems

Sometimes the conveyor belt breaks down, or the operator puts the pages in upside down, or out of order. If that happens, the anchor can continue the story by reading from the script on the desk—glancing down and looking up, a sentence at a time.

When experienced anchors suddenly stumble, it's usually a clue that something has gone wrong with the TelePrompTer. A few seconds later, when the prompter problem is fixed, they'll go back to looking at the camera.

How To Speak TV, Print & Radio

The TelePrompTer monitor is reflected by an angled sheet of glass in front of the camera lens.

Computerized TelePrompTers

TV newsrooms are now being computerized. In those systems, the conveyor belt is eliminated. Reporters write their stories at video display terminals. The lines of type the anchor reads are generated by a computer. The TV set under or over the camera is actually a computer monitor. The copy of the script in the anchor's hand came out of a computer printer, not a typewriter.

The best anchors glance down at the script on the desk each time they turn a page. They give the illusion that they read the entire page, memorize it, and then recite it to you. If they don't look down occasionally, the viewer begins to wonder why the anchor never looks at the pages being flipped. Maybe they're in braille?

Story Keys

To make a copy story more visually interesting, a graphic of some kind is "keyed" in the upper corner, over the anchor's shoulder. The graphic is inserted electronically, in the control room. You know, of course, the drawing, or picture, is not actually there in the TV studio. If it's a story about a postal workers' strike, there may be a postage stamp, or a mailbox in the "key." A copy story about a murder may "key" a gun, or a knife.

This is part of television's constant effort to show you something while they talk. It helps you understand and pay attention. You should do the same thing when you talk to the Kiwanis Club or the County Commission. Speakers who have nothing visual to illustrate their points make it hard for us to concentrate. We daydream if we have nothing to look at while the speaker drones on.

Invisible Weather Maps

The same electronic gadget that keys a graphic over the anchor's shoulder is used to make a blank wall look like a weather map. This is one of the most interesting electronic illusions the first time you visit a TV studio for a live newscast.

The meteorologist works in front of a blank wall that is painted muddy blue or bright green. At home, you see a map of the area, the state, or the nation on the wall. It's not really there.

How Chroma-Key Works

The Chroma-Key device electronically merges two sources of video. The camera shooting the weathercaster is tuned to be blind to the color on the wall. The picture it takes is a cutout of the forecaster. The picture is blank everywhere else.

Another video source is fed into the Chroma-Key. It can be videotape, slides, or a live radar scope. The Chroma-Key inserts into the map video the camera cutout picture of the weathercaster.

Electronic Cookie Cutters

Imagine two sheets of cookie dough. A cookie cutter (the studio camera) stamps out the image of the forecaster. The rest of that dough is thrown away. The same cookie cutter then stamps out the same image on the second sheet of cookie dough. This time, you throw away the cookie and keep the remaining dough. There is a hole in the sheet of dough—the silhouette of the forecaster.

Then the cutout from the first sheet (the forecaster) is inserted into the second sheet of cookie dough (the weather map). It is done so seamlessly we think the weathercaster cutout and the map are all part of the same sheet of dough.

Smoke and Mirrors

When the forecaster is pointing to a storm system over the Great Lakes, the Great Lakes are not there. On each side of the set, where viewers can't see them, are TV monitors showing what we're seeing at home. The forecaster appears to be looking at the map on the wall.

Instead, the forecaster is watching a monitor. If the finger pointing to the Great Lakes is actually over Arkansas, you can see on the monitor where you're pointing, and make a correction.

Live Remotes Do It, Too

At some stations, the same device is used when anchors are talking to reporters doing live remotes from the field. The anchors talk to what looks like a TV monitor. The monitor is actually a screen painted the same blue or green used for the weather segment.

The studio camera shoots over the shoulder of the anchors, and the Chroma-Key inserts the reporter doing the remote into the screen the anchors talk to. The anchors have a small monitor viewers can't see. They can view the reporter in the field as they have their two-way conversation.

Why Blue or Green?

The blue color was originally chosen because it was the one color most absent in human skin tone. Later equipment worked better with a shade of green. Occasionally, anchors will have something in their clothing that is too close to the Chroma-Key color.

An anchor's tie or scarf with the same blue or green as the Chroma-Key will make that part of the anchor invisible. We will see the weather map where the tie or scarf are. Just as though the anchor had a window in that part of the body.

This same equipment is often used in commercials. A pair of hands holding the product seem to be unattached, floating in air. They're actually at the end of a sleeve that is Chroma-Key color. The arm disappears. We only see the hands and the product.

Voice-Over Story Formula

In a voice-over story, the anchor begins to read the story on camera. About 10 seconds into the copy, the director in the control room switches the picture from the anchor to videotape of what the anchor's talking about. The anchor continues to read, live, while you watch videotape. The tape may have sound with it, played very low. This is called *natural sound*. The anchor voice is *over* the picture and any background sound on the tape.

As the anchor talks about last night's Academy Award winner, you see the actor accepting the statuette. If the tape is used with natural sound, you will hear, softly, in the background, the applause when his name is pulled from the envelope.

Voice-Over to Sound

In the voice-over-to-sound formula (V/O to SOT), the anchor begins the story on-camera, just as before. The story becomes V/O as you watch the actor accept the Oscar. Then the anchor stops reading. The sound on the tape is turned up, full volume, and you see and hear the actor thanking his mother, his father, his mistress, his director, and his dog.

For this kind of story, everything must be timed precisely. After the copy is written, a producer with a stopwatch takes it to the anchor, who reads at a normal pace. They time from the point where the live voice-over begins—to where the actor in last night's ceremony will speak on videotape. The voice-over section of tape is edited to run exactly as many seconds as it takes for the anchor to read the copy.

The Countdown

When the anchor reads the copy during the newscast, the director in the control room punches a stopwatch as the voice-over tape begins to roll. The anchor must read for exactly 16 sec-

The director has the entire newscast timed to a split second. As an anchor reads, voice-over, the director calls out the countdown to the floor crew.

onds. If the reading is too fast, there will be a hole of silence between the anchor's voice and the actor's. Read too slowly, and the anchor will drown out the beginning of what the actor says.

The director works with a microphone and headset. The anchor wears a hidden earphone. The floor crew in the studio all have headsets. By flipping a selector switch, the director can talk to anyone in the studio. As the anchor reads the voice-over section of the story, the director watches the stopwatch and begins a countdown to the floor manager. Ten—nine—eight—seven . . .

Watch My Fingers Count

The floor manager hears the countdown on his headset. He holds up fingers, dropping a finger as each second ticks by. The anchor can see the finger countdown beside the TelePrompTer. When the countdown reaches five seconds, the anchor will hurry a little, or slow down, to finish the voice-over script a split second before the sound-on-tape (SOT) begins. When the Oscar winner finishes thanking everybody, the anchor comes back on camera to begin another story.

V/O—SOT—V/O

The voice-over to sound-on-tape to voice-over (V/O-SOT-V/O) is a variation of the same formula. The anchor begins with a copy story, on camera. This is a typical script:

The floor manager hears the countdown on his headset and relays seconds remaining before sound-on-tape. The anchor must finish reading just as the last finger drops.

ANCHOR LIVE	THE CITY'S GARBAGE COLLECTORS SAY THEY'LL STRIKE AT MIDNIGHT UNLESS THE CITY COUNCIL GOES ALONG WITH THEIR DEMAND FOR A FIFTEEN PERCENT PAY INCREASE.
V/O (Videotape of meeting)	THE GARBAGE COLLECTORS' UNION MET AT TWO A.M. THIS MORNING, AND WOUND UP WITH A UNANIMOUS VOTE, SETTING THE WALKOUT DEADLINE.
SOT (Union president)	"The Council says we don't care about our city. Well, I say they don't care about us. We're human beings. We have to eat, too."
V/O (Mayor entering City Hall)	THE MAYOR HAS CALLED AN EMERGENCY MEETING OF THE CITY COUNCIL TO-NIGHT IN A LAST-DITCH EFFORT TO STOP THE STRIKE.

If the story is more complicated—getting the mayor's point of view, for instance—it will usually be handled by a reporter, who will "package" the story in Sony Sandwich form.

The Lead-In

On the air, the Sony Sandwich is introduced by the anchor. The anchor copy is called the lead-in. It is a headline, designed to tell you generally what the story is about, grab your attention, and make you want to listen to what the reporter is about to say.

The reporter's entire story is on videotape, both sound and picture. That is why, once edited, it is very difficult to change the length. In the Sony Sandwich formula, the reporter begins by giving viewers the basic facts while we see videotape—V/O NAT SOUND. This is bottom of the sandwich. The bread. It is 15 to 25 seconds thick. The interview is in the middle, followed by the top of the sandwich—another 15 to 25 seconds of reporter narration.

In the story scripted below, the beginning natural sound will include sirens and the crackle of the fire under the reporter's voice.

Scripting the Story

The notations at the left side of the script are like stage instructions for a play or movie script. It is a blueprint that shows how the story is built. The newscast director needs that blueprint if the story is read live. With the script, a videotape editor can build the story on tape while the reporter who wrote it does something else.

This is what the script will look like:

ANCHOR LIVE	FIVE PEOPLE ARE DEAD, THREE OTHERS MISSING AS THE RESULT OF A FIRE THAT SWEPT THROUGH THE UPPER FLOORS OF A DOWNTOWN ROOMING HOUSE LATE THIS AFTERNOON. REPORTER DEBBIE DARLING SAYS ARSON IS SUSPECTED.
DARLING V/O NAT. SOUND (flames) (man jumping)	THE FLAMES RACED SO QUICKLY THROUGH THE THIRD FLOOR OF THE OLD WOODEN BARCLAY HOUSE, FIREMEN SAY EVERYONE ON THAT FLOOR DIED. ABOVE, FROM A FOURTH-FLOOR WINDOW, A TERRIFIED MAN JUMPED TO HIS DEATH BEFORE FIREFIGHTERS COULD RAISE THEIR LADDERS.
(carrying people out)	THERE WERE DRAMATIC RESCUES THAT KEPT THE DEATH TOLL FROM CLIMBING EVEN HIGHER.
(*Now the meat of the sandwich*) SOT (woman in blanket)	"The smoke was so thick I couldn't see anything. I knew I was dead. Then this fireman knocks the door down, and he throws me over

his shoulder, and goes running right through
the flames. He saved my life."

(And the bread to
top it off)
DARLING V/O
NAT. SO.
(Covered bodies)
(More fire)

THE NAMES OF THE DEAD HAVE NOT
BEEN RELEASED. FIRE INSPECTORS SAY
THE SPEED
AT WHICH THE FLAMES SPREAD MAKES
THEM BELIEVE IT WAS SET BY AN ARSON-
IST. WE'LL HAVE A FULL REPORT TONIGHT
AT ELEVEN.

(Darling with fire
chief)

I'M DEBBIE DARLING, EYEWITNESS NEWS.

INSIDE THE MEDIA

NEWSPAPERS

Extra! Extra! They're Not Reading About It!

The newspaper industry is very worried these days about its failure to grow. Daily newspaper circulation has decreased slightly in the last 20 years. In that same period, the number of households in the United States grew 42 per cent. A number of different studies clearly show the percentage of Americans who read a daily newspaper is steadily shrinking.

They Don't Have Time

People surveyed say they don't have time to read the newspaper any more.

A study by the Newspaper Advertising Bureau Inc. shows 19 per cent of the adults in households subscribing to a newspaper do not get around to reading it on a typical day.

That same study shows two out of three people watch TV news on a typical day, with average viewing time 58 minutes. Half those who see TV news tune in more than one newscast. And 45 per cent of those surveyed said they heard news on the radio during a typical day.

Reading a newspaper takes effort and concentration. Television viewing requires no energy. You can do something else while TV delivers news.

Declining Percentages

Other studies by the Associated Press Managing Editors Association showed 73 per cent of the population read a daily newspaper in 1967. By 1988, the figure was 51 per cent. Among adults

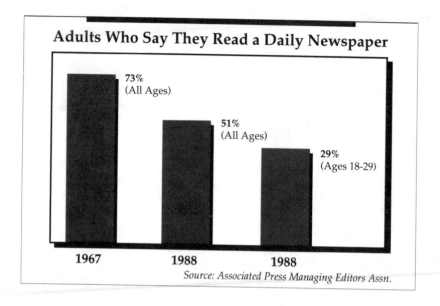

Adults Who Say They Read a Daily Newspaper

73%
(All Ages)

51%
(All Ages)

29%
(Ages 18-29)

1967   1988   1988

Source: Associated Press Managing Editors Assn.

age 18–29, only 29 per cent said they read a newspaper on week-days.

The competition of television is just part of the problem. Other reasons for the drop in readership—

Illiteracy. A large segment of the population does not read well enough to tackle a newspaper. Publishers have launched a nationwide effort to sponsor and encourage programs that teach adults to read.

A mobile population, with few ties or personal identification with the local community. They do not care very much about what is happening in the community. Newspapers in this country have traditionally covered local news. Other developed nations have national newspapers. The closest America has is *The New York Times, The Wall Street Journal, The Christian Science Monitor,* and a newcomer—*USA Today.*

Expanding options for using leisure time.

Women working outside the home. Housewives were once a major segment of newspaper readership. With a job outside the home, surveys show women still shoulder household chores, too. Free time is scarce. Newspaper reading is one of the things they drop.

The Good News Is Sunday

The brighter side of newspaper circulation is Sunday newspapers. While it hasn't kept pace with the growth in households, Sunday newspaper circulation increased 26 per cent between 1970 (49.2 million) and 1992 (62 million), according to *Editor and Publisher.*

One theory for the increase in Sunday circulation is more time to read it, on a day when you don't have to go to work. How do you know how many people buy a newspaper? The Audit Bureau of Circulation (ABC) is the national source for certifying how many newspapers and magazines are sold.

Audit Bureau of Circulation

The ABC serves the same purpose as broadcasting rating services. It tells newspaper advertisers how many people they will reach if they buy newspaper or magazine ads.

Critics often say the print media sensationalize "to sell newspapers." That was true in the days of the afternoon paper, purchased on the street to read on the subway or bus after work. And it's still very true for the tabloids. They count on headlines about movie stars' sexual exploits with aliens from UFOs to make you curious enough to buy while you wait in the check-out line at the supermarket.

But most newspapers are bought, sight unseen. Delivered to homes and offices, paid for in advance. For many of those subscribers, too much sensationalism will make them cancel their subscriptions.

Most Readers Subscribe

Today, only 18 per cent of newspaper readers will buy the paper from a rack or newsstand, according to the Newspaper Advertising Bureau. Seventy-two per cent of newspaper readers are subscribers. The remaining 10 per cent read a paper someone else bought. "Pass-along readers," the trade calls them.

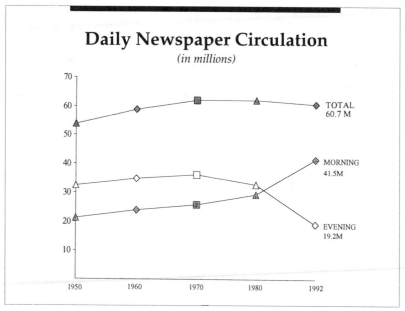

Daily Newspaper Circulation
(in millions)

Source: Editor and Publisher

Here are circulation figures compiled by *Editor and Publisher*:

Year	Morning	Evening	Total M&E	Sunday
1950	21,266,126	32,562,946	53,829,072	46,582,348
1960	24,028,788	34,852,958	58,881,746	47,698,651
1970	25,933,783	36,173,744	62,107,527	49,216,602
1975	25,490,186	35,165,245	60,655,431	51,096,393
1980	29,414,036	32,787,804	62,201,840	54,671,755
1985	36,361,561	26,404,671	62,766,232	58,825,978
1990	41,311,167	21,016,795	62,327,962	62,634,512
1992	41,469,756	19,217,369	60,687,125	62,067,820

As you can see from the figures, afternoon papers are responsible for the flat circulation figures. Morning sales have grown while afternoon sales steadily declined in the last 20 years.

The last deadline for afternoon newspapers is about 1 p.m. Why read news that is four or five hours old, when you can catch the 5 or 6 p.m. newscast and be up-to-the-minute?

Newspapers by Fax

To counter the lag time and compete with broadcast news, 10 newspapers in 1989-90 began offering an abbreviated version of their next edition by facsimile. The number of faxed newspapers is growing. The price is high, but expected to drop as more subscribers for the fax version sign on.

The Number of Dailies

In 1950, there were 322 morning papers, 1,450 evening newspapers. In 1992, the count was 571 morning papers, 1,042 evening newspapers.

Most American newspapers are fairly small. Only 16 per cent have circulations of more than 50,000.

The Five Largest Papers

ABC figures for 1992 show the five largest, in circulation, are:

The Wall Street Journal	1,795,448
USA Today	1,418,477
Los Angeles Times	1,177,253
The New York Times	1,110,562
The Washington Post	791,289

One of the most dramatic changes in newspapers is the growth of newspaper chains. Traditionally, newspapers were small-town, family-owned, with deep community ties. No longer.

The Big Newspaper Chains

Today, 76 per cent of all daily papers in America are owned by newspaper groups. Those chains account for 82 per cent of total circulation.

A third of the nation's newspapers are owned by 20 companies. The largest, in terms of newspapers owned in 1992, were:

Thomson Newspapers, Inc.	124
Gannett Co., Inc.	81
Donrey Media Group	56

Knight-Ridder, Inc.	28
The New York Times Co.	25
Newhouse Newspapers	26
Dow Jones & Co. Inc.	23
Scripps Howard Newspapers	21

Circulation for the Chains

The largest chains, in terms of average daily circulation, are:

Gannett Co., Inc.	6,021,123
Knight-Ridder, Inc.	3,764,185
Newhouse Newspapers	3,081,203
Times Mirror Co.	2,797,631
Dow Jones & Co., Inc.	2,406,536
Thomson Newspapers, Inc.	2,301,351
The New York Times Co.	2,134,345
Scripps Howard Newspapers	1,618,937

Competing Papers

The number of cities with separately owned, competing newspapers is rapidly shrinking. In 1988, there were 102. In 1990, the count was 43. By early 1993, only 29 cities had competing newspapers. In about half of those cities, competition was kept alive through joint operating agreements (JOAs).

In a JOA, the larger newspaper (usually a morning newspaper) agrees to print the evening paper on its presses and use its circulation department to distribute the afternoon paper.

In most JOAs, the advertising departments are also merged. The editorial and news staffs for the two papers remain separate, distinct, and competitive. The efficiency created by using the same plant, trucks and advertising staff is the only way the smaller newspaper can survive.

The Cost of a Newspaper

In most cities, what you pay for a daily newspaper doesn't even cover the cost of the blank paper it's printed on. In 1991 the average price of a daily newspaper was 35 cents; the average price of a Sunday paper, 91 cents, according to the Newspaper Association of America.

Newspapers live or die by advertising profits, not what they

Where Advertisers Spend Their Money

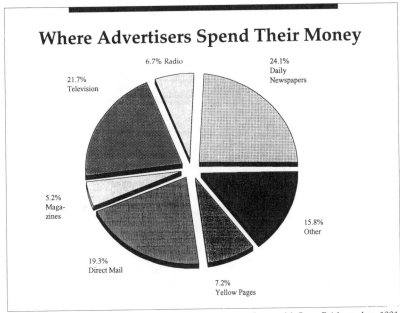

Source: McCann-Erickson, Inc. 1991

get from the people who buy the paper. The advertising rates, of course, are based on circulation. So the more papers they sell, the more they can charge their advertisers.

Advertisers spend more on newspapers than any other medium, but television and direct mail keep gaining on them. For 1991, McCann-Erickson, Inc. reports, 24.1 per cent of all advertising dollars were invested in newspaper ads. Television commercials accounted for 21.7 per cent of advertising expenses nationwide, followed by direct mail, 19.3 per cent; telephone directory yellow pages, 7.2 per cent; radio, 6.7 per cent; and magazines, 5.2 per cent.

Weekly Circulation

The number of weekly newspapers has declined slightly in the last 20 years, but their circulation has doubled. A large part of that increase is the explosion of free weeklies, designed to appeal to neighborhoods and offer inexpensive advertising.

In 1970, there were 7,612 weeklies in America with a total circulation of 27.9 million. In 1992, there were 7,417 weeklies with a total circulation of 54.6 million. Those newspapers had an average circulation of 7,358 copies per week.

How To Speak TV, Print & Radio

INSIDE THE MEDIA

PRIVACY

Get Out of Here . . .
And Leave Me Alone

Many suits against the media now claim invasion of privacy, not libel. Because of its cameras, lights, microphones—and the networks' national audience—television can be much more intrusive than print. Jurors in suits against the media have strong feelings about their own personal privacy. The concept—at first glance—seems simpler to a jury than libel. Privacy verdicts—even more than those in libel suits, depend on how the jury feels about the circumstances in each case.

It's Not In the Bill of Rights

Personal privacy is a new legal concept in this country that is still developing. The Bill of Rights protects citizens against unreasonable search and seizure. But that is a protection from government abuse—not private enterprise, or individuals. We inherited criminal trespass from British Common Law, but the idea of a right to privacy in your personal life was not conceived until the 1890s.

In the 1950s, electronics leaped far ahead of the old laws regulating wiretaps. A comprehensive federal statute to protect the privacy of conversation was not adopted until 1968. There still is no statutory privacy protection from a telephoto lens.

Physical Trespass

Trespass is physical intrusion onto your property. It is a criminal act.

Invasion of privacy by a reporter or photographer can occur when they broadcast or publish what they saw and heard while they were physically trespassing. The effect of the story or picture is to bring thousands—perhaps millions—of people into your home or business, where they have no right to be. Since you can't prosecute all of them (you don't even know who they are), a suit provides a way to financially punish the media outlet that ushered those hordes of people through your private property.

Shooting vs. Showing

Shooting a picture, and publishing or broadcasting it, are two different kinds of intrusion. If the picture taken by a trespasser is never shown to anybody else, then a simple trespass took place. But once the picture is shown to others, the trespasser has brought other people inside your space, invading your privacy.

An invasion of privacy can also occur without pictures or physical trespass, if a journalist tells the world something about your life that is very intimate.

Let's go back now to trespass—physical intrusion—and work forward to the latest electronic eavesdropping devices.

Where Cameras Can Go

A photographer has the same freedom of movement as anyone else. If you can walk down the sidewalk, so can a television or print photographer. We have public places in this society where anyone can go, unless a state of emergency is declared—streets, parks, subways, beaches, public buildings.

We sometimes give the news media special access so they can represent the public and report what happens. At a major trial, for instance, seats are reserved for the media and some spectators are shut out. Reporters and photographers are allowed beyond police lines at disasters so they can see, record and photograph the victims and the rescue effort.

There are some public places where citizens have access but cameras and microphones are barred. Television cameras were not allowed to cover proceedings in the U. S. House of Representatives until the 1970s. The U. S. Senate allowed camera coverage of its committee hearings as early as the 1950s (McCarthy, Kefauver), but did not allow daily, continuous coverage of proceedings in the Senate chamber until 1986.

Cameras in Courtrooms

By early 1993, 46 states permitted cameras in their courtrooms. Federal courts still banned cameras, but a three-year experiment was underway to let cameras cover appellate arguments in two U. S. Circuit Courts (New York and San Francisco); and civil trials in five selected U. S. District Courts (New York, Washington, Pennsylvania, Massachusetts, Michigan and Indiana). The experiment ends June 30, 1994. The U. S. Supreme Court will then decide whether to allow cameras in lower federal courts on a regular basis.

Opponents of cameras in courtrooms argue that the camera affects witnesses and jurors. That doesn't apply in appellate courts, where there are no witnesses and no jury. Nevertheless, in late 1989 the Supreme Court justices voted against letting cameras cover their proceedings. Chief Justice William Rehnquist had said during his Senate confirmation hearings that he would consider letting TV cover Supreme Court sessions. During their confirmation process, Justices Souter, Kennedy, O'Connor and Thomas said they favored TV coverage. Reportedly, cameras will not be allowed to cover their sessions until the nine justices unanimously approve.

Semi-Public Places

There are semi-public places, privately owned, but open to the public. Stores, restaurants, bars, offices. Anybody can walk in. There is an understood, open invitation.

In a truly public place, a reporter or photographer cannot invade privacy. When they walk off the sidewalk into a semi-public place, the rules shift.

Le Mistral, Inc. v. CBS
61 A.D. 2d 491, 402 N.Y.S. 2d 815, 3 Med L. Rptr. 1913 (1978)

Most cases now seem to indicate a still photographer or TV camera crew can come in, shooting, but must leave if the owner of the semi-public place tells them to. This would apply to almost any place of business. The owner of a restaurant in New York City won a large privacy suit judgment against CBS, claiming that a television crew refused to leave, created a scene, and frightened some of his customers. Witnesses disagreed on how long the camera crew tarried, but the jury felt they overstayed their welcome.

The CBS crew had entered the restaurant with a health inspector, hoping to videotape unsanitary conditions in the kitchen. The restaurant manager could not stop the health inspector, but argued that the inspector's right of entry did not include the right for a TV crew to tag along. The jury agreed.

If You Go, the Camera Can

Again—the camera crew has the same right of entry as the general public. The photographer has the legal right to walk into the reception area of a doctor's office, but can't barge past the receptionist into the examining rooms, where patients have their clothes off.

In semi-public places, the outcome of a privacy suit may hinge on the behavior of the two antagonists. Juries tend to rule against people who are loud or obnoxious, and act like bullies. If a television crew enters your place of business and you ask them to leave, the nicer you are—and the pushier they are—the better your chances of winning a privacy suit.

If they leave when they're asked to, they've met the privacy and trespass guidelines. The longer they refuse to leave, the more they interfere with the operation of your profession or business, the better your case.

The Most Private Place

The most private place is the home. Here, criminal law says you commit a felony—not just trespass—if you enter without an invitation, even if the door is unlocked. Because of that long tradition that holds privacy of the home so sacred, many successful suits for invasion of privacy involve intrusion there.

Unless there is a "Do Not Enter" sign at your front gate, no trespass is committed if someone enters your property and knocks on the front door of your home.

Martin v. Struthers
319 U.S. 141, 149 [63 S.Ct. 862, 87 L.Ed. 1313] (1943)

Once they knock and are asked to leave, they become trespassers if they refuse. A rented home—or a hotel room—carries with it the same sort of privacy rights as a home you own.

In the past, reporters and photographers have frequently been invited by the police to accompany them on raids in private homes. On a Saturday night, a police department called to ask if my station would like to go along on a big gambling raid. It was a slow night, and the assignment editor jumped at the chance.

Our crew went to the police briefing. It looked like World War III. The SWAT team was ready. Flak jackets, and automatic weapons. The target was a private home. Watches were synchronized, and the home surrounded. A team of officers knocked on the front door, announced that they had a search warrant, and barged through the door into the living room.

The Penny-Ante Poker Raid

Our photographer was right behind them, camera rolling.

Inside the house was a group of senior citizens playing penny-ante poker. A penny-ante criminal case that never went anywhere. But for some reason, we broadcast a story that included the embarrassed faces of card players.

The homeowner sued my station for invasion of privacy. The argument was very similar to the Le Mistral Restaurant case. The search warrant gave the *police* the right to enter the home, the plaintiff's attorney argued. But it did not give a TV crew that same right.

Eventually, the suit was dropped. But our attorney—one of the nation's experts in media law—suggested that in the future, we might be more careful about barging into private homes with the police. Juries in the future, with the perception that the media have become too powerful and too pushy, might establish new law.

Electronic Eavesdropping

Most states passed laws against wiretapping in the 1920s and '30s. But they were often more concerned with the bootlegging of telephone service than with personal privacy. The proudest achievement of a well-known professional wiretapper was tapping into the Associated Press Sports Wire so his bookie client could have instant game scores and race results. The police accidentally discovered the tap, and prosecuted him.

Two- and four-party telephone service was common in most American homes through the 1940s. Most people just assumed someone might be listening to their conversations. Privacy is not a big concern if you don't expect it.

Wiretaps

A wiretap is a physical connection to a communications line—tapping into the wire that carries information. You can tap into a telephone line, a teletype line, a cable TV line and hear or see what the person at the other end of the line is receiving. One of the most vulnerable spots for industrial espionage is a telephone line that carries computerized information from one office to another.

There are no provisions in the law for private citizens to wiretap. **Wiretapping by individuals is always illegal.** The early laws let police agencies wiretap with little control or supervision as part of a criminal investigation.

Bugs

Federal law enforcement agencies were required to get approval from the U. S. Attorney General before they could wiretap. Then, in the early 1950s, the first small "bugs" were created. Law enforcement began using them on a massive scale. There was no requirement that they be reported, and very little law governing their use.

A Microphone Transmitter

A "bug" is a small combination microphone-radio transmitter. It is easy to hide, and much more intrusive than a wiretap. In a car or a room, it intercepts conversation and transmits it to a radio receiver. A "bug" can be designed to pick up not only conversation in a room, but also both ends of a telephone conversation from that room. Some of them use house current, or the voltage in the telephone line, and never need their batteries replaced. Most "bugs" have a limited range. The receiver must be located within several blocks to pick up their signal.

The invention of miniaturized electronics opened up new worlds of possibilities for privacy invasion. Their widespread use by law enforcement, as well as private investigators engaged in industrial espionage, became a major issue in the early 1960s. Congress passed in 1968—as part of its Omnibus Crime Bill— national standards for electronic eavesdropping.

The Federal Law

Simply stated, federal law says if you participate in a conversation, you may record it. But if you plant a microphone, tape recorder, or "bug" to intercept a conversation that you cannot hear, then you have committed a serious federal crime.

Under this law, police agencies must get court approval to intercept conversations if they—or their informants—are not participants. The court approval is an electronic search warrant. If a police officer goes before a judge with sworn information that you have contraband hidden in your home, the judge issues a search warrant. It gives the police the right to go into your home and search for evidence of a crime.

In the same way, if a police officer has sworn information that you are about to have a conversation that would become evidence in a criminal investigation, the judge can give the officer permission to "search" that conversation with a wiretap or a "bug." The officer must certify that conventional investigative techniques will not work; that the electronic eavesdropping is a technique of last resort.

State Eavesdropping Laws

Federal law gives states power to pass more stringent eavesdropping regulations, if they choose. About a third of the states have made it a crime to secretly record conversations, even if you participate in that conversation. In those states, it is a felony to record your telephone calls—to record any conversation whatsoever—unless everyone whose voice is intercepted knows the microphone or "bug" is picking up the conversation.

In states that have not adopted more stringent laws, you may record your telephone calls without telling the other person, if you use a suction cup or other inductance pickup that does not physically tap into the telephone company wires. You can wear a small recorder to tape conversation. In those states, reporters can secretly record what you say and use it later in their stories.

In the more stringent states, reporters cannot secretly record your voice. If a recorder is in use, they must tell you.

Skirting the Law

Illinois forbids secret recording, but "60 Minutes" came up with a clever way to get around the law. They rented a storefront in Chicago and put a sign in the window announcing a doctor's office would open there soon. Representatives from about a dozen laboratories dropped in to solicit business for blood and urine tests. There was a hidden microphone, wired so the "doctor" could turn it on and off. When the laboratory owners talked, the mike was off. The laboratories were offering kickbacks. Send us your business, and we'll give you a cut, under the table.

Read My Lips

A hidden camera photographed the kickback negotiations. The audience heard the "doctor" say something like, "Now, let me get this straight—if I send you all my Medicare blood tests, you'll kick back 25 percent?"

The sound went dead, and you saw the lab man nod his head. You couldn't hear the answer, but it was easy to read his lips as he said, "That's right."

Visual Eavesdropping

So far, there are no laws establishing visual privacy similar to audio privacy. If a telephoto camera lens outside can see you inside your home or business, it has not invaded your privacy. The theory seems to be—if you don't close the blinds, you can't blame your neighbors for watching you undress.

But if a secret camera were hidden inside your home or business to photograph things the reporter couldn't see with the doors and blinds closed, most judges and juries would probably feel your privacy had been invaded.

Personal Privacy

Intrusion into your personal life is another matter. It often involves some kind of physical trespass, but not necessarily.

The concept was first proposed in December, 1890 in a *Harvard Law Review* article written by two young lawyers who had roomed together in Cambridge—Samuel Warren and Louis Brandeis. Brandeis would later become one of the legendary justices of the U. S. Supreme Court. Warren's family was prominent in Boston society. They threw lavish parties. It was the heyday of Yellow Journalism. The press gossips constantly pestered the family and tried to crash their parties.

The Right To Be Left Alone

Warren and Brandeis published their novel idea in the *Harvard Law Review* essay. It is time, they said, to create a new area of law in America that would guarantee the right of personal privacy. Their definition is still used today: Personal privacy is the "right to be left alone."

Their idea took a long time to catch on. As late as 1950, most states still had no laws specifying personal privacy rights. Many still have none, perhaps because they are difficult to define. The lines keep changing.

In Public, No Privacy

In a public place, you have almost no right of personal privacy. If the general public can see it, a news camera can shoot it.

Suppose a young child has been hit by a truck. The mother is sitting in the street, holding the body, sobbing hysterically. The truck driver, sitting at the curb, is going into shock. His face is gray and he is having trouble breathing. A police officer is trying to help him.

A news photographer arrives and begins shooting closeups of the mother and child and the truck driver.

Does the photographer invade their privacy?

At this point in our history, no.

Police-Media Conflicts

This kind of incident often leads to major confrontations between the police and the news media. Officers, with feelings of human compassion, step in to stop the photographer. Sometimes, they seize the camera and arrest the photographer for interfering with an officer by ignoring an order to stop shooting.

The officer has no legal right to stop the photographer. It is a public place. No criminal trespass is occurring. But sometime in the future, the civil law could change. Jurors and judges angry with the intrusions of the news media might decide that the mother and truck driver in this moment of great tragedy and grief have *the right to be left alone.*

In the early days of television, cameras broadcasting baseball games showed people in the bleachers who were supposed to be at work. When they got into hot water with their bosses, they sued, claiming invasion of privacy. The courts held that if you are in a public place, you have no privacy protection from a camera that catches you playing hooky, or with a person who is not your spouse.

Libel & Privacy Differences

Let's look at the differences between libel and privacy.

Suppose you are about to be promoted to the presidency of a department store. A reporter discovers that 40 years ago, when you were 15, you were caught shoplifting in that same store. If the story is published or broadcast, there is no question it will damage your reputation. The embarrassment could even stop your promotion. But you can't win a libel suit, because it's true.

Public Good vs. Privacy

You might be able to win a privacy suit. In deciding whether damages should be paid, the judicial scale tries to balance the public good that is accomplished by publishing or broadcasting information, against the damage that is done to the individual whose privacy is invaded. Examples:

Briscoe v. Readers Digest Assn.,
4 Cal. 3d 529, 93 Cal. Rptr. 866, 483 P. 2d 34 (1971)

The *Reader's Digest*, in a long-running series on organized crime, includes a brief reference to a man who had been convicted of a crime as a young adult. The story does not focus on him. His case is simply used to illustrate a point. His wife and children, his employer, his friends knew nothing of his criminal past before the article was published. He sues for invasion of privacy, and wins. He argues he paid his debt to society, became a productive citizen, lived an exemplary life after he left prison. Any public good that was served by publicizing that part of his early life, he maintains, was far outweighed by the damage it did to his personal privacy. The court agreed.

A Final Exam Quiz

A question from my final exam, when I was an adjunct professor:

A woman calls you with a story tip. Every Saturday night, she says, the people next door throw a very wild party. They leave all the doors and windows open. From my back bedroom, you can look into their house. By 10 p.m., they are drunk and rowdy. By midnight, they are naked and obscene. Some of them are holding a white powder to their nose and snorting it.

I've called the police with no results, your caller says. How would you like to come sit in the dark, in my house, and take pictures of what goes on next door?

Questions

Question A: If you accept the invitation and shoot into the house next door, have you invaded the privacy of the people at the party?

Question B: If you publish or broadcast those pictures, have you invaded their privacy?

Answers

Answer A: Shooting the pictures will not invade their privacy. You were not trespassing when you shot the pictures. If someone chooses to undress in front of an open window, and you watch, you can't be accused of being a peeping Tom.

Answer B: The best test answer I had from a student was one which said, "If it's just a bunch of naked people, you may invade their privacy. A jury might decide their privacy outweighed any public benefit from publishing the pictures. But if one of the people in your pictures is the police chief—or the governor—that's something else." The outcome of a privacy suit in this example will hinge on the jury's weighing personal privacy vs. public good.

Senator Eagleton's Past

U. S. Senator Thomas Eagleton of Missouri in 1972 becomes the Democratic vice-presidential candidate, running with George McGovern. A newspaper reporter discovers that Eagleton, years earlier, had been a patient in a mental institution. The story causes Eagleton's withdrawal from the race. But there is never even a suggestion that he sue for invasion of privacy. Why? Because he is a public official. Like libel, privacy law offers little protection to public officials.

Gary Hart And Donna Rice

U. S. Senator Gary Hart of Colorado was the front-runner for the Democratic nomination in 1988. There were recurring rumors that Hart had an active sex life outside his marriage. The rumors became so strong, Hart challenged the media to follow him and prove whether the rumors were true or false. Acting on a tip, the *Miami Herald* followed model and actress Donna Rice when she flew from Miami to Washington, D. C. While they did not have photographs of Hart and Rice together, their story suggested the two had spent the night in Hart's Washington townhouse.

Hart attacked the newspaper for scurrilous, slanted reporting; said he had done nothing immoral, and planned to continue as a presidential candidate. But when the *National Enquirer's* front page the next week showed Rice on Hart's lap during a weekend boat trip to Bimini, Hart's campaign collapsed and he withdrew from the race.

The stories sparked a national debate on whether political candidates have the "right to be left alone" in their private lives.

Attitudes Change

There was a time when certain parts of public officials' lives were private. As a result of polio, it was extremely difficult for President Franklin D. Roosevelt to rise from a sitting position. He had to be carried in the arms of a servant when he left the White House, then placed in the presidential limousine. At his destination, the servant would lift him out of the car and hold him up while another servant locked his legs in steel braces.

FDR's Handicap

Once on his feet, with his braces locked, he could walk stiffly, slowly, with the aid of two canes. The process was never photographed. Throughout his presidency, news photographers avoided pictures that showed how handicapped he was. It was considered a matter of personal privacy.

Look at the difference during Ronald Reagan's term in office. In network stories, the nation was given nightly diagrams of his colon and his prostate during his surgery and post-operative care. We learned more about his private parts than we really wanted to know.

Where's Lyndon?

Before John F. Kennedy was assassinated, Washington reporters began to wonder if they should report on Vice-President Lyndon Johnson's private life. Bored, alienated from Kennedy, Johnson drank a lot. He had an eye for the ladies, and frequently disappeared in the afternoons. Suppose something happened to the President, the reporters asked themselves. If there was a national emergency, would anybody know where to find the Vice President? And if they did, would he be in any condition to make critical decisions?

Johnson became President, got back into working trim, and the stories were never written. The reporters were relieved. Most reporters and public officials were men, and men had a gentlemen's agreement not to talk about certain things.

The Stripper's Swim

The dam that held back stories on politicians' sex lives broke the night Rep. Wilbur Mills, a longtime alcoholic, got into a spat with his stripper girl friend, Fanne Foxe. She jumped into the Tidal Basin and onto the front page of nearly every newspaper in the country. From that point on, it seemed that nothing in a politician's private life was sacred. We were besieged with stories about the sex lives of former presidents. Since President Lyndon Johnson showed us his scar after his gall bladder operation, we expect major political figures to show us their stitches. After a fund-raising dinner, we almost demand to hear them belch.

Public People: Less Privacy

It is not so extreme, but the same kind of attitude exists about government employees. The rule of thumb seems to be: the higher the official, and the more contact with the public, the less privacy. Police officers and school teachers probably have less privacy than government auditors or secretaries, on the theory that their private lives can affect the quality of their public work.

Outside government, the more visible you are, the less privacy you can expect. Officers of a major labor union or corporation expect to give up some of their privacy. Lawyers who represent famous clients or try newsworthy cases become public persons, along with entertainers and professional athletes.

We are still trying to decide just how far the media should go in invading private lives.

Cantrell v. Forest City Publishing Co.
419 U.S. 245, 95 S.Ct. 465, 42 L.Ed.2d 419 (1974)

In Ohio, a newspaper reporter and photographer return to an area that had been devastated by a flood. Their story focuses on one family. The children, at home alone, let the newsmen into the house. They tell them how the flood has changed their lives. The reporter never sees the mother. But in his story, he fudges, and includes a sentence about how tired she looks. He gives the clear impression that she was present during the interview. In deciding that the family's privacy was invaded by the story, the court makes a special note of the reporter's deception.

Privacy and Curing Cancer

In California, a Life magazine reporter goes to the home of a naturopathic "doctor" and feigns symptoms of cancer. The "doctor" wires the reporter to a gadget with flashing lights and tells her she is feeling bad because she ate rancid butter. He even gives her the exact day on which she ate the butter. While she is receiving his diagnosis, her "husband," a *Life* photographer, is shooting pictures with a hidden camera. He is wearing a "bug" that transmits the entire procedure to a prosecutor parked up the street in a van. When the prosecutor arrests the "doctor," *Life* magazine is there to photograph the bust. The pictures taken inside the house are featured in an article on quack doctors.

Dietemann v. Time, Inc.
449 F.2d 245 [9th Cir.] (1971)

The naturopath sues for invasion of privacy. He wins the case, as well as the appeal. In upholding the verdict, the appellate court makes it clear that it simply does not like the idea of reporters coming into people's homes with hidden cameras and microphones, acting as agents for the police.

Barging in with the Police

A television crew is invited along on a raid at a remote school for problem children. The prosecutor has obtained a search warrant, based on information that sex and drugs are part of regular activities at the school. The police barge in before dawn, pulling frightened kids out of their beds and ransacking their rooms. The camera catches everything. The officers show bags of unidentified substances, but the script leaves little doubt they found the drugs.

Green Valley School, Inc.
v. Cowles Florida Broadcasting, Inc.
327 So.2d 810 (1976)

In the end, the police do not have a case. The television station loses a suit for privacy invasion. Here again, the facts are messy. The script is clearly written from the prosecutor's point of view. Witnesses say the officers used the television camera to intimidate people as they were being questioned. The seized pills shown in the story turn out to be tranquilizers; the apparent marijuana, herbal tea.

Fla. Publishing Co. v. Fletcher

340 So.2d 914, 2 Med. L. Rptr. 1088 [Fla. S. Ct.] (1976), cert. denied 431 U.S. 930 (1977)

A fire kills a young girl, at home alone. Her bedroom burns, and when firemen remove the body, her silhouette remains in the charred floor. A fire inspector, who does not have a camera, asks a news photographer to take a picture of the room and the unburned spot where the girl died. It is a dramatic shot, and the newspaper publishes it.

The mother sues for invasion of privacy, saying the fire inspector had no right to bring the photographer into her home, and the newspaper had no right to invade her life by publishing a picture that causes her so much pain. At the trial, a jury finds the newspaper guilty of privacy invasion. On appeal, the verdict is overturned.

The lines are difficult to draw. Verdicts in one state disagree with those in another. It is new law, growing and being shaped each time a jury wrestles with the facts in a specific case.

To Recap

Let's recap—
- If it's true, you can't win a libel suit.
- If the story is false, and you're a public official or a public person, you can win a libel suit only if you prove the media outlet had malice—that is, knew it was false, and ran it anyway; or they were sloppy reporters and demonstrated reckless disregard for the truth.
- True or false, a story can invade your privacy.
- You have no privacy from a camera in a public place.
- If you are in a private place, a photographer shooting with a telephoto lens does not invade your privacy.
- Broadcasting or publishing what is shot with that telephoto lens *can* invade your privacy if a court decides your privacy outweighs any public good served by the publication or broadcast.

- Photographers can come into a privately owned place where the public is invited, but can become trespassers if the owner asks them to leave and they refuse.
- Federal law does not prohibit secret recording of telephone conversation by people who participate in those conversations, but about a third of the states have more stringent laws that prevent *all* secret recording by private citizens.
- Spreading facts about your past—and intimate portions of your present—may do more personal damage than public good, and therefore become an invasion of your privacy.

Invasion of privacy verdicts are returned when a jury feels, "They shouldn't do that. I wouldn't like it if they did that to me. That person had a right to be left alone."

INSIDE THE MEDIA

RATINGS

Will They Know I Switched From Opera to Wrestling?

Television is probably America's most fiercely competitive industry. Very slight shifts in the number of people watching your station or network can mean millions of dollars. It is an industry constantly in metamorphosis, looking for some new game or gimmick that will entice a few more people away from the competition. If the audience wants a little more sex, a little more violence, that's what it gets. Each producer is constantly trying to guess next season's fad or fashion, hoping to invent a show or character or situation that will play to the appetite of that fleeting, fickle audience.

Spinoffs

Once a show becomes a success, there is a stampede to copy and clone it, hoping to squeeze every penny of profit out of the idea before it gets stale and the audience moves on to whatever turns them on. "All in the Family" becomes "Archie Bunker's Place," until the audience eventually becomes weary of the characters and dwindles away. "Happy Days" breeds "Laverne and Shirley"—"The Cosby Show" begets "A Different World." Sometimes the spinoffs work. Sometimes they don't.

At the top, television news is controlled by the same people who program entertainment. They are always looking for the magic formula that will seduce people away from the competition. If they suspect the audience wants more flash and trash, then flash and trash becomes the lead story.

From city to city, television news is as varied as radio station formats. There are newscasts anchored by gray-haired veterans as bland and dated as elevator music.

Hard Rock News

In other markets, young, hyper anchors almost shout stories in a style similar to hard-rock radio. It doesn't matter so much what the words say, so long as you keep the rhythm and beat. Keep it frantic.

"The City Manager's Secret Agony! Tape at Eleven!"

"A Psychic Says UFOs Will Disrupt The Governor's Inauguration! I'll Talk With Her Live, at Five!"

How do you know how many people are watching? How do you know they'd rather learn about a new diet than the defense budget?

Ratings Set the Price

As a general rule, the cost of commercial time on television is based on how many people will see the advertising. There are no hard and fast rules. The price is based on what the market will bear. It has to be competitive with other forms of advertising.

Thirty seconds of commercial time in a small town, after midnight, can cost as little as $10. In a major city, a locally-produced special in prime time may charge as much as $15,000 for half a minute. Thirty-second network commercials in prime evening hours average about $75,000.

In early 1983, the last installment of "M*A*S*H" set a new record—$450,000 for each half-minute of commercial time. But the record didn't stand very long.

$1.7 Million Per Minute

Super Bowl telecasts contain the most expensive commercial time on the tube. Price to advertise during the 1993 Super Bowl broadcast was $850,000 for a 30-second spot. It keeps going up.

Thirty seconds during the 1987 game cost $600,000; 1988, $650,000; 1990, $700,000; 1992, $800,000. Spots toward the end of the game are usually cheaper than those at the beginning, but NBC in 1993 charged $850,000 per unit throughout the game, and sold out well in advance. The national economy affects sales. At the last minute in 1992, CBS had to offer advertisers special deals on other commercial time to sell all its Super Bowl spots.

Buyers don't always get what they pay for. The runaway score at Super Bowl XXIV in 1990 (San Francisco 49ers, 55; Denver Broncos, 10) drew a smaller audience than any Super Bowl since 1969.

Top Prices, Poor Show

Ratings showed the average audience for the three hour and 25 minute 1990 show was 39 per cent of American households. At least part of the 1989 game had been watched in 43.5 per cent of all the homes in America.

Broadcasting Magazine reported that CBS sold national advertising for the 1990 game with no promises on the size of the audience.

Some local stations, however, had promised a minimum audience in their market for local spots during the game. They had to make other advertising time available to those advertisers at reduced prices because of the game's low ratings.

The industry calls those "make-good" commercials. The station or network makes good its promise to deliver a certain number of people per dollar spent on a commercial.

Nationwide, advertisers spend about $26 billion per year for commercial time on TV. Radio advertising totals about $9 billion. (See **INSIDE THE MEDIA/Newspapers** for advertising in other media)

The Ratings Game

How do they know they're getting the audience they pay for? Ratings.

The entire economic foundation of television and radio in this country is based on a very inexact science. Broadcast rating services use various systems to measure how many people are listening or watching at any given time.

They sell their results to broadcasters and advertising agencies. They, in turn, sell advertising based on those statistics.

But the process has always been questioned. It was used because that's all there was. The entire system is undergoing revolutionary changes. Nobody is sure yet whether the new technology, introduced in the fall of 1987, will be more accurate than the old systems.

Nielsen and Arbitron

Two companies—A. C. Nielsen and Arbitron—have historically been the major ratings services. They constantly monitor how many people have their sets turned on, and which shows they're tuned to.

Until 1987, the rating services used three basic techniques to measure the audience:

- Telephone surveys.
- Viewer diaries.
- Viewing meters.

For all three methods, the rating services develop small, random samples that are supposed to accurately reflect the audience. Arbitron's specialty was large telephone surveys. Nielsen developed the technique of selecting representative families, giving them a diary to log what they watch.

Family Diaries

The families are supposed to make an entry every 15 minutes when the set is turned on, showing which station is on, and who's watching. Once a family agrees to keep a diary, their viewing habits are monitored for long periods of time. Their identity is a secret, to avoid any outside influence on their choice of shows.

But diary-keeping is a real chore, and there was always a suspicion that some families in the sample weren't as precise as they should have been.

TV Meters

In 1972, Nielsen began using viewing meters in New York City to supplement its telephone surveys and viewer diaries. The company selected households in the same statistical way it chose a family for a telephone call or a diary.

The family gives its permission for the rating service to connect a meter to its TV set.

Any time the set is turned on, the meter automatically keeps a record of which station it is tuned to. By 1993, the metering technique had spread to 29 market areas that contain 51 per cent of all the television viewers in the United States. The meters are connected by telephone lines to computers, so that instant ratings can be tabulated. They are on 24 hours a day, year-round, not just during "sweeps" periods.

"Voting" A Show

In some ways, meters are much more accurate than telephone and diary reports. Rating services learned over the years that people in viewing samples have a tendency to cheat. If they have a favorite series, they "vote" for it, reporting that they watched it, even if they didn't.

Viewers also tend to tell the rating service they watched shows they think they *should* watch. They may say they saw a National Geographic Special or a symphony concert when they were really watching wrestling.

Meters eliminated the inaccuracies of diaries in families that have literacy or language problems; or families that get sloppy, and fill out their diaries at the end of the week, relying on memory to report what they watched.

But meters have their own inaccuracies. They report viewers if a set is turned on, even when nobody is watching.

Meters Increase Viewing

When a family gives permission for a meter to be installed, they seem—for a while—to watch a lot more television than the norm. There's a subtle psychological effect. Their inclusion in the sample makes families feel like their choice of shows has suddenly become more important. That tendency to increase viewing time slacks off after several months.

The families aren't told this, but the rating services usually don't start tabulating their viewing until that early period of heavy TV watching has passed.

Independent stations seemed to be the big winners when meters replaced diaries and telephone surveys. One study showed daytime ratings for independents doubled after meters were installed. The analysts could only guess why.

The Meter Mystery

Under the diary systems, people may not report using independent stations' re-runs to baby-sit small children. The re-runs of classic sit-coms like "I Love Lucy" and "The Honeymooners" may be more entertaining—even if you've seen it five times before—than the current crop of programming.

Another explanation could be that they don't want their spouses or parents to know how much time they spend watching daytime television, and simply don't report their viewing accurately in the diaries.

Meters seemed to make little difference in audience numbers during prime time, from 8 to 11 p.m. But after 11 o'clock, one study showed the ratings of independent stations 42 percent higher. That late-night difference is harder to explain than the daytime discrepancy between diaries and meters.

People Meters

For advertisers, WHO is watching is just as important as HOW MANY are watching. You don't advertise beer in a children's show, or toys on "20/20." And so the technology was created to tell you exactly WHO and HOW MANY are watching in your carefully selected sample group.

Nielsen began testing people meters in 1986. The people meter is very much like a remote-control TV device. A complex gadget is attached to the TV set. When the set is turned on, the people watching must push a button on the remote device to "log in." Each member of the family has a personalized button. If someone new comes into the room to watch TV, or if someone leaves, they're supposed to use the remote control to tell the meter.

Time to Push the Button

If the station is changed, a light flashes. Each person watching must "log in" again. Using a remote control to quickly see what's on the other stations won't require a new tally if the set is returned to the original station within 45 seconds. Longer than 45 seconds requires a new roll call of viewers. If the set stays on for many hours without a change of stations, each company has a formula that drops that family from the viewer count that day. Even with these people meters, the set could be on for several hours, with nobody watching, and still show viewers who weren't there. But you can't go back two hours later and "vote" a show. In effect, this type of people meter is an electronic diary.

People meters are subject to cheating, too. One member of the household can log in absent family members. But they narrow the ways in which participating families can fudge.

In the fall of 1987, Nielsen and a competing British company—AGB Television Research—began daily people-meter ratings.

The first results knocked the industry for a loop. People meters brought in some numbers that didn't coincide with any of the older rating methods. In the first weeks, the people meters gave "The Cosby Show" 10 to 15 percent fewer viewers than diaries or the old meters. "Miami Vice" did better with people meters than with the other systems. "The Today Show" had been the clear leader in morning television under the old rating system. With people meters, "Today" was neck-and-neck with "Good Morning America."

People Meters Disagree

In some time slots, there were significant differences between Nielsen, Arbitron and AGB results. If your show fared poorly, you blamed it on a bad sample of viewers.

There was a belief that young adults who were more familiar with computers and other electronic gadgetry would be more conscientious and adapt quickly to people meters. Some experts direly predicted that people meters would cause a sharp shift in programming to appeal only to young adults.

Age Affects Meters

But some carefully controlled experiments showed viewers over 50 were much more accurate in pushing the people meter buttons. Children loved the people meter responsibility at first, but seemed to quickly tire of the chore, and stop pushing the buttons.

Overnight, subscribers are able to get 40 different kinds of demographic breakdowns on viewers as well as total numbers.

There are other problems with the metering systems. They do not deal accurately with videocassette recorder use, and about 65 per cent of American households had VCRs by 1990.

Viewers Away from Home

And what about metered families who are away from home watching television? In 1989, Mediamark Research, Inc., set out to estimate the number of people who are not measured by the ratings systems.

In one project for ABC, Mediamark found huge numbers of college students uncounted. Many college students are hooked on daytime soap operas. In one case, the uncounted audience was higher than the measured audience, Mediamark said.

Other studies show at least 10 per cent of the "Monday Night Football" audience is in bars, which are not metered. Travelers in hotel rooms watching television are uncounted. So are hospital patients and people at the beach, using the estimated 10 million battery-powered TV sets in America.

The rating services are working on it.

ScanAmerica

To compete with Nielsen, Arbitron in 1987 developed still another rating service it called ScanAmerica. Participating households reported everything they bought to ScanAmerica, so the service could correlate buying patterns with TV commercials watched. But ScanAmerica was too complex and burdensome for the families it measured. The service folded in September, 1992.

A few months later, Arbitron announced it was working on a new, portable device about the size of a telephone beeper that sample viewers would carry with them all the time. It would somehow record whether they were watching TV, and which program, no matter where they were.

There is another major problem in the people meter systems—remote control devices that allow viewers to rapidly jump back and forth between channels. Or "zap" the commercials to peek at what the other stations were offering. And digital sets that allow you to see several stations on the same screen at the same time.

Measuring the Zappers

So a Seattle firm—R. D. Percy & Co.—came up with still another, more sophisticated kind of people meter. It measures, second-by-second, what a household is watching. Percy hoped to be able to tell advertisers which commercials were "zapped" by remote control, and which commercials viewers stuck with, even if they'd seen it a hundred times.

Percy's technology includes an infra-red device that can sense the number of people in front of a TV set. If a new person comes into the room, or someone leaves, the people meter asks for a new log-in to determine exactly who's out there. But the Percy service—like AGB Television Research—suspended operations after several months. The costs and technical problems overwhelmed them.

Translating the Numbers

Radio and TV programs are measured in two ways:

Rating—the percentage of homes in a market area that watched or listened to a show. This figure is technically the percentage of *homes who have radio or TV* that watched. In most communities, more than 99 per cent of the homes have at least one radio and TV set. So the rating number is really the percentage of households who watch or listen to a show. The ratings are tabulated for local market areas as well as nationwide.

Share—the *percentage of households with their sets turned on* who were tuned to a particular program. The station's share of the audience at any given time.

The TV industry has another term in its jargon—HUT Numbers. Households Using Television. The spread of people meters may create another term—PUT Numbers. People Using Television.

If a town has 100 households and five are watching television—but all are watching the same show—then that show will have a 5 Rating/100 Share. Five per cent of the homes are watching that show. But 100 per cent of the people watching TV at the time are watching that show.

A program with a 12 Rating/26 Share was watched by 12 per cent of the households who own TV sets and by 26 percent of the households who were using TV during its time slot.

Prime Time Ratings

Rating numbers go up during prime time (8 to 11 p.m.) when more people watch television. Share numbers in any market total 100, no matter how many people are watching.

Radio audiences are generally highest during "drive time"— rush-hour traffic periods, when large numbers of people listen as they commute between home and work.

In addition to the rating and share figures, the services traditionally reported detailed demographic information on the people watching, by age, sex, ethnicity, education, income level, and number of people in the household who were employed. They report whether the households have cable or pay TV.

Special Services

If a subscriber wants to know more about the audience, it can arrange for the rating service to expand the information on each household in the sample. All this can be useful to advertisers who want to target a certain audience, but it's expensive. This kind of detailed information is routinely included in the people meter ratings.

The "Sweeps"

The standard rating periods take place four times a year—in November, February, May and July. You'll notice local newscasts promoting themselves a lot more during the rating "sweeps," trying to improve their numbers so the sales departments can increase the price of advertising. At many stations, special reports and series are broadcast only during the sweeps.

Because meters and the new people meters operate year-round, the hyping of shows during sweeps could eventually be eliminated.

Advertisers are particularly interested in 18 to 49-year-olds. They're the consumers in our society—the ones who earn more, and spend it more freely. A newscast ranked second in terms of total audience can charge more for its advertising time if the ratings show it outdraws the Number One station in 18 to 49-year-old viewers.

High-Priced Anchors

Slight shifts in audiences mean millions of dollars. If a network show increases its ratings just one point, that means another two and one-half million people watched the broadcast and absorbed its commercial messages. That's why on-air "talent"—particularly anchors and sportscasters—are paid so much.

A popular anchor or sportscaster who moves to a competing station can sometimes bring the fans to the new station and cause dramatic shifts in ratings. Most rating changes are much more gradual. Humans are creatures of habit. Changing their viewing or listening patterns takes time.

It's not unusual now for a popular anchor in a major local market to earn a quarter to a half-million-dollars, plus all kinds of "perks"—a chauffeured limousine to commute between home and work; an extravagant expense account and clothes allowance, a reporting assignment outside the country at least once a year, where the entire family gets to go along.

"Hi, Dan."

Network anchors are even more pampered.

Television is an unusual medium. Its anchors have more celebrity status than anyone except the President of the United States. Walk a movie star and Dan Rather down the same sidewalk, and many more people will recognize Rather. More than just recognize him—they'll speak, wave, call him Dan. They think they know him on a personal basis. If you questioned them, they'd have a complete personality in mind, all based entirely on their perceptions of him from his visits in their living room every evening.

The ability to create that kind of relationship with viewers is an extremely valuable commodity. Rather is reportedly the highest-paid anchor in the industry, earning about $3 million per year.

Shooting Craps

Because the ratings are so critical and so fluid, television news is in a constant state of flux. If the ratings get stuck or go down, you change the format or the pacing or the people.

It's like shooting craps. If the new anchor or weather fore-caster or news director doesn't bring the ratings up, fire them, one at a time, and try another roll of the dice. Keep changing people until you hit a winning combination. Most on-air talent have a contract that guarantees their salary for two or three years. If the ratings are truly bad, stations and networks will often tell the talent goodbye, but continue to pay their salary for the contract period.

Consulting firms charge small fortunes to study newscasts and newscasters, looking for the magic formula that will increase ratings. They lock test viewers in a room, show them videotape, and then debrief them on what they saw, what they like, what they remember.

Consultants

The consultant tells the station to fire the sportscaster. He's not macho enough. Get a meteorologist who's also a stand-up comic. Change the anchor's haircut, or clothes. Build a new set that looks like a space station. Have the talent talk to each other more during the newscast. Make it look like they truly enjoy each other's company, and what they're doing.

There are millions of combinations to try, always in pursuit of some subtle effect that will make more people switch to a station—particularly 18 to 49-year olds. Once a prescription works in one city—like the "happy talk" formula in the 1970s—the consultants race from station to station across the country, selling their new cure for ratings sickness.

The Magic Elixir

And, like magic, it works. For a while. Until some other consultant comes up with another elixir that will lure viewers.

The process never stops.

All this may seem terribly phony and money-grubbing. But it is the way the system works. Capitalism and free enterprise in their purest forms.

Television is not going to disappear. The candidate who chooses to run a whistle-stop campaign from the back of a Pullman car instead of using TV spots will wind up in some obscure train yard, with nobody listening.

INSIDE THE MEDIA

TECHNOLOGY

What Will They Think of Next?

Technology is changing the news media in dramatic ways. The advent of television began the decline of the evening newspaper. Cable TV was originally designed to get TV into remote areas broadcast signals could not reach. But by 1993, cable was delivering dozens of channels to 61 per cent of the homes in America. With so many choices, the network audience is shrinking dramatically. The future of networks as we've known them is in doubt. (See **INSIDE THE MEDIA/Networks**)

Other, newer technology is also threatening the cable industry. As this book goes to press, a major battle is underway in Congress over whether telephone companies should be allowed to deliver TV programming and other high-tech services.

Cable vs. Phone Company

Why have two wires coming into your home, the telephone companies argue—one for cable, one for telephone—when one fiber optic cable can deliver both and much more. In addition to telephone service, fiber optics can provide a greater number of TV and radio channels than current cable TV technology; computer data banks; inter-active message services; home banking; travel reservations; shopping—and a lot more that hasn't been invented yet.

The capacity of fiber optics is so huge, for instance, it could provide TV shows and movies on demand, rather than having to wait until a scheduled broadcast time. You could call a central library, tell them what you want to watch, and it would be on your home screen immediately. That kind of service would also eliminate the corner videotape rental store.

Breakthrough for Cable

In late 1992, several companies announced a major breakthrough in transmitting data over copper wires. By digitalizing the data (the way computers do) and compressing it, the companies claim existing copper cable can carry almost as much data as fiber optics. Having 500 channels in your cable TV service would be possible with either technology.

The court order that broke up AT&T in 1982 and the 1984 Cable Television Act prevented telephone companies from delivering TV signals, except in rural areas that have no other cable TV service available.

Courts and Congress

In 1991, an appellate court ruled that telephone lines could be used to transmit information services and TV programming. As this book goes to press, telephone companies are in court asking for the right to create their own programming, not just transmit it for others. The right to become true cable TV companies. The potential for services through new technology is so great, there is enormous pressure for Congress to write new law.

Still other technology is ready to compete with both cable TV and the telephone companies. All of the services that can be provided through fiber optics can also be transmitted by satellite.

Satellite Saucers

The big problem—until now—was the size of the antenna dish. To receive and transmit by satellite in the early days, the dish had to be about eight feet in diameter, and mounted in concrete to make sure there was a steady shot between the dish and the orbiting "bird."

But satellite systems are now perfected that use a receiving antenna less than two feet in diameter. A dish small and light enough to clip to a windowsill. Several companies are already delivering TV programming through the compact satellite system. More are under construction. Radio programs direct from a satellite instead of your local station are also in the works.

Classified Ad Competition

Newspapers have watched some of their advertisers defect to competitors using new technology. Classified real estate advertising has been hurt by computer-generated books of listings that Realtors publish weekly or biweekly.

Realtors are also using videotape to help prospective buyers narrow their choices. No need to spend money on classified ads for those clients.

In some states, cars, trucks and boats are advertised in free or low-cost weekly publications available in convenience stores.

To compete, newspapers in some cities now offer a special 10-day classified ad rate for boats and cars. If it doesn't sell in 10 days, they'll run your ad free until it does sell.

Fax Newspapers

Another new innovation is facsimile delivery of tomorrow's newspaper, made possible by the sudden spread of fax machines across America.

That service is being refined, so you can order just a page or section by fax. Sports scores or stock prices. And have it before the six o'clock news.

Inter-active Video Catalogs

Just over the horizon is an even greater threat to both newspaper and TV advertising—inter-active video catalogs.

Suppose your lawn mower or washing machine breaks. You go inside and dial up the Video Mart catalog. An attractive salesperson pops up on your TV screen.

"Hi," the salesperson says. "Welcome to Video Mart. If you know which section you'd like to browse in, dial that number on your telephone now. If you don't know the section number, here's an index."

The Miss America Pitch

You punch in the number for lawn mowers. Instantly, a tape of a former Miss America is playing on your screen. Dressed in a bikini, she's strolling behind a self-propelled mower. She turns off the mower and begins to give the sales pitch, explaining this model's features.

"Like to have one like this?" she coos. "Well, you're lucky. It's on sale today. Just $399.95. Punch in your Video Mart credit card number now and we'll deliver it before dark."

How can conventional advertising compete? What will happen to the economic base that provides newspapers and TV programs? Hard to predict. Stay tuned.

Radio's Good-Bad News

Technology has helped and hurt radio news.

Cellular telephones offer a marvelous way for radio reporters to relay on-the-scene stories to their stations for live broadcast.

But local news stories produced by the radio station staff are disappearing. Local news is very expensive, compared to canned music and national news.

With satellite technology, an absentee owner can now operate a radio station with one employee in the studio. All programming is delivered by satellite, broadcast live or taped for later broadcast.

The station owner needs someone to turn on the transmitter at the beginning of the broadcast day, turn it off at night. The fewer employees at a radio station, the higher the profit.

Look, Ma, No Hands

It's even possible to operate a station now with nobody there. It's all done by remote control. In 1989, a company in Colorado was created to monitor radio stations' technical operations by satellite.

Engineers in Colorado watch a control panel that duplicates the gauges and dials in the control rooms of client stations across the country. From Colorado, they can turn on a local radio station's transmitter anywhere in the hemisphere, fine-tune the station's signal, and choose the source of taped or satellite-delivered programming.

Alarms sound in Colorado if a serious problem develops. The Colorado company than calls the station owner, who sends a live engineer down to fix it.

Less Radio News

Most radio news is now packaged in another part of the country and beamed to the local station for re-broadcast. Locally-produced radio news is very rare. News of any kind is also dwindling on American radio.

One reason is television's ability to broadcast sound and pictures live from the scene of a breaking story. In the old days, that was radio's edge in the news business. As soon as a radio reporter reached the scene, with a two-way car radio or a borrowed telephone, his account could be broadcast live. Most TV stations now have helicopters on call to fly reporters and photographers across town or across the state, where they can immediately beam pictures and sound back to the station for live broadcast. Radio has lost its exclusive.

Another damaging blow to radio news was CNN Headline News, which is all-news radio with pictures. A new development is round-the-clock cable TV news services which cover local and regional news. The first was launched on Long Island, New York, in December, 1986. As this book goes to press, there are five others in operation. Orange County, California began in 1990; Washington, D.C., in 1991; New York City and Boston in 1992; and Chicago in early 1993. There were plans to build a local all-news channel that would cover the entire state of California, beginning in late 1993.

Radio News and Market Size

As community size increases, a smaller percentage of radio stations carry news. Dr. Vernon Stone at the University of Missouri School of Journalism was commissioned by the Radio and Television News Directors' Association to survey the status of radio news in America.

In 1992, Stone found that 13 percent of radio stations nationwide had no news operation of any kind. In metropolitan areas of more than a million people, 19 per cent of the radio stations had no news. In communities of between 250,000 and one million, 21 per cent had no news. Radio news' last stronghold is communities of less than 250,000 people, where all but 10 per cent of the stations still broadcast news.

The entire financial base of broadcasting depends on audience ratings. Technology in that field is also undergoing dramatic changes. (See **INSIDE THE MEDIA/Ratings**)

The USA Today Revolution

When *USA Today* first appeared, veteran newspaper people hated it. It was very different. Strange. Television on paper. The world's largest high school newspaper. McPaper.

But most other American newspapers have now adopted much of the look and printing technology that *USA Today* pioneered.

Lots of color and graphics. Short, bright stories, simply told. *USA Today* is now the nation's second largest newspaper, in terms of circulation. And it grew that big from a dead start while other newspaper sales failed to grow at all.

Newspapers by Modem

The newspaper as we've known it—delivered to your home or office each morning—may not be economically possible in the very near future. We'll still have printed news. But it will be delivered to your computer through a modem.

While the coffee is perking, you'll have a list of stories on the monitor, and check the ones you'd like to read. You can also choose the length and detail for each story. The stories will be printed on your own printer by the time you sit down for breakfast.

This kind of service is already available through a number of computer services. You pay according to the time and length of stories requested. The transition from old-style newspapers to this new form will take place when more newspaper advertising is siphoned away to other media, and when enough newspaper readers own home computers. (See **INSIDE THE MEDIA/ Newspapers**)

SEMINARS
On-Camera Training in Media Skills & Strategy

Author Clarence Jones conducts seminars nationwide for professionals and executives in government and private industry. He also consults with organizations on specific media problems or projects.

If you'd like more information on those seminars, the standard information package includes a list of workshop modules that can be custom-tailored to fit your group. Complete the form below and mail to:

Video Consultants, Inc.
5220 S. Russell St. # 40
Tampa, FL 33611
(813) 832-4137.

Yes, I'd like more information on Clarence Jones' seminars in news media skills and strategy.

I'm interested in: (check those that apply)

____ Basic news media relations.
____ News media strategy.
____ Interview skills.
____ Organizing and managing in-house media relations staff.
____ Creating and implementing media policy.
____ Crisis management.
____ Using the media to lobby a specific issue.
____ Becoming more pro-active about media coverage.
Other _____

My field is   ____ Assn. Management   ____ Health Care
(check one)   ____ Business   ____ Human Services
                      ____ Education   ____ Law/Courts
                      ____ Government   ____ Law Enforcement
                      Other _____

Send seminar information to:

Name _____

Organization/Title _____

Street or PO Box _____

City _____ State _____ Zip _____

BOOK ORDER FORM

If You'd Like More Copies

If you'd like more copies of this book, use the order form below. We offer discounts for carton-lot orders. A carton contains 32 books.

For less than a full carton within the United States, the following shipping and handling charges apply for U. S. Postal Service delivery, book rate.

COPIES		COPIES	
1	$2.00	6–10	$ 7.00
2	$3.50	11–20	$ 9.00
3–5	$5.00	21–32	$11.00

****

MAIL TO:

Video Consultants, Inc.
5220 S. Russell St. # 40
Tampa, FL 33611

I need _____ copies of "How to Speak TV, Print & Radio" at $17.95 each.

_____ copies X $17.95 .... $_____

Plus postage and handling from table above ... _____

Fla. orders add state sales tax—$1.17/copy ..... _____

TOTAL ENCLOSED .... $_____

Name _____

Street or PO Box _____

City _____ State _____ Zip _____